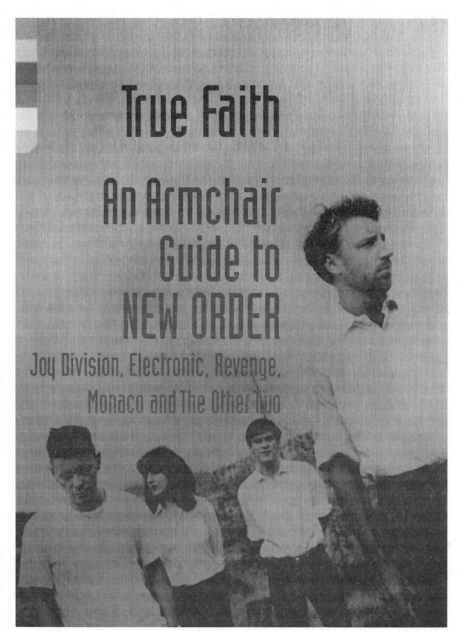

True Faith

An Armchair Guide to NEW ORDER

Joy Division, Electronic, Revenge, Monaco and The Other Two

First edition published in 2005 by
Helter Skelter Publishing
South Bank House, Black Prince Road, London SE1 7SJ

Copyright 2005 © Dave Thompson

A CIP record for this book is available from the British Library

ISBN 1-900924-94-3

TRUE FAITH:

An Armchair Guide To NEW ORDER

Joy Division, Electronic, Revenge, Monaco and The Other Two

By Dave Thompson

with additional input from David Sultan

Helter Skelter Publishing, London

Author's Note

TRUE FAITH: THE ARMCHAIR GUIDE TO NEW ORDER represents the largest and most complete discography ever published around the life and times of Joy Division, New Order, Revenge, Electronic, the Other Two and Monaco, reviewing and documenting the historical and musical background to the band's entire catalogue of singles, albums, remixes, compilations and more.

Based upon years of avid collecting and listening, the book also utilises material from four interviews conducted with individual members between 1991 and 2001, together with further first-hand material dating back to the late 1970s. Other sources, including quotes and excerpts from press encounters elsewhere, are acknowledged in the text and in the bibliography at the end of the book.

How to Use this Book

For hopefully obvious reasons, *TRUE FAITH: THE ARMCHAIR GUIDE TO NEW ORDER* is laid out chronologically by year, with all entries then following, again, in chronological order. Although the emphasis is on material considered to have been released officially, a small number of bootlegs are also noted. Within these parameters, the following headings should be similarly self-explanatory. But, just in case....

SINGLES: Includes 45rpm, 10-inch, 12-inch, EP and CD single releases, including collaborations with other artists. Bootlegs are featured, but by no means exhaustively. Original release, reissue and chart data (if any) is also included. Joy Division, New Order releases and all associated spin-offs (Be Music Productions, Revenge, Electronic, the Other Two, Monaco) are listed sequentially.

Finally, in general, only basic UK catalogue numbers are given – any given single might well appear in a dozen different permutations, with some tracks (usually remixes) exclusive to one pressing, but others common to all of them. Rather than double the size of the book with repetitive lists and largely similar numbers, all versions of each single are rounded up into one entry, identified by the most simple of the many catalogue numbers.

ALBUMS: Includes LP, cassette and CD full length releases, including collaborations with other artists and Various Artist compilations featuring newly recorded material. Again, a handful of bootlegs are noted. Original release, reissue and chart data (if any) is also included.

LIVE: Concert recordings listed by date of original show where known. Performances by associated spin-offs (Revenge, Electronic, the Other Two, Monaco) are not included.

STUDIO: Unreleased studio material, or recordings subsequently released on compilations and anthologies (detailed in appendix II), listed by date of original recording where known. Undated material is listed either following the main chronological sequence, or where it would seem to fit in regard to the band's repertoire of the time. When in doubt, performances are dated to the year in which the song was first recorded. Material by associated spin-offs (Revenge, Electronic, the Other Two, Monaco) is not included.

SESSION: Specially recorded material cut for radio/TV broadcast. Broadcast recordings by associated spin-offs (Revenge, Electronic, the Other Two, Monaco) are not included.

MISC: Factory Records catalogue numbers assigned to non-musical items. From the outset, label chief Tony Wilson recognised the record collectors' need to be constantly challenged and entertained by the hobby, and, particularly through its first five years of activity, the Factory catalogue interspersed records with a plethora of other oddities, ranging from label stationery and posters, through to real estate – FAC 51 was the Haçienda nightclub, built and operated by Factory from May, 1982, and soon to become the focal point for Manchester nightlife; FAC 98 was the hairdressing salon opened in the Haçienda's basement in October, 1983. Even more bizarre was FAC 99, New Order manager Rob Gretton's dentistry bill, paid for by Factory after he was beaten up by associates of the band A Certain Ratio.

For ease of reference/cross-reference, every Joy Division and New Order song is individually numbered according to year (the first two digits – 77, 78, 79 etc) and by the release's position within the above sequence. Unreleased songs known to have been recorded at listed events are noted UNR (UNRELEASED). Subsequent (live, radio or rerecorded) appearances of the same song receive a new number. However, alternate recordings/mixes from original session, or commercial remixes of a previously released recording, when issued under the original title, retain the original number, suffixed a, b, c etc.

Releases by associated groups – Revenge, Electronic, the Other Two and Monaco – are also numbered according to their own internal sequence. Replacing the numerical prefix, Electronic releases appear with the prefix *e*; Monaco *m*; the Other Two *o*, Revenge *r*.

Further material is included in the appendices: (I) Compilations and Anthologies; (II) Tributes and Related Releases; and (III) Unofficial Live Recordings/ Gigography.

Introduction

'The fiddler stood in the doorway.... He was bent and thin: he limped: his voice was old: there looked to be no strength in him. He stretched out his fiddle bow.... "I shall not harm you. Take the end of my bow... the stairs are dangerous".' – Alan Garner, *Elidor*

Summer, 1976 was a great time to be in Manchester, and even greater times were around the corner. Returning home from the FA Cup Final, United manager Tommy Docherty, 'The Doc,' didn't even try to apologise for his side's defeat against Second Division Southampton. Rather, he reminded us that, just two years before, the worst United side in living memory had tumbled out of the top flight for the first time since the war, yet still came close as Christmas to scooping the double in their first season back.

Now he was demanding that we look to the future and, in front of several tens of thousands of witnesses, insisted we'd be back next year. And who would dare to doubt him? And who would want to? Even on the blue side of the City, there was a certain civic pride to be taken from the speed with which United bounced back – all the more so since it was City who sent them down in the first place. And they had their own cause to celebrate as well; their own trip to Wembley, a couple of months earlier, saw City drill out a memorably unmemorable (forget the game, check out the silverware) League Cup win, to ensure that for only the second time ever, both Manchester sides would be marching into Europe next year.

Football unites in ways that other pastimes can only dream of. Place a Bay City Rollers fan in the same room as a Black Sabbath freak, and the only common ground they'll find is that both are bipedal mammals. Put a United supporter in with a City nut, though, and provided they don't try to kill each other first, they have a stronger, longer bank of memories shared than the average married couple. And, from those united memories there came a sense of an undivided future. A Rollers fan and a Sabbath freak could never form a band together. But a United supporter and a City nut? It was happening all the time.

The clutch of squats that rotted a few streets away from the Oldham Road were a case in point. The name of the street – like the street itself – is long forgotten; long since marked down for demolition, and deserted by its rightful tenants, a row of terraced houses simply waited in mute anticipation of the wreckers balls that swung a few roads away – when the wind was in the right direction, you could hear it going about its business, and the knowledge that this street's lifespan could be measured in weeks... maybe even days... was tangibly etched into every blind window.

'Grass grew in the cobbles, and in the cracks of the sidewalk.' Author Alan Garner's *Elidor*, that mystical binding of past and present, reality and fantasy, fear and something even greater than fear, starts out in a street like this... maybe even the same street... 'off to the right up Oldham Road.... Doors hung awry. Nearly all the windows were boarded up, or jagged with glass. Helen looked through [one]. "This room's full of old dustbins!" she said.'

And so it was. But this was not *Elidor*, this was not fantasy. There was no castle, no mound, no unicorn... there wasn't even a derelict church at the end of the road, and no phantom fiddler to draw you in. This, by the standards that the western world so proudly proclaims its moral supremacy, was life at the thinnest edge of squalid survival, where the outside toilet was a hole in the ground and the plumbing was a cup to catch the drips condensing on the walls; where the bugs behind the wallpaper made the posters look alive, and a rope hanging down through the hole in the floor was considered safer than the stairs.

But that's not to say there was no music. Every one of the squats had its own resident musicians, every one of those musicians had his own resident dream. And every couple of weeks, one of them would bang on a few doors and ask if anyone wanted to come hear his band, rehearsing in a basement somewhere, auditioning at a pub or... and this was the big one... stepping out at one of the handful of clubs that still preferred live music to the disco automaton.

There, too, there was a sense that good times were just around the corner. Tommy Docherty didn't speak only for his football club that May afternoon; or, maybe he did, but his words were relevant in a larger context as well. All across Manchester, even within those dingiest quarters where a dying Labour government's legacy of homelessness, poverty and unemployment had all-but sucked the soul out of everything, the dream of renewal flickered fitfully into life.

United may not have been the spark that lit it, but they were certainly the breeze that fanned it to life. In 1974, after two seasons spent flirting with the unthinkable, the not-so-long-ago Champions of Europe had crashed through the floor of the First Division, not quite leaking goals as they went – they rarely lost a game by more than one – but rarely scoring them, either. As of Christmas Day, the side's joint top scorer was goalkeeper Alex Stepney. But a season out of the limelight became a season of ambitious rebuilding and fearless resurgence. 1975 saw United sweep almost arrogantly, and certainly ruthlessly, to the Second Division Championship and, the following year, they finished third in the League and second in the Cup. Relegation was the best thing that could have happened to the club because, it's only when you touch rock bottom that you can really begin to climb out again. And Manchester itself had touched rock bottom, politically, economically, culturally. It was time to begin the rebounding.

There were catalysts aplenty – the day after Dr Feelgood passed through town, rehearsal rooms echoed to the chunka-thump of bruised R&B; when the Hot Rods made it north, a dash of adrenalin was poured into the pot. Graham Parker, ferocious in his Angry Motown phase, added soul and passion to the brew, and a host of lesser lights – the Pub Rocker alumni that was barely scraping by in London – returned home wondering why every city's audience couldn't be as responsive and as raucous as Manchester.

Latter-day rock historians, sometimes born-and-bred in the city, bond with Mafioso intensity on the insistence that it was the Sex Pistols who awakened the slumbering beast that was Manchester rock; that it was the London quartet's first local show, at the Lesser Free Trade Hall on June 4 that ignited the latent dreams of the cold northern souls. But weeks, if not months before a pair of local art students, Pete Shelley and Howard Trafford, convinced Malcolm MacLaren to let them play promoters for an evening, pockets of brittle musical belligerence were rising up everywhere. Most had no name, many had no instruments, some had no idea at all what it was they actually wanted to do. The only thing they did know was the Doc hit the nail on the head.

We'll be back.

A hundred people paid 50p a pop to see the Pistols and history, again, insists that they more than got their money's worth. Faces who'd simply passed one another in a club somewhere found they had something new to bond over; acquaintanceships that might never have got out of bottom gear were suddenly turbo-thrust into top. And back in those decaying squats in a derelict street, where at least a handful of the Pistols' witnesses returned shaken and breathless at the end of the night, there was the knowledge that something new, something magical, had entered their lives; that perhaps *Elidor* had come true after all; that maybe they'd just met the fiddler after all. And the wild dance was about to commence.

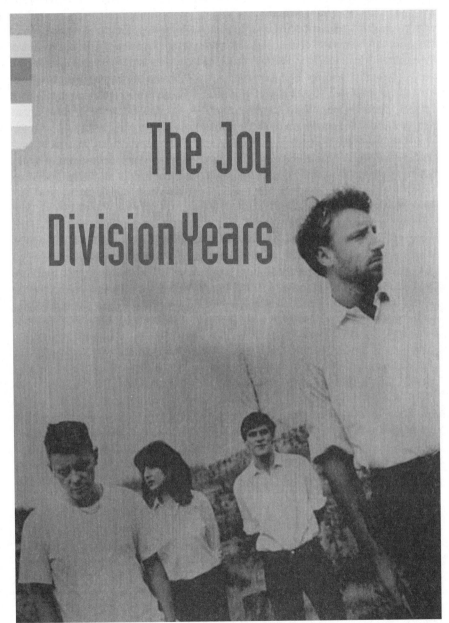

The Joy
Division Years

1977

'Seeing the Sex Pistols showed me that it was more about spirit than virtuosity,' onlooker Bernard 'Sumner' Dicken recalled. He went to the show with his best friend Peter Hook (the pair had known one another since they were 11, almost a decade before), and another mate, Terry Mason. '[Terry] read somewhere about the Sex Pistols having a fight onstage, and he dragged us down to see them.'

Not one of the trio expected much more from the evening than another object lesson in why you should never believe what you read. Instead, they discovered a way of life. 'I loved music,' Sumner continued, 'but the lifestyle was appealing [as well] – escaping from the 9 to 5 existence with 2 weeks holiday a year and a boss and [a] job you hate. Almost complete personal freedom was very appealing.'

Peter Hook agreed. 'The thing about punk to me, was... the great thing about being a kid is that you always think the way you do things is the right way, and the way your parents do it is wrong, your bosses are wrong. So, being in a group and making your own music and being Indy was quite important, because you're really making your mark on the world. Everybody wanders around at 17 and 18 going "ooh. I hate me parents, I hate me bosses," and it was a wonderful way of doing things for yourself.

'It was a real triumph, it broke the mould, which is a nice thing and, for me, it meant a period of self freedom. I found what I wanted to do with life and, luckily life found what it wanted to do with me. It was a building and a growing period; it's when I became what I considered an adult, it's when my life was formed, and that was down to punk, and it was down to a kind of self politics – "I'm not out to change the world," and I wouldn't think for one minute that me standing here in Didsbury could change the world. But it changed my world, and I'm very happy about that and, as we went on, I was very happy with the things we did and the things we achieved.'

The Pistols returned to Manchester in July, playing this time to an audience that hearsay had swollen to gargantuan proportions and, within weeks, Manchester suddenly seemed alive with new bands.

Slaughter and the Dogs, the Worst, the Fall, the Buzzcocks, the Drones, Ed Banger and the Nosebleeds... some of them had been around, in form if not fact, long before the Pistols turned up; others were hastily thrown together in the scalding white heat of the London group's aftermath. Some came tearing out of the squats, finally awakened to the directions that their anger and suffering had been building towards; others rose out of more comfortable surroundings, where mundanity, not misery, was the greatest curse in life.

But all represented a ferocity and sense-of-purpose – musically and culturally – that the local music scene had not witnessed in years, not since the early 1960s, when Manchester was the northern heart of the British Beat Boom, and bands like the Mindbenders, Herman's Hermits, the Whirlwinds, the Sabres and the early Hollies pounded out a sound to rival even the Beatles and the Stones.

That was the legacy with which every young band in the city had been confronted since then, the wise and wizened old club owners who yawned at the most earnest solicitations because they were there when the Twisted Wheel and the Oasis really swung, and they'd not heard anything so exciting since then. As what history quickly came to call 'Punk Rock' took hold – in Manchester, Liverpool, Birmingham, Bognor, in any city where the kids had the eyes to see what was going on, and the wits to make sure they became a part of it – that generation of club owners was to be swept aside as thoroughly as the bands they still espoused. And, as they tumbled out of view, an entire reality shifted.

Before he saw the Pistols, 'I thought a rock gig was Led Zeppelin at Earl's Court,' 19-year-old Ian Curtis confessed. Now, however, he knew it was something else entirely, something that was within reach of anybody who cared to touch it. As the local live circuit began to clog with bands; and the Electric Circus, swift to establish itself as *the* primal punk venue in Manchester, switched from a barely-getting-by rock palace at the smelly end of Collyhurst Street, to the steaming centre of noise, excitement and energy; so Curtis threw himself into the melee. And, as the weeks passed and the shows began to blur into one another, he realised there were certain people that he seemed to bump into every night.

Peter Hook and Bernard Sumner had noticed Curtis as well. The day after seeing the Pistols, Hook had purchased his first bass guitar; now he and Sumner, already an aspiring guitarist, were strumming away together, amplifying their stumblings through the pick-up of Sumner's gran's gramophone player. They were, Sumner confessed, 'crap,' but that was scarcely a consideration. What mattered was that they were doing *something* and the only cloud on their horizon, as 1976 sped towards its conclusion, was the absence of anyone else to do it with.

There were a few 'rehearsals' with a schoolfriend, one Martin Gresty, but he was never cut out to be a lead vocalist and quickly faded from view. Other friends and names were mentioned, but they rarely went beyond the realm of wishful thinking. An ad in the window at the Virgin Records store encouraged little more than a succession of singers and drummers passing through, 'space cadets' one and all, as Hook put it. 'We just seemed to attract complete lunatics.'

Even Ian Curtis seemed out of the duo's league, as they learned that he had his own 'sort of band,' an unnamed combo that time alone would reveal to be as shorthanded as Hook and Sumner's. 'It was just him and a guitarist messing about,' Hook later said. '[But] we were a guitarist and a bassist, so it just didn't seem to fit.' One night, however, Curtis wandered over and mentioned that his guitarist had just split the group. Days later, Hook, Sumner and Curtis were rehearsing together at the Black Swan pub in Salford.

They worked hard. Over the next four months, the trio wrote and rehearsed a mass of music, the bulk of it dominated by Curtis' own choice of interests and influences, a gamut that ran from the conventional godheads of Iggy Pop and the Velvet Underground, through to the harsher realities of Throbbing Gristle. Sumner recalled, 'we used to get Kraftwerk albums, and David Bowie's *Low*… music like that, and we'd educate ourselves. So, when we came to writing our first songs, it would be "what sort of song shall we write?" I remember one time, Ian brought in Iggy's *The Idiot* (a hot new release in March 1977) and we played "China Girl" and said, "yeah, let's write something like this." And it didn't come out sounding anything like "China Girl," but that's what stimulated us to start.'

Still a three-piece, the group began casting around for gigs even before they found a drummer or a name. In the event, both appeared within days of one another; within days, too, of the group's first ever live performance, at the bottom of the bill when the Buzzcocks and Penetration played the Electric Circus on 20 May, 1977.

Drummer Tony Tabac filled the empty space at the back of the stage; 'The Stiff Kittens' filled the gap at the bottom of the posters. It was a name gifted to the group by Buzzcock Pete Shelley – he'd been carrying the name around for months now, delightedly telling friends that it was *the* greatest name for a band. Curtis, Hook and Sumner weren't so sure – having already toyed with calling themselves Pogrom or Gdansk, they had now settled on 'Warsaw,' apparently out of deference for one of the lengthy instrumental tracks ('Warszawa') on side two of the latest David Bowie album, *Low*. Like *The Idiot*, like Throbbing Gristle, that album painted itself into precisely the same musical corner that the trio were intent on occupying themselves.

Not, as it transpired, that either name mattered on the night. Somewhere down the line, the quartet's very presence had been omitted from the posters, to be replaced by that of the slightly-better-known Birmingham outfit, the Prefects. Journalist Mick Middles later remarked, '[the] notion that [Warsaw] were, in fact, the Prefects prevailed throughout the gig…' – even, apparently, to people who had already seen the Prefects in the past. 'The bands did look, if only to the inebriated eye, strikingly similar.'

NME's Manchester correspondent Paul Morley was not deceived. Reviewing the show, he wrote of Warsaw, 'there is a quirky cockiness about the lads that made me think, for some reason, of the Faces. Twinkling evil charm. Perhaps they play a little obviously, but there's an elusive spark of dissimilarity from the newer bands that suggests they have plenty to play around with; time, no doubt, dictating tightness and eliminating odd bouts of monotony.'

According to Sumner, incidentally, 'It's a popular misconception that we were called Warsaw. We were never called Warsaw. At our first concert we changed it to Joy Division.' Hook, on the other hand, insists that Warsaw in fact remained a going concern for a few months, but agrees it was but a passing fancy.

The new name, Curtis' suggestion, was taken from a trashy Holocaust novel he had picked up, titled *House Of Dolls* – there, the 'joy division' was the area within the concentration camp where the more attractive female prisoners were sent to work as unpaid prostitutes; one of the group's earliest songs, 'No Love Lost,' also drew its inspiration from the same book. Neither was Curtis in any doubt as to the effect the new name would have. At a time when British street politics were being utterly riven by the rise of the racist National Front, and Punk had already made it clear that its own internal beliefs were in direct opposition to the Front's, any invocation of Nazi sympathy was a dangerous move. But it also grabbed attention and, at that stage, that was the most important thing.

That first show, and the handful that followed, were tentative, nevertheless. '[It] was a bit like playing on the moon,' Sumner shuddered. 'I felt as if I was miles away and wondering what I was doing there and why.' He was brought back to earth two nights later, when the band's second show, at Rafters, was all but wrecked by equipment malfunctions.

Concentrating their efforts on Rafters and the somewhat more unconventional

Squat (so named for the student-occupied premises in which it was sited), the group gigged sporadically through the summer, their reticence exacerbated by their problems they were having finding a drummer. Tabac departed, to be replaced by one of Sumner's schoolfriends, Terry Mason. When he didn't work out, Steve Brotherdale stepped in, moonlighting from his regular combo, the Panik, and promptly trying to lure Curtis away to that band.

It was mid-July before Joy Division finally found a player who fit, Stephen Morris, by which time the band had garnered their first slice of true infamy, after Curtis – mid-set at another disappointing Rafters show – took a leaf out of Iggy Pop's old textbook, and started carving at his own legs with a broken glass. Whereas Iggy's antics ultimately became a pillar of his own legend, however, Curtis' half-hearted thrusts drew no more than an embarrassed silence from the watching handfuls (Wednesdays at Rafters were rarely that crowded), and the night's subsequent infamy apparently owes more to the awe of people who *weren't* there, than the response of the people who were.

Morris auditioned for the band at the Abraham Moss Centre in Crumpsall and, initially, impacted the watching musicians only as the most nervous person they had ever encountered. Only once he started to play did he loosen up; only afterwards, as he fell into an almost brotherly conversation with Curtis, did he open up. However Morris was too late to join the band at Pennine Sound Studios in Oldham, where they were to cut their first ever demo tape. Stephen Brotherdale filled the drum stool for those demos only.

(STUDIO) Pennine Sound Studios, Oldham, 18 July 1977
UNR Inside The Line
UNR Gutz
UNR At A Later Date
UNR The Kill
UNR You're No Good For Me
ORIGINAL RELEASE: On bootleg: *Dal Cuore Della Città/From The Centre Of The City* (Stampa Alternativa)
COMMENTS: The sound of a rudimentary band whose ambitions are clearly far more advanced than their playing abilities. Familiar from a slew of bootleg releases over the years (the *Ideal Beginning* EP and the *Warsaw* CD are the best known), the five tracks are little more than imaginative rentapunk, with Curtis still a long way from finding his (or any other) voice and Hook's already distinctive bass the only real 'clue' as to the group's identity. Indeed, so dominant is his instrument that the strongest point of comparison is surely the Stranglers, were they to be shaved of their Doors-like keyboards.

The group's youth and inexperience shine through everywhere, in the 'misunderstood/ bored youth' lyric of 'At A Later Date'; in the earnest guitar thrash that dissects 'Gutz'; in the crunchy nihilism of 'The Kill.' But they have a firm grasp on the rabble-rousing tendencies of period second-division punk, lacing every song with at least one heartfelt chorus and even, punctuating 'Inside The Line,' a nice line in shouted 'hey's. The D-I-Y production, meanwhile, is only heightened by the absolute failure of the group's obvious attempts to meld mood and momentum – the near singalong 'You're No Good For Me' opens with an almost anthemic guitar chime, then crashes into a trough of shouted lyric and stumbling bass distortion, both of which conspire to derail what might, in any other hands, at least have given the likes of the Users a run for their money.

(LIVE) Electric Circus, Manchester, 2 October 1977
7701 At A Later Date
ORIGINAL RELEASE: Various artists live album *Short Circuit: Live At The Electric Circus* Virgin VCL 5003 (10inch LP) April 1978
COMMENTS: The Electric Circus, a long established rock'n'roll club that had since fallen on hard times, redesigned itself as a Punk Mecca of sorts and, from barely scraping by in July 1976, it was filled to the gills by September. Within a year of its rebirth, however, constant police attention had pushed the Electric Circus to the brink, and the club formally set its closure for 2 October, with Virgin Records despatching a mobile recording studio north to Collyhurst Street, to preserve the proceedings for posterity.

The label's motives may not have been wholly historical. Six months earlier, the Harvest label scored a sizeable hit with its own documentary record of the Covent Garden Roxy, recorded at what was widely predicted to be that august venue's final few nights.(In any event, it simply underwent a change of management and, maybe, scruples).

Even more importantly, Manchester was sparking, everywhere you looked. Tommy Docherty had been right – one year on from defeat in the Cup Final, Manchester United were back at Wembley, defeating Liverpool to take the trophy. And, as local sport returned to the top of one tree, so local music had ascended to the top of another. The Buzzcocks were already signed to United Artists; Slaughter and the Dogs had gone to Decca. The Rabid local label was barking ferociously. Other cities had their scenes, of course. But Manchester had a veritable industry, the cream of which was turning out to bid the Electric Circus farewell: the Panik, the Negatives, John the Postman, Manicured Noise, the Drones, John Cooper Clark, the Worst, the Fall, Joy Division and – for the first time on any stage, Magazine, the new band led by ex-Buzzcock Devoto.

They alone would be rewarded with a full length Virgin Records contract. But a handful of the others did score abbreviated versions, as the label grabbed six bands, eight songs and ten inches of vinyl, and put them altogether as *Short Circuit*.

Released in April 1978, *Short Circuit* featured one Joy Division track and, if one remembers that they had still to play their 15th concert; remembers, too, that the group's eventual vision was still far out of their musical reach, Joy Division's performance is not, in truth, especially removed from the Pennine Sound Studios version of the same song (the rabble-rousing 'At A Later Date'), cut three months earlier. But that is scarcely a recommendation. The group still had an awful lot of growing to get on with.

(SINGLE) *An Ideal For Living* EP
7702 Warsaw

7703 No Love Lost
7704 Leaders Of Men
7705 Failures
ORIGINAL RELEASE: 7-inch ltd edition of 1,000: Enigma PSS 139 – June 1978; reissued 12-inch ltd edition of 1,200: Anonymous ANON 1 – October 1978

COMMENTS: Still scarcely gigging, Joy Division returned to Pennine Sound Studios in December 1977, to cut their first single... an EP, in fact... for self-release on their own Enigma label. And it was a sign of just how quickly the band was advancing that *An Ideal For Living* found Joy Division effortlessly escaping the scratchy punk of their first stirrings and blurring instead in the direction of what the music press was then terming New Musik – jagged rhythms, a convolutedly ragged danceability, jerky funk for and from the same musical mindset that brought you the early Gang Of Four, Wire, London Zoo and so forth.

Its greatest downfall in that sense, as the band themselves acknowledged, was the somewhat crunchy sound quality of the finished item. Nevertheless, the strength of the performance rings through.

'Warsaw' and 'Failures' are the harshest of the four songs on the EP; the exquisitely-titled 'Leaders Of Men' and the two-minute instrumental passage that opens 'No Love Lost' the most prescient, both in terms of dynamic and in the latter's eventual willingness to experiment – unexpected drum breaks, odd stereo and echo, and a precipitously unexpected conclusion all make the track stand out. And, had the story ended here, *An Ideal For Living* would be one of those records that collectors haul out as an example of a band that really should have gone onto greater things. Precisely what those "greater things" might have been, however, could never be fathomed from this EP alone.

'Our first single got bad... I mean UNFAVOURABLE, but, I thought, very well written, reviews,' Ian Curtis reflected. 'One compared it to John Lennon, another to Stockhausen... the comparison between the two was quite good!'

Revelling in the still controversial connotations of their name, meanwhile, Joy Division not only remained unrepentant, they deliberately set about raising the temperature even further. *An Ideal For Living*, arrived draped in a picture sleeve splashed with a photograph of a Hitler Youth laddie banging a drum, while a German soldier aimed a gun at a child. Delve inside, and the very title 'Leaders Of Men' seemed to flirt with a similarly unsavoury, fascist mindset.

But, beyond the hysterical response that such material was intended to provoke, the group's fascination with wartime imagery can be looped back to any number of sources. Sumner later recalled spending school holidays with grandparents whose attic was a treasure-trove of World War Two era memorabilia, and he readily points out, 'that kind of stuff does make an impression. You do become fascinated by the era. At the time I was a 20-year-old kid. I actually didn't know about politics – I'm just not into politics.' And, even though the band was happily playing benefits for Rock Against Racism, still Sumner reels, 'I [even] used to get accused of having a fascist haircut!'

1978

Working around the release of *An Ideal For Living*, Joy Division spent the first half of 1978 gigging with increasing regularity around Manchester. They opened the year at Pip's, one of the Bowie/Futurist type discos that were then springing up around the country (and which would soon give birth to the entire new Romantic movement); Rafters and the Mayflower hosted other performances. But the group remained a tentative phenomenon, as liable to self-destruct on stage as play a set that anyone enjoyed.

In April, on a bill that featured just about every unsigned group in the city, they famously bombed at the Stiff Test/Chiswick Challenge travelling talent show, and similar disappointments became part and parcel of the Joy Division experience. Nevertheless, these first months saw the group do enough to impress at least a handful of crucial outsiders.

The first was Martin Hannett, at that time working with the booking agency Music Force. He caught the band for the first time at Salford Tech, opening for Slaughter and the Dogs, and recalled being impressed as much by their fortitude under fire, as by their music – 'the PA broke down, and Steve and Hooky busked for about 15 minutes.'

Another early convert was Rob Gretton, a DJ at Rafters. He first saw the band at the Stiff/Chiswick challenge and, no matter how poorly the band are said to have performed, he thought 'they were the best group I'd ever seen. There was something really weird about them. They were smart, punky, but not scruffy; it was unusual. And the music was absolutely wonderful.' Flattered by Gretton's enthusiasm, Sumner invited him to attend one of the band's rehearsals, albeit without telling his bandmates who 'this big grey-haired guy with glasses' actually was; the ensuing misunderstandings and confusion notwithstanding, Gretton would become the band's manager soon after.

The group could also bank on the support of at least one journalist and, by summer 1978, the ever-watchful Paul Morley was eagerly comparing Joy Division to Siouxsie and the Banshees, and *not* because of any misunderstood imagery – that band, after all, had had their own brush with the emotive whack of Nazi symbolism. Rather, he sensed in Joy Division's now firmly gestating sound, the same cinematic iciness that was the Banshees' calling card; the same disregard for the conventions and niceties that were now punk's own stock-in-trade; and an absolute refusal to do anything that didn't feel 'right.'

Joy Division themselves paid little attention to such praise, nor to the lashings of hindsight with which certain people subsequently regarded the group's earliest strivings. As Hook pointed out, 'pinpointing the direction the band would take is just a very highbrow way of saying they'd listened to us jamming, and said "that sounded good".'

Neither were outsiders the only fans who were truly forced to use their imagination when it came to isolating a Joy Division sound. The band, too, were constantly on guard for any moments of prescient magic that might filter through their rehearsals and jams. 'Because we didn't have tape recorders in those days,' Hook continues, 'the only place it was recorded was in your head.'

It was Curtis who paid the most attention to the noise of the band. 'Ian used to spot the riffs,' says Hook. 'We'd jam; he'd stop us and say "that was good, play it again." He spotted "24 Hours," "Insight," "She's Lost Control," all of them. If it hadn't been for his ear, we might have played it once, and then never again. You didn't know you'd played it half the time. It's unconscious, but he was conscious. It was all down to chemistry, we just clicked, we complemented one another, and we just went from strength to strength.'

One early reward for this chemistry arrived in May, when RCA Records' Manchester rep, Derek Brandwood, approached the band to discuss whether they would be willing to record a 'punk' version of the northern soul classic 'Keep On Keeping On,' a musical dream he had nurtured all year. The group agreed – but only they can tell whether or not they truly *agreed*.

The session itself was financed by another RCA staffer, Richard Searling, and his partner, John Anderson of Grapevine Records; Joy Division's first ever record contract was signed with their production company. (They would buy themselves out again for 1,000 pounds, later in the year.)

(STUDIO) Arrow Studios, Manchester, 3-4 May 1978
7801 The Drawback [incorrectly referred to as All Of This For You on a bootleg]
7802 Interzone
7803 Shadowplay
UNR Failures
UNR Ice Age
UNR Leaders Of Men
UNR No Love Lost
UNR Novelty
UNR Transmission
UNR Walked In Line
UNR Warsaw
UNR Keep On Keepin' On
ORIGINAL RELEASE: Box set *Heart And Soul*. All on bootleg *Warsaw* (RZM 200)
COMMENTS: The planned cover of 'Keep On Keeping On' was the first item on the agenda – and the last thing on the band's mind. 'We tried to do it,' Sumner pledged, 'but we're fucking hopeless at cover versions.' Instead, the band learned the riff, and transformed it into their own song, 'Interzone,' as Joy Division utilised the five day session to record their own mini-album.

Perhaps the most intriguing aspect of the resultant demo is discovering the band's own awareness of their abilities and potential. Songs that would not survive Joy Division's earliest days tend, for the most part, towards clattering punk or a ferocious mutant dance – and include new, marginally less frenetic renderings of the four songs already featured on *An Ideal For Living*. Those that would live on, on the other hand, are already clearly recognisable, even if the active imagination can conceive of some remarkable comparisons. Anyone who has ever wondered what might have happened had the early (*Three Imaginary Boys*-era) Cure tried their hand at 'Shadowplay,' for example, need only step this way.

But, give or take the occasional burst of over-exuberance, future favourites 'Transmission,' 'Novelty' and a distinctly Damned-like 'Ice Age' are all more or less fully-formed, with the former further distinguished by some genuinely intriguing sound effects twittering away beneath the band. '["Transmission"] was our first great song,' Hook enthused later. 'We were doing a soundcheck at the Mayflower and we played [it]; people had been moving around, and they all stopped to listen. I was thinking, "what's the matter with that lot?" That's when I realised….'

The demo itself 'sounds very young,' Hook mused two decades later. 'The demos sound very, very young, someone trying to find their feet, not very confident in what they're doing. But we got old very quickly, and that was down to chemistry. There's a million things in groups that happen, but its all down to chemistry, if the people that you're working with grow with you, then the world's your oyster or whatever. But if you're with people who hang back like you find in most bands, or people aren't as good as the others…. We all just clicked, maybe not personality wise, but certainly music wise, and we just went on and built from there. I knew that whatever I played, Bernard would be playing something just as good, and Ian would be singing something just as good and Stephen would be drumming something just as good, and it would be great. And you relied on that for consciousness.

'It's a funny thing to look back and, even though we didn't get on personally… we were always at each others throats, it was always a struggle… the thing was, we made great music. There's no better way in the world of getting back at somebody than singing about what a cunt they are, while they're standing next to you, putting the anger and the venom into your music. I think, because we were young and because we were trying to find ourselves, if anything, you always hurt the people you love and the people who are closest to you, even when you know you shouldn't, I think it was like that.'

(SESSION) Radio Manchester – 25 July 1978

COMMENTS: Although the band was interviewed on this appearance, opinions are divided over whether they also performed "live" versions of all four tracks from *A Design For Living* (as stated in the *Heart And Soul* liner notes), or if the DJ simply aired the original EP, as a listener to the original broadcast insists.

(LIVE) Band On The Wall, Manchester, 4 September 1978
UNR Walked In Line
UNR She's Lost Control
UNR Shadowplay

UNR New Dawn Fades
UNR Day Of The Lords
UNR Insight
UNR Disorder
UNR The Only Mistake
UNR I Remember Nothing
UNR Sister Ray

COMMENTS: It is indicative of just how quickly the band was now moving that, of the 11 songs they recorded, only two ('Walked In Line' and 'Shadowplay') were performed that night – the remainder of the set comprised apparently new/recent compositions, with 'She's Lost Control' now widely considered the stand-out number in their repertoire ('our *second* great song,' deadpanned Hook).

Ironically, in view of Curtis' own eventual fate, the song told the story of a woman he met during a spell spent working at the local job centre; according to Sumner, 'she had epilepsy and lost more and more time through it. Then one day she just didn't come in any more.' Curtis assumed she'd found a job. It was only later that he discovered she had suffered an epileptic fit and died.

The inclusion of 'Sister Ray,' a semi-regular in the musicians' repertoire for the next decade, meanwhile, testifies to a confidence that few other bands of the era could lay claim to. The Velvet Underground were indeed one of the Punk era's most sainted and, therefore, covered bands. But it was a brave acolyte indeed who stepped beyond the 'Waiting For The Man'/'White Light White Heat'/'Sweet Jane' axis, with even 'What Goes On' not truly impacting in anybody's live set until *after* Bryan Ferry covered it, in late 1977.

'Sister Ray,' 17+ minutes long in the Velvets' own repertoire and, in terms of feel and flavour, the quintessential VU cut, was a courageous step for any group to take, but Joy Division took it regardless, eschewing their own inbred aversion to covers by first, trimming the performance down to a manageable six to eight minutes, then by genuinely rewiring (as opposed to simply restating) the original's improvisational passages.

Several underground recordings of the song's performance exist, leading up to the one officially released take (on the compilation *Still*), each of which depicts the band as capable of improvisatory brilliance as the Velvets themselves were. A little cattily, one might also note that the Sisters Of Mercy's live rendition of the song, as hatched a couple of years later, was based more in an appreciation of Joy Division, than a love of the Velvet Underground.

(SESSION) *Granada Reports* (TV) 20 Sept 1978
7804 Shadowplay
ORIGINAL RELEASE: VHS *Punk* (Vision 50366) 1992
COMMENTS: According to legend, the first Tony Wilson, host of Granada TV's *So It Goes* rock show, ever heard of Joy Division was when he received a note from Curtis, describing him as 'a fucking cunt' for not having yet put the group on the air.

Wilson responded by going to see the band live, and later admitted 'it took just 20 seconds to convince me that… this was a band worth investing in.' He told

Rolling Stone, 'In early '78, I went to this gig in Manchester where every local band played. Fifteen bands played, and I thought, "None of these is really *it*",' Wilson recalls. 'Then Joy Division came onstage and played two numbers. And I thought to myself that the reason they're different is that they're onstage because they have something to say.

'The other bands are onstage because they want to be musicians. It's as different as chalk and cheese.'

Wilson adopted the band on the spot, and quickly acted to satisfy Curtis' demand for exposure. Shot for Wilson's *Granada Reports* news magazine, this earliest television show performance catches the fresh-faced Curtis in fiery form, his dishevelled robot dancing and daring pink shirt a distinct counter to his bandmates' heads-down anonymity. A smidgeon of atmosphere is layered over the spot, incidentally, via negative images of highway scenes taken from a recent instalment of the *World In Action* news show.

(SINGLE) various artists EP – *A Factory Sample*
7805 Digital
7806 Glass
ORIGINAL RELEASE: 2x7-inch compilation Factory FAC 2 – December 1978
COMMENTS: In August 1978, Roger Eagle, owner of Liverpool's Eric's club, contacted Wilson, in his role as the self-styled guru of the Manchester scene, to discuss a joint venture, a record label that would pinpoint both the best of the two cities' musical output, and highlight their bitterly earned independence from the London scene that still, in the pages of the press and the ears of radio, dominated British rock.

The projected label broke down before its first release was even finalised – indeed, that is why it broke down. Eagle's vision was of a budget-priced LP length compilation, introducing a clutch of bands in the spirit of the legendary record label samplers of years gone by – Island's *You Can All Join In*, CBS's *Fill Your Head With Rock* and so forth. Wilson, on the other hand, imagined a pair of 7-inch singles with grandiose packaging that, in itself, was an event before you even heard the music.

When they realised that they couldn't even agree on this issue, the pair knew they were unlikely to see eye to eye on anything else. Eagle returned to his own Eric's label; Wilson inaugurated Factory, soon to become one of the dominant independents of the age and, even in its infancy, a remarkable venture.

Wilson's gameplan, Hook told *Top Of The Pops* magazine, was simple. 'To make a record you need a record company – that was Factory. You need a record producer, which was Martin Hannett. You need someone heavy-handed to make them all work together. You need a graphic designer – that was Peter Saville – to do the sleeves, and you need a guy who owns the studio – Peter Brierly from Cargo Studios. And then all you need when you got them five is the group! So then Tony went out and got a group. Us.'

With this team in place, Factory debuted in December 1978 with, as Wilson intended, a double 7-inch. A limited edition of 5,000 copies, *A Factory Sample* featured two tracks apiece by Joy Division, Durutti Column and Cabaret Voltaire, and three from John Dowie.

Hannett produced them all. In the 18 months or so since he oversaw his first ever recording sessions (a long-forgotten effort by Albertos' frontman C.P. Lee's Greasy Bear project, followed immediately by the Buzzcocks' rather more epochal *Spiral Scratch* EP), Hannett had established himself as *the* Mancunian producer; indeed, he'd even scored a hit single that summer, behind Jilted John's 'Jilted John.' Now he was to work that same magic on Joy Division – or was he?

Recorded at Cargo Studios, Rochdale, on 11 October 1978, Joy Division's contributions to the *Factory Sample* swing from the metronomic shuffle of 'Digital' to the agitated handclap-along of 'Glass.' But 'Martin didn't give a fuck about making a pop record,' Sumner recalled.' All he wanted to do was experiment. His attitude was that you get a load of drugs, lock the door of the studio and you stay in there all night and you see what you've got the next morning. And you keep doing that until it's done. That's how all our records were made. We were on speed, Martin was into smack.

'Bernard and I were very down to earth,' Hook continued, 'and [Hannett] was, like, from another planet. He was just this really weird hippy who never talked any sense at all. At least, I never knew what he was talking about anyway. Still, you had a rapport with him. He used to say to Rob [Gretton], "Get these two thick stupid cunts out of my way". In the studio, we'd sit on the left, he'd sit on the right and if we said anything like, "I think the guitars are a bit quiet, Martin," he'd scream, "Oh my God! Why don't you just fuck off, you stupid retards." It was alright at first, but gradually he started to get weirder and weirder.'

All four of the acts on the *Sampler* would become Factory staples. But only Joy Division would become a landmark, not only for the label but, as their reputation spread and their sound began filtering into even a limited consciousness, for the post-Punk scene in general. Reflecting on his first ever studio encounter with Joy Division, Hannett himself simply stated, 'it was heaven sent.'

(LIVE) Hope & Anchor, London, 27 December 1978
COMMENTS: With their northern fame now rising, Joy Division played their first London gig two days after Christmas, before a small crowd in the tiny basement of Islington's Hope and Anchor. The music press greeted them with glee – already primed by Paul Morley, the *NME* heralded the group's arrival with a cover story. But the show itself was a let down and the entire affair might have been forgotten were it not for events on the journey home.

Trying to sleep in the back of the band's Transit Van, Sumner suddenly became aware of Curtis tugging at his sleeping bag. He tugged back, and the two began to struggle, with Curtis, all the while, wrapping the sleeping bag around his own head.

Taking his turn at the wheel, Morris pulled the van over to the side of the road, watching with mounting concern as Curtis, still encased in the sleeping bag, began lashing out with his fists, slamming them against the windows with increasing fury and then, just as suddenly, diminishing strength. Finally, as he calmed, Morris restarted the van, and drove to the nearest hospital.

Back home, Curtis' own doctor placed him on a waiting list to see a specialist; meanwhile, the fits continued. One day he returned home from walking the dog, looking as though he had been beaten up. On another occasion, he slipped into a zombie-like silence from which he could not be aroused. Both events were seizures, extremities that matched the wild mood swings that his newly prescribed medication could so easily set off. 'The whole thing about epilepsy,' Peter Hook reflected years later, 'they can treat it so much more easily these days. Back then, it's amazing the guy didn't rattle, he was taking that many pills.'

(LIVE) Middlesbrough Rock Garden – 14 Sept 1977
UNR Leaders Of Men
COMMENTS: Guest-hosting Piccadilly Radio's *Last Radio Programme* on 9 June 1990, Peter Hook aired three Joy Division recordings: 'Heart And Soul' from *Closer*, a live 'Wilderness,' recorded at the Factory in 1979, and this otherwise unknown performance.

1979

(SESSION) *John Peel Show:* recorded 31 Jan 1979; broadcast 14 Feb 1979
7901 Exercise One
7902 Insight
7903 Transmission
7904 She's Lost Control
ORIGINAL RELEASE: EP *The Peel Session 31.1.79*, Strange Fruit SFPS 013 – November 1986
COMMENTS: Destined to become one of Joy Division's most loyal supporters, DJ Peel aired his first session by the band on Valentine's Day, 1979. It is a remarkable sounding offering, as BBC producer Bob Sargeant and engineer Nick Gomm allow the band to strip back completely, layering echo over the vocals and drums, and emerging with a sparse sound that, building on the breakthrough of 'Digital' and 'Glass,' for the first time captures the 'true' sound of Joy Division.

Aired in a month that also saw debut sessions from the Piranhas, Laura Logic, Joe Jackson and the Monochrome Set (plus repeat visits from the Undertones, the Molesters, Prag Vec and the Wasps), Joy Division's performance was broadcast alongside the latest by Generation X, making their third appearance with four astonishingly lackluster new songs. Indeed, no matter how hard Billy Idol and the boys huffed and puffed, simply hearing their efforts… 'Paradise West,' 'Love Like Fire,' 'Night Of The Cadillacs,' 'English Dream'… alongside Joy Division's reinforced nothing so much as how fast, and how dramatically, the entire musical landscape had shifted in the mere 26 months since 'Anarchy In The UK' first ushered Punk into the limelight.

Remembering the group on his 1987 *Peeling Back The Years* retrospective, Peel admitted that he was not immediately receptive to Joy Division. 'The first of the Post Punk bands [all] seemed to be coming out of Manchester, which is something I deeply resented, because I was fiercely partisan in Liverpool's favour, so I resented the fact that the best and the most interesting bands seemed to be coming out of Manchester.'

He never dreamed, therefore, 'that Joy Division were a band I was going to prefer above any others,' but he did acknowledge their presence among 'a whole handful of bands that I was enjoying at the same time. I always think of them in a rather romantic way, as being introspective and rather Russian.... I read somewhere that that kind of introspection was classed Russian, and [listening to them] always makes me feel at least slightly Central European.'

(STUDIO) Eden Studios, London, 4 March 1979 – Genetic Records demos
7905 Insight
7906 Glass
7907 Transmission
7908 Ice Age
UNR Digital
ORIGINAL RELEASE: Box set *Heart and Soul*
Gigging through early 1979, and with Factory still an uncertain prospect, Joy Division found themselves feted by both Radar Records, the newly-established home to Elvis Costello and Nick Lowe; and producer Martin Rushent's Genetic set-up. With the promise of a 40,000 pound advance hanging over their heads, March saw the band in London, cutting four songs with Rushent by way of a demo.

Rushent's track record, as the distinctly commercially-minded producer of Buzzcocks, Generation X, 999 and the Stranglers, might have set off some alarm bells, although the first and last of those bands both had moments in their music that looked vaguely towards where Joy Division were heading – the 'cocks' 'Something's Gone Wrong Again' and 'Why Can't I Touch It,' in particular, both evinced Pete Shelley's own love of the Kraftwerk/Bowie edge that fired Curtis' most immediate musical dreams, and that was the energy that Rushent brought to these sessions.

The end result is a considerably brighter-sounding, but no less compulsive, Joy Division, most apparent on the revised vision of 'Glass,' which sheds its ironic handclaps, but compensates with renewed pace, the guitars chiming with police siren urgency over the clattering percussion. 'Insight,' with its synthetic drum booms, is less satisfying (or, maybe, just too gimmicky), but 'Transmission' would be absolutely electrifying if only Curtis' vocal did not sound so querulous. (As yet unheard on either official or unofficial release, a final mix of 'Digital' does exist, though it was inexplicably left off *Heart And Soul*.)

Ultimately, the session can be termed a success, if only because the band had yet to record anything that surpassed it – that, of course, would happen in a couple of months time, after the band opted to follow manager Rob Gretton's advice, and wait for Tony Wilson's Factory to get off the ground. In the meantime, Peter Hook insists, 'all I remember about Martin Rushent is, he had a big boil on his bum.'

(LIVE) Bowdon Vale Youth Club, Altrincham, 14 March 1979
7909 She's Lost Control
7910 Shadowplay

7911 Leaders Of Men
UNR Insight
UNR Disorder
UNR Glass
UNR Digital
UNR Ice Age
UNR Warsaw
UNR Transmission
UNR I Remember Nothing
UNR No Love Lost
ORIGINAL RELEASE: *Joy Division: Substance* VHS. Entire concert as above on bootleg *Death* (P7)
COMMENTS: This raw, handheld footage of the opening three numbers, shot by Malcolm Whitehead, was included within the 17 minute film premiered as Factory FAC 9 at the Scala Cinema on 13 September 1979.

(ALBUM) *UNKNOWN PLEASURES*
7912 Disorder
7913 Day Of The Lords
7914 Candidate
7915 Insight
7916 New Dawn Fades
7917 She's Lost Control
7918 Shadowplay
7919 Wilderness
7920 InterZone
7921 I Remember Nothing
ORIGINAL RELEASE: Factory FACT 10 – June 1979

UK CHART POSITION: 30 August 1980 – #71 (1 week)
COMMENTS: Recorded at Strawberry Studios, Stockport with Martin Hannett in April 1979, Joy Division's debut album, explained Peter Hook, 'was recorded in three days, mixed in two, and then you were back tending the garden. Joy Division were very prolific as a group, two songs a month was the general thing. We'd practise for three hours, then out of there.'

It seems peculiar now to recall that, though the album was released to a hail of critical astonishment, sales were initially poor. It would be another year-plus before the record actually charted, but if you actually travel back to May 1979, there can be little shock at that. With chilling irony, *Unknown Pleasures* was held up by *Sounds* as the last record you'd play before committing suicide, beneath a headline howling 'Death Disco' – John Lydon's Public Image Ltd would later turn that title into an extraordinarily unlikely hit single, but for now, it was Joy Division's territory alone. *Melody Maker*, meanwhile, compared the album to a tour of Manchester, 'endless sodium lights and semis seen from a speeding car, vacant industrial sites... gaping like teeth from an orange bus.' Yeah, let's see Gary Numan follow *that*.

All, however, were in agreement over one thing: that Joy Division were, quite simply, the most depressing band ever to walk the earth. 'It was very unsettling,' Peter Hook reflected two decades later. 'To go from being nothing, to being lauded as one of the darkest groups known to man, was a trifle confusing.' He never understood, he continued, 'why people thought we were so miserable, because I thought it was quite exciting.'

So did Curtis. Seated with his bandmates, all he would say, in the same soft-spoken monotone he always adopted for interviews, was that things were not always what they seemed. 'Some people have said [our music] is all about death and destruction. But it isn't really. There are other things. None of the songs are about death and doom; it's such a Heavy Metal thing, that.' And Joy Division were anything but heavy metal.

Nevertheless, doom and gloom remained an easy mantle to wrap around Joy Division's shoulders, particularly once one bunkered in with Curtis' lyric, and the almost uncanny coil that the music wrapped around them; it was no surprise at all, then, to see names like Peter Hammill, Richard Strange and (in later critical retrospectives) Nick Drake dropped as potent forebears of Joy Division's art.

Like them, Joy Division were distinctly English romantics who understood the emotional equation that gave them that distinction in the first place; like them, Joy Division's music possessed an innate changeless timelessness; like them, the group operated from a position of absolute isolation. Six years earlier, reviewing Drake's *Pink Moon* swansong, *Zig Zag* magazine remarked, 'The album makes no concession to the theory that music should be escapist. It's simply one musician's view of life at the time, and you can't ask for more than that.' That same observation was echoed time and time again as *Unknown Pleasures* made its presence felt.

'It's funny, isn't it,' mused Peter Hook. 'Americans have this thing where they can sing about what a beautiful day it is. Whereas with the English, it's always a really rotten day.' John Cale, discussing the commercial failure of Nico's *Marble Index* album, once opined, 'it's an artefact. You can't package suicide.' Joy Division, it seemed, suddenly proved that you could. You just needed to be very selective about the kind of wrapping paper you used.

Unknown Pleasures retains its power to shock. In 1995, Wire's Bruce Gilbert was interviewed for *The Wire* magazine's *Invisible Jukebox* feature, where sundry artists are asked to comment on a random selection of songs, without being told who or what they were. 'Wilderness' was included within Gilbert's sequence and his first question was 'is this new?' Of Joy Division themselves, however, he was in little doubt as to their import. 'Ian Curtis was clearly a poet with his sights set on a higher plane... of activity within music, but using music as a commercial avenue to do what he wanted to do. Inescapably the album was significant. This is music done with intent. This is not messing around, this is not fun.'

A lot of that effect, it transpired, was Hannett's doing. 'We played the album live,' Sumner reported, 'loud and heavy.... We felt that Martin toned it down, especially with the guitars. The production inflicted this dark, doomy mood over the album; we'd drawn this picture in black-and-white, and Martin had coloured it in for us. We resented it, but Rob loved it, Wilson loved it and the press loved it, and the public loved it; we were just the poor, stupid musicians who wrote it.'

The sleeve – as distinctive an icon of its age as the prisms bedecking Pink Floyd's *Dark Side Of The Moon* are of theirs' – was designed by Peter Saville, igniting a relationship that would persist for the next quarter-century, ensuring his work has become as instantly recognisable as the music it accompanied. From the script on the label to the classically inspired typefaces and motifs which hung, often in absolute isolation, on the cover, Saville created an iconographical panoply that remains one of the most splendid, and most slavishly imitated of the last 25 years.

(ALBUM) various artists – *EARCOM 2*
7922 Autosuggestion
7923 From Safety To Where...?

ORIGINAL RELEASE: Various artists compilation (Fast Products 9B – Oct 1979)

COMMENTS: Additional material recorded during the Strawberry Studios sessions in April 1979 was gifted to the second in the Fast label's series of avant-rock showcases – an admirable idea, regardless of the quality of much of the music therein. In terms of both name recognition and musical execution, Joy Division stand head and shoulders above the other acts featured on *Earcom 2* – Middlesbrough's Basczax ('Karleearn Photography' and 'Celluloid Love') and the Thursdays ('Dock of the Bay' and 'Perfection'); that said, however, neither of their contributions could be accused of over-working the band's reputation.

The extraordinarily over-long 'Autosuggestion' is little more than a drum pattern, over which Curtis croons, and ghostly guitars scrape and keen; it has a certain atmospheric quality, mantric to a point, but even the band seem to tire of it after five minutes or so, picking up the pace for one final run through the circuit, and then dribbling out on a dying drumbeat.

'From Safety To Where...?' is similarly sparse, a brief (under two-and-one-half minutes) sketch that sounds more like a band *trying* to be Joy Division, than Joy Division themselves. Already, it seems, the group had created its own cliché. Thankfully, they had also already proved themselves capable of eclipsing it.

(STUDIO) outtakes
7924 Exercise One
7925 The Kill
7926 Ice Age

7927 The Only Mistake

7928 Walked In Line

ORIGINAL RELEASE: 7924-27 on compilation *Still*; 7928 on box set *Heart And Soul*.

COMMENTS: Still more *Unknown Pleasures* outtakes, sprinkled with an unspecified amount of 'post-production' prior to their eventual release.

The inclusion of these five tracks on *Still* has ensured they stand as proud amid the Joy Division canon as any of the music released during the band's own lifetime. For many people, after all, that package was the first Joy Division album they ever bought, while a version of 'Exercise One' was granted the additional fillip of opening the group's first ever John Peel session.

'Exercise One' is, in fact, the strongest track here, as one of the group's most satisfyingly threatening rhythms reaches a level of intensity that makes a nonsense of its omission from *Unknown Pleasures* itself. The thrashing live favourite 'Ice Age,' too, draws new strength and power from the studio set-up, with only Curtis' less-than-convincing vocal, and a somewhat pedestrian drum pattern spoiling the party. Hook and Sumner, on the other hand, combine for a fabulous backdrop, as urgent and electrifying as any other. 'The Only Mistake,' too, impresses, a piece of deliberately-building menace with Curtis' vocal so deeply buried within the mix that it is of no more prominence (and no less dynamism) than the guitars that scratch flesh around it.

The reappearance of 'Walked In Line' (dating back at least to the RCA demos if not earlier), is entertaining, although scarcely informative – this *uber*-monotonous track, in particular, is absolutely out-of-place in the hands of Joy Division *c*1979, perhaps explaining why it would be almost 20 years before the performance finally saw an official release (on *Heart And Soul*), though a remixed version was released on *Still* in 1981.

(SESSION) Piccadilly Radio, 4 June 1979

7929 These Days

7930 Candidate

7931 The Only Mistake

7932 Chance (Atmosphere)

UNR Atrocity Exhibition

ORIGINAL RELEASE: Box set *Heart And Soul*; 'Atrocity Exhibition' on bootleg *Atmosphere* (Atmos 104)

COMMENTS: The absence of the Piccadilly Radio take on 'Atrocity Exhibition' from *Heart And Soul* deprives listeners of experiencing one of the finest-ever performances of the song, climaxing one of Joy Division's own greatest broadcast sessions.

With the band opting to eschew a simple recounting of the album's greatest bits, in favour of a clutch of new songs and old heroes (*Unknown Pleasures* is represented by 'Candidate' alone), there is an abandoned electricity to the broadcast that even *Unknown Pleasures* cannot match; while Piccadilly producer Stuart James sensibly flinches from trying to recreate Martin Hannett's trademark sound, in favour of a wide open approach that is all the more effective for the claustrophobia that remains at its heart.

The album out-take 'The Only Mistake' is rough and impassioned, 'These Days' sharp and punky. And, while it is true that the heavy echo that drapes Curtis' vocal on the surprisingly brief 'Candidate' could have been applied a little more carefully, you would need to search long and hard to find a more potent version of the newly-composed 'Atmosphere,' broadcast under its original title of 'Chance,' and, with the keyboard doing its best to ape a viola, bleeding the group's love of the Velvet Underground from every pore.

(LIVE) The Factory, Hulme, 13 July 1979
7933 Dead Souls
7934 The Only Mistake
7935 Insight
7936 Candidate
7937 Wilderness
7938 She's Lost Control
UNR Shadowplay
7939 Disorder
7940 Interzone
7941 Atrocity Exhibition
7942 Novelty
7943 Transmission

ORIGINAL RELEASE: Box set *Heart And Soul*; 7943 on the *Atmosphere* single FACD 213 – June 1988

COMMENTS: The earliest concert to have been officially released in its entirety, the Factory show is a stark reminder of just how different a beast the live Joy Division was, when compared to its studio counterpart. At a time when idols Kraftwerk were taking live music to its iciest limit yet, Joy Division remained in thrall to the crash and clatter of their instrumentation, a roughshod roar that did not lose, but certainly camouflaged the stark simplicity of the recorded sound.

Speed, not space, was the essence of the live Joy Division sound, as the band sensibly realised that it was excitement, not introspection that the majority of gig-goers wanted at that time. Popular history likes to imagine Joy Division concerts as events of near-religious intensity; in fact, the group's live following was among the most raucous and dance-hungry of the age, and the live set reflected those needs, with thundering drums, whooping guitars, and a tempo that wouldn't have looked out of place at Brand's Hatch.

Occasional tracks – the ever-stately 'Insight' and 'She's Lost Control' paramount among them – cannot be distracted from their purpose. But 'Atrocity Exhibition' and an almost panic-stricken 'Interzone' seem to race past at twice their familiar pace, remembering the Punk band that Joy Division used to be, rather than the monumental icon they were set to become. So *should* 'Novelty,' introduced by Curtis as 'a very old song… some of you might remember it'; in fact, it emerges one of the highlights of the recording – and is that a premonition of 'Love Will Tear Us

Apart,' dancing around the guitar pattern? Probably not, but hindsight can play tricks on the ears regardless.

The sound quality here is not the best, although it is certainly an improvement on a lot of the similar-era tapes out there. The hint of distortion around the vocals readily translates to an edge of desperation, and the stereo mix crudely approximates the stage set-up itself. Turn it up, close your eyes… and you can almost sense the Massed Hordes of Pogo bearing down behind you.

(STUDIO) Central Sound, Manchester, July 1979
7944 Dead Souls
7945 Something Must Break version 1/count-in intro
7946 Something Must Break version 2
UNR Transmission
UNR Novelty
ORIGINAL RELEASE: Box set *Heart And Soul*; Transmission and Novelty on bootleg *Atmosphere* (Atmos 104)
COMMENTS: The group's first attempt to record a new 45 saw them return, once again, to the RCA demos, to draw out 'Transmission' and 'Novelty' as the cuts-most-likely-to-cut it. The session as a whole, however, appears to catch the group on an off-day. Neither track packs more than a modicum of kick, with 'Transmission's 'dance to the radio' refrain sounding positively anaemic. 'Novelty' is a little more lifelike, but only a little (the vocal is hopeless); and, with 'Dead Souls' similarly failing to get off the ground, the band scrapped the entire exercise and booked themselves into Strawberry Studios instead, to have another go.

The inclusion here of 'Something Must Break' version 2 is tentative – assigned to the Central Sound sessions within the *Heart And Soul* liners, it has also been dated to the Strawberry Studios sessions a few days later (below). The count-in was (correctly) edited out when mastering *Still*).

(SINGLE) Transmission
7947 Transmission
7948 Novelty
ORIGINAL RELEASE: Factory FAC 13, Nov 1979
COMMENTS: Recorded at Strawberry Studios, July/August 1979, and a vast improvement on the Central Sound effort. 'Transmission' is especially dynamic – written, one assumes, around the premise that British radio cannot resist any song that mentions radio (no matter how damning that mention might be – Elvis Costello's 'Radio Radio' is a case in point), the song simultaneously throbs and thrusts around a magically dislocated vocal, while Curtis sounds as though he, himself, is singing through the ether, shedding the shadows only when it comes to the song's maddeningly infectious refrain.

Martin Hannett's production, meanwhile, pulls out all the sonic stops – this is the *biggest* sounding Joy Division record yet, and its failure to do more than gnaw the wasteland just below the Top 75 remains one of those mystifying quirks with which

British chart history abounds.

Finally, legend insists that Joy Division were remixing 'Transmission' for release on the same night that Manchester's Victorian sewer system collapsed, drenching the city in a stench that dated back 100 years. As *The Face* put it, 'To hear Joy Division then was to feel something of the agony of the times.'

(SESSION) Granada TV *What's On* (broadcast July 20, 1979)
UNR She's Lost Control
COMMENTS: Often confused with the version of the same number performed for the BBC cameras two months later, this appearance has never resurfaced on either an official or unofficial release.

(LIVE) Prince Of Wales YMCA, London, 2 August 1979
UNR Dead Souls
UNR Disorder
UNR Wilderness
7949 Autosuggestion
UNR Transmission
UNR Day Of The Lords
UNR She's Lost Control
UNR Shadowplay
UNR Atrocity Exhibition
UNR Insight
ORIGINAL RELEASE: Box set *Heart And Soul*; Entire concert as above on bootleg *Shadowplay* (TAKRL 1404)
COMMENTS: Was that really Echo and the Bunnymen who opened? Or three other nervous Liverpudlians with a temperamental drum machine and a clutch of songs that really weren't that distinguishable from one another? Turned out the band was still to play its twelfth gig at the time, and they sounded a lot better on *John Peel* a fortnight later. So maybe this was just an off-night.

Joy Division, on the other hand, were a revelation, setting up shop with a mesmeric 'Dead Souls,' then going hell-for-leather through a set that was designed for maximum impact. The one cut culled from this show for an official release, 'Autosuggestion,' itself suggests a considerably tamer evening than reality recalls; and a considerably quieter crowd. On the night, it was difficult to tell who was louder, the band or their followers, a dilemma that also marked out the group's next major London show, at the Electric Ballroom on 31 August.

Scritti Politti, the Monochrome Set and A Certain Ratio were gifted the unenviable task of warming up the audience and, with the arguable exception of the latter, it was apparent that none of them especially warmed to the task. The biggest crowd Joy Division had ever appeared before – in excess of 1,200 – was restless throughout all three sets, reserving its energies for the headliners' eventual appearance; an honour that the band repaid with a similarly energetic performance. Several bootlegs of this performance exist, although few boast anything beyond a muddy blurge of noise in lieu of fidelity.

(SESSION) BBC2 TV *Something Else*; recorded 1 September 1979, broadcast 15 September 1979
7950 Transmission
7951 She's Lost Control
ORIGINAL RELEASE: VHS *Substance;* CD *The Complete BBC Recordings*
COMMENTS: Curtis adapted to his illness, just as Joy Division adapted to their reputation of harbingers of a doominess darker than death itself, subconsciously, but nevertheless effectively, incorporating his seizures (or at least, their appearance) into his stage act. 'During the set's many "peaks",' *Sounds* journalist Mick Middles wrote, 'Curtis often loses control. He'll suddenly jerk sideways and, head in hands, he'll transform into a twitching, epileptic-type mass of flesh and bone.' And just as suddenly, he would recover again. It was an unsettling display, all the more so since his comrades were never certain exactly what was going on. Was he simply dancing? Or was this the real thing?

Nobody could be sure. When Joy Division appeared on *Something Else*, the BBC switchboard was swamped by viewers complaining about Curtis' appearance, with opinion divided over what they were offended by – the fact that he looked so stoned? (He wasn't.) Or his tasteless impersonation of an epileptic fit? But, even as the band tried to keep Curtis' condition to themselves, the singer's onstage behaviour continued to attract attention. Years later, Bernard Sumner detailed one evening when some fans approached Curtis with one simple question: 'are you the singer that has fits?' 'I felt like fucking killing them,' he admitted.

(SESSION) Radio 1, *Rock On*, September 1979
UNR Interzone
UNR Shadowplay
COMMENTS: While the session remains strangely unavailable, though some sources believe these were the album versions, an accompanying interview, between host Richard Skinner, Ian Curtis and Stephen Morris, was included on the *Complete BBC Recordings* album.

Topics include the 'isolation' of Manchester ('it has been quite a good thing because... we're apart from everything, we've got to develop in our own particular way in our own environment'); the lack of visiting A&R men ('I don't think they can afford the train fare'); ambition ('when you first start, everybody wants to be the next Beatles'); and the newly ascendant Gary Numan's recent insistence that 'Machine Rock' was going to be the next big thing. 'With all due respect to Gary Numan, I don't agree with classifying anything. What we do is what we do.'

(LIVE) Futurama Festival, Leeds, 8 September 1979
UNR I Remember Nothing
UNR Wilderness
UNR Transmission
UNR Colony
UNR Disorder
UNR Insight

UNR Shadowplay
UNR She's Lost Control
UNR Atrocity Exhibition
UNR Dead Souls

COMMENTS: Joy Division cemented their status at the forefront of the post-Punk underground with headline appearances at two festivals in late summer 1979. First, on 27 August, the northern twin towers of Factory and Liverpool's Zoo Records pooled the cream of their individual rosters for the Leigh Festival, a gathering of the black raincoated clans that featured Joy Division, Echo and the Bunnymen, The Teardrop Explodes, Orchestral Manoeuvres In The Dark, A Certain Ratio, the Distractions and Elti Fits, and was intended – of course and as usual – to spotlight the north-western corridor's independence from the London industry.

Two weekends later, Joy Division co-headlined the Futurama Festival at Leeds' 5,500-capacity Queen's Hall and, there, the brief was somewhat less parochial. The brainchild of local promoter and F Club owner John Keenan, Futurama was custom-designed as the first national event to specifically acknowledge the widening schism in the Punk/New Wave consciousness, the fact that a vast aesthetic difference had developed within the musical culture, and a massive audience wanted to hear all it had to offer.

Setting the pattern for four future events, Futurama was spread over two days, 8th/9th September 1979. Joy Division closed the first night, space rock veterans Hawkwind, enjoying a new lease of life as parents of a neo-psychedelic strand of anarcho-Punkoid offspring, headlined the second. Lurking elsewhere on the billing were Cabaret Voltaire, the Expelaires (featuring future Sisters Of Mercy/Mission bassist Craig Adams, and Red Lorry Yellow Lorry's Dave Wolfenden), the Fall, Orchestral Manoeuvres In The Dark and Public Image Ltd, playing only their fifth ever live show.

Reorganising the Leigh Festival set ('Leaders Of Men' and 'Interzone' were both dropped for Futurama, to be replaced by 'I Remember Nothing,' 'Wilderness' and 'Atrocity Exhibition'), Joy Division triumphed over them all. And then the following night, they were back down the pub.... (As New Order, the musicians would return to the fourth and final Futurama in 1982.)

(SINGLE) *Licht Und Blindheit*
7952 Atmosphere
7953 Dead Souls
UNR Ice Age

ORIGINAL RELEASE: Sordide Sentimental 33002 – March 1980

COMMENTS: It was Genesis P Orridge who suggested Joy Division cut a single for release on the French Sordide Sentimental label, and the unique arrangement of their 'deal' with Factory enabled them to do so. Any other label, as Hook pointed out years later, would have barricaded the group behind red tape, and refused to even consider their moonlighting for a 'rival' concern. Factory welcomed the opportunity to allow the group to spread its wings further.

Recorded at Cargo Studios, Rochdale, Oct-Nov 1979, 'Atmosphere' is up there alongside 'Transmission' as the greatest Joy Division 45 of them all – although a less 45-like song could scarcely be conceived. Shedding the overt Velvetisms of its Piccadilly Radio airing, the song emerges now as a modern hymn, the stately church-like keyboards and Curtis' evangelical vocal merging to majestic effect. A couple of years on, the Cure would forge an entire album, *Faith*, around many of the same motifs and moods that created 'Atmosphere,' and emerged with an album of equal incredible beauty. The difference was, the Cure needed an entire album to make the point. Joy Division achieved it with one song. 'That was the best track that Martin ever mixed,' Sumner enthused later. 'I thought it was beautiful.'

'Dead Souls,' too, has a drama that Joy Division had never previously approached; that outstrips the live and (unreleased) studio versions that preceded it, and indicates just how quickly band and producer (Hannett, of course) were moving forward.

The single was issued in March in a limited edition of 1,578 copies, packaged within a three-page colour gatefold sleeve, with a panegyric text written by Jean-Pierre Turmel, a painting by Jean-Francois Jamoul and a photograph by Anton Corbijn. The limited nature of the single itself was great for future collectors. In terms of actually *needing* to be heard, however, 'Atmosphere' did the band a shocking disservice.

(LIVE) Plan K, Brussels, Belgium, 16 October 1979
ORIGINAL RELEASE: Slow motion, silent footage from this show appears within the *Here Are The Young Men* video.
COMMENTS: Joy Division's first ever European concert, the opening night of a new art centre in the Belgian capital, was also the night when Curtis met Annick Honore, the woman for whom he would soon be leaving his wife of four years, Deborah, and six-month-old daughter Natalie.

(LIVE) Manchester Apollo, 27 October 1979
7955 Dead Souls
7956 Love Will Tear Us Apart
7957 Shadowplay
7958 She's Lost Control
7959 Wilderness
ORIGINAL RELEASE: VHS release *Here Are The Young Men* (Factory FACT 37) includes 1-4; 'Wilderness' (performed immediately following 'Dead Souls' on the night) available on the promotional *Substance* VHS.

(LIVE) Manchester Apollo, 28 October 1979
7960 Day Of The Lords
7961 Transmission
7962 Sound Of Music
7963 Walked In Line
7964 I Remember Nothing
ORIGINAL RELEASE: VHS release *Here Are The Young Men* (Factory FACT 37)

COMMENTS: October saw the launch of perhaps the most eagerly awaited tour of the autumn season, as the Buzzcocks set out in support of their newly released third album, *A Different Kind Of Tension*, and took Joy Division along for the ride.

It was, of course, a colossal mismatch. Although the headliners had certainly progressed from the purebred power-pop of their earliest strivings, still their audience flocked to the theatres in search of the string of peerless hits with which the Buzzcocks had assaulted the charts of the past 18 months. Joy Division, on the other hand, remained an unknown quantity outside of the immediate environs of their cultish following – and their live sound was *never* going to live up to the promises that the music press habitually made on their behalf.

And so it proved. Beyond the hardcore faithful who flocked to each show, audience reaction to the opening act tended towards the dismissive; it was only, again, in the pages of the music press that Joy Division truly 'blew the Buzzcocks offstage,' although it must be confessed that the Buzzcocks turned in their own fair share of dodgy showings as the tour progressed.

Bootleg recordings exist of every night on the tour, the sound quality varying considerably of course. The best hail from the two Manchester Apollo shows, utilizing the soundtrack to footage shot by Buzzcocks manager Richard Boon (on half-inch videotape), and highlighted by what now stands as the earliest officially released rendering of 'Love Will Tear Us Apart.'

(LIVE) Bournemouth Winter Gardens, 2 November 1979
7965 I Remember Nothing
UNR Love Will Tear Us Apart
UNR Wilderness
7966 Colony
UNR Insight
7967 These Days
UNR Digital
UNR Transmission
UNR Atrocity Exhibition

ORIGINAL RELEASE: Box set *Heart and Soul*; Entire concert (as above) released on bootleg *Bournemouth* (TAKRL 1405)

COMMENTS: From all accounts, this was one of the finest Joy Division performances of the entire Buzzcocks tour, a status confirmed by the *Bournemouth* bootleg, and then given wider credence by the inclusion of three tracks from the show on *Heart And Soul*. A very crunchy sound quality literally shoves the band into your face, with 'Colony' emerging especially raw.

(SESSION) *John Peel Show*: recorded 26 Nov 1979; broadcast 10 Dec 1979
7968 Sound Of Music
7969 Twenty-Four Hours
7970 Love Will Tear Us Apart
7971 Colony

ORIGINAL RELEASE: EP *The Peel Session 26.11.79,* Strange Fruit SFPS 033

– November 1987

COMMENTS: Joy Division's second Peel session highlighted a month otherwise dominated by the first ever broadcast by Public Image Ltd (December 17); the band's four songs were aired alongside a session by Lene Lovich, making her own second appearance on the show.

With their thoughts now firmly focused on their already-gestating second album, Joy Division premiered four relatively new songs at the session – all had featured in the band's live set throughout the Buzzcocks tour, although this was their first ever airing in the studio. As such, the four sound somewhat weaker (and, certainly, more tentative) than they would eventually become, although even this early in its lifespan, 'Love Will Tear Us Apart' has 'future classic' stamped all over it, the signature keyboard line and so-buoyant rhythm utterly dismissing Joy Division's reputation as a bunch of moody buggers. No-one, at this time, could even have began to imagine just how much emotional baggage would be affixed to the song before the next year was out.

(LIVE) Les Bains Douches, Paris, 18 December 1979
UNR Passover
UNR Wilderness
7972 Disorder
7973 Love Will Tear Us Apart
7974 Insight
7975 Shadowplay
7976 Transmission
7977 Day Of The Lords
7978 Twenty-Four Hours
UNR Colony
7979 These Days
7980 A Means To An End
UNR She's Lost Control
UNR Atrocity Exhibition
UNR Interzone
UNR Warsaw

ORIGINAL RELEASE: *Les Bains Douches, Paris, 18 December 1979* (NMC FACD2.61) – 2001; entire show (as above) on bootleg *Live In Paris* (JD 1984).

COMMENTS: A live French radio broadcast captured nine songs from what was, by now, a fairly characteristic Joy Division set, as *Unknown Pleasures* continued its slide out of the group's affections, to be replaced by the material that would comprise *Closer*.

Announcing plans for the recording's first official release in 2001, Tony Wilson explained, 'We are doing *Les Bains Douches* if we find a good version of the gig; always seems to be some strange French woman who has a good copy but no-one can find her.' He also spoke of an accompanying CD-Rom, packaged in a limited edition (2,000 copies) tin. 'The CD-Rom is more of a CD-plus.. who knows, but there are visuals to go on it from the gig.' It was also supposed to include a short film called *Exercise One*.

Both on bootleg and the official release, the sound quality does not deny the recording's origin as a radio broadcast – clear and clean, it nevertheless suffers from a certain compression, a squashiness, in fact, that ensures that *Les Bains Douches, Paris, 18 December 1979* is unlikely to be the listener's first choice when it comes to deciding which Joy Division live album to listen to next.

'My only memory [of this night] is of a grand, red-carpeted staircase,' wrote Tony Wilson in the CD liner notes. 'It was some swank Parisienne nightclub where the boys hopped off to after searing the Bain Douche. And wasn't some shit English band on that night at this swank club? Was that [the] night one of our lot pissed on Spandau Ballet from the balcony?'

1980

(LIVE) Paradiso, Amsterdam, 11 Jan 1980
8001 Passover
UNR Wilderness
UNR Digital
UNR Day Of The Lords
UNR Insight
8002 New Dawn Fades
UNR Disorder
UNR Transmission
UNR Love Will Tear Us Apart
UNR These Days
UNR A Means To An End
UNR Twenty-Four Hours
UNR Shadowplay
UNR She's Lost Control
8003 Atrocity Exhibition
UNR Atmosphere
UNR Interzone

ORIGINAL RELEASE: *Les Bains Douches, Paris, 18 December 1979* (NMC FACD2.61); entire concert on bootleg *Amsterdam* (Factory PRO 1) and on *Live In Amsterdam* (Rarities & Few RMCD1112).

COMMENTS: 'Welcome to the atrocity exhibition' – with those words, Ian Curtis kicks off one of the finest of all Joy Division bootlegs, 1981's *Amsterdam*, a set greeted by the *LA Reader* as 'staggering... a good antidote to [the then newly released] *Movement*... it shows how rugged and moving Joy Division could be on a good night.'

Originally recorded for a Dutch VARA radio broadcast, the tapes suffer from a slightly thin sound quality, but – as the *Reader* continued – '*Still*'s version of "Sister Ray" is delectable, but I'd trade all of that record's live tracks for the version of "Love Will Tear Us Apart" on *Amsterdam*. That song, and much of the rest of the bootleg, goes a long way toward proving how awesome and how frightening inspired rock music can be.'

(LIVE) Effenaar, Eindhoven, Netherlands, 18 January 1980
8004 Digital
8005 Colony
8006 New Dawn Fades
8007 Autosuggestion
8008 Dead Souls
UNR Love Will Tear Us Apart
UNR These Days
UNR Ice Age
UNR Disorder
UNR Day Of The Lords
UNR Shadowplay
8009 Atmosphere
UNR Warsaw
ORIGINAL RELEASE: 8004-07 on VHS release *Here Are The Young Men* (Factory FACT 37); 8008-09 on *Les Bains Douches, Paris, 18 December 1979* (NMC FACD2.61); entire concert (as above) released on the bootleg *A Christmas Of Joy Division* (Santa Claus 002) and Concert 18 Jan Effenaar (Hawkeye 008)
COMMENTS: The video footage is excellent, and the bootleg's a lot of fun as well, a two-pronged assault that makes you truly appreciate just what a great gig this must have been. An all-time best live rendering of 'New Dawn Fades' draws out one of Curtis' most impassioned vocals.

(LIVE) Warehouse, Preston, 28 February 1980
8010 Incubation
8011 Wilderness
8012 Twenty-Four Hours
8013 The Eternal
8014 Heart And Soul
8015 Shadowplay
8016 Transmission
8017 Disorder
8018 Warsaw
8019 Colony
8020 Interzone
8021 She's Lost Control
ORIGINAL RELEASE: *The Fractured Music Archive Volume One: Preston 28 February 1980* (New Millennium FACD 2.60) 1999
COMMENTS: Of all the Joy Division live shows to have been released officially, Preston is one of the strangest – not through the quality of sound or performance, both of which are fair enough, but for the equipment meltdown that transformed, briefly, the concert into chaos. They got away with the mounting problems for the first three songs but, as 'The Eternal' wound down, Curtis had to admit, 'I'd like to apologise for everything.' And so the band 'play around for a little while' while the repairs are carried out, and 'Heart And Soul' finally kicks off,

beauty in the face of absolute adversity.

'This is not a memento, this is a gig,' warn the liner notes. 'This is not a souvenir or shifty "not the best of." This is a gig. This is not bootleg chic, this is just a gig.' And later, apparently from one of the horses' mouths, 'Equipment malfunction. Mostly no function. Preston... worse [expletive] gig we ever did. Complete breakdown of bloody everything. A shambles.'

(LIVE) Lyceum, London, 29 February 1980
8022 Incubation
8023 Wilderness
8024 24 Hours
8025 The Eternal
8026 Heart And Soul
8027 Love Will Tear Us Apart
8028 Isolation
8029 Komakino
8030 She's Lost Control
8031 These Days
8032 Atrocity Exhibition
ORIGINAL RELEASE: *No More Ceremonies*: Italy, Primo Records WK 46 – 2004

∞ No More Ceremonies ∞

COMMENTS: Prior to sundry bands' recent obsession with self-bootlegging entire tours, then releasing discs of each night to the slavering fanatics, there can be few periods in the life of any comparatively unknown group that have been so exhaustively documented as Joy Division at the end of 1979/beginning of 1980. Even Bruce Springsteen had to sell a few million albums before the tapers started out-numbering the dancers, but one of the most potent memories of a Joy Division gig at this time involves the serried ranks of silent young men who jostled for the best position at the back of the hall, and loudly hushed anyone who dared even glance in the direction of the microphone pinned to the lapel.

The tapers were rarely disappointed. New songs were entering the set at a considerable rate, while the group's own policy of altering the set list on a nightly basis meant you could catch them five or six nights running, and rarely hear the same songs more than thrice. Still, the scattershot release policy engendered by this stockpile does grow wearisome after a while, and one longs for the day when someone sits down and compiles the ultimate 'here's one of every song' live anthology. Or 'one of every gig.'

Between the end of the Buzzcocks tour, at London on 10 November, and the beginning of the *Closer* recording sessions in March, the group played 20 shows, 11 on the continent and the remainder around the UK, leading up to this triumphal headliner at the London Lyceum. With the release of *No More Ceremonies* in April 2004, bringing an at least quasi-legal face to a performance that has existed on bootleg for almost quarter-of-a-century, fully one-quarter of those shows were now at least partially represented on CD and, while supporters could argue that each caught the group as it pursued the transition between studio LPs, cynics could ask precisely how much catching the band now required?

There could, after all, be few fans who truly welcomed another go-round for the same old songs, especially as the sound quality didn't even try to improve on the original murky boots. One for collectors and the avid have-it-alls, but the view from halfway back in the auditorium, with a couple of noisy neighbours having a natter throughout, isn't really worth the bother.

Except for one moment. 'The Eternal' serves up one of Curtis' most haunted observations, of the mongol child that grew up down the road from him in Macclesfield. Some 15 years later, Curtis saw him again – 'Ian had grown from five to 22,' explained Sumner. 'But the kid looked the same.'

(STUDIO) Pennine Sound Studios, Oldham, January 1980
8033 Sound Of Music
8034 These Days
8035 Love Will Tear Us Apart (version one)
ORIGINAL RELEASE: 8033 on compilation *Still*; 8034 on Fac 23; 8035 on FAC 2312 – not only on 12" but also on original UK 7" FAC 23 which had three tracks.

(STUDIO) Strawberry Studios, March 1980
8036 Love Will Tear Us Apart (version two)
8037 She's Lost Control (12-inch version)
ORIGINAL RELEASE: 8036 on Factory FAC 23; 8037 on FACUS 2

(SINGLE) Love Will Tear Us Apart
8036 Love Will Tear Us Apart (version two)
8034 These Days
8035 Love Will Tear Us Apart (version one)
ORIGINAL RELEASE: FAC 23: 28 June 1980 – #13 (9 weeks); reissue 29 October 1983 – #19 (7 weeks)
COMMENTS: There was never any doubt that 'Love Will Tear Us Apart' would be the group's next single; the only question was, were they able to do the song justice? The first attempt, at Pennine Sound, certainly didn't come up to scratch; just as they had with 'Transmission,' the band was forced to relocate to Strawberry before they finally hit on the sound they wanted. The Pennine take would be held back for a bonus track on the eventual (posthumous) 12-inch single, where it joined the 7-inch b-side, 'These Days'; the excellent five minute recut of 'She's Lost Control' that was recorded alongside the Strawberry 'Love Will Tear

Us Apart,' meanwhile, appeared on the back of the next Joy Division single, a reissue of 'Atmosphere.'

For better or worse, 'Love Will Tear Us Apart' is frequently described as the quintessential Joy Division song, although listened to dispassionately, and with no reflection on the tangled skeins of Curtis' own private life, it is difficult to understand what all the fuss is about. Frequently overlooked, after all, is the humourous subtext of the lyric, as Curtis purposefully set about writing a scathing rebuttal of the Captain & Tenille's 'Love Will Keep Us Together.'

His own personal dilemmas might indeed have been reflected in the song's examination of a crumbling relationship, as he and wife Deborah parted after five years, and Curtis pledged his heart, instead, to new love Annik Honore. But the jaunty keyboard line that travels behind the melody is as sweet as cheesecake; and, though the title would soon become Curtis' epitaph, the song stands as his most lasting legacy .

(SESSION) Love Will Tear Us Apart (promo video)
8036a Love Will Tear Us Apart
ORIGINAL RELEASE: *Here Are The Young Men*
COMMENTS: A video, the group's first, was shot for the single on 28 April 1980. 'It was meant to be very professionally made,' Sumner recalled. 'Unfortunately, the sound guy didn't turn up, so we had a silent video. A pop video without the pop. They had to graft the record on in the end, which is why you see some rather nasty editing.' A smattering of post-production overdubbing adds some distinctive variations to the familiar version of the song.

(ALBUM) *CLOSER*
8038 Atrocity Exhibition
8039 Isolation
8040 Passover
8041 Colony
8042 A Means To An End
8043 Heart And Soul
8044 Twenty-Four Hours
8045 The Eternal
8046 Decades
ORIGINAL RELEASE: Factory FACT 25 – July 1980

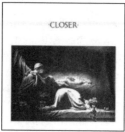

UK CHART POSITION: 26 July 1980 – #6 (8 weeks)

COMMENTS: 'Most bands don't make a great second album; usually most bands make a shite second album, but Joy Division actually made a great second LP,' breezed Peter Hook.

Recorded at Britannia Row Studios, London, March 1980, but unreleased until July, a respectful six weeks after Curtis' death, *Closer* caught Joy Division in high spirits.

'We were very happy,' affirmed Hook. 'Apart from Ian's illness, of course. We were going up in popularity, the songwriting was going up, we were having fun!' – and then he paused as though aware that he had uttered some dreadful blasphemy. 'It's like people used to say to us when they'd meet us, "oh God, Joy Division are so serious, yet you're all here having a game of football, and drinking beer and shouting after girls, you shouldn't be like that, you should be...." But when you're alone, you *can* be like that, you're completely different to how you are in the group. When you're in the group you were very serious.

'The music had that effect, it brought out the professionalism and the seriousness, but when you come out of the group, it's like coming out of school. We'd go bananas, and I could never understand why people didn't understand that aspect of it.'

Producer Hannett himself ranked *Closer* among his all-time finest creations. 'Professionally speaking Magazine's *The Correct Use of Soap* was the best. [But] *Closer* [was] the most mysterious. That album was made as closed as possible, kabalistic, locked in its own mysterious world....'

One non-musical memory sticks out from the sessions. Hook says, 'I can remember U2 coming to the studio when we were doing *Closer*. U2 were the best copyists. They were very Joy Division-esque, they were desperate to meet Joy Division, they'd got Martin Hannett in to do their next record, and they came to see us. And God, they were just like little kids. I was only 22, so they were like 16. And you dismiss them, you forget about people, and all of a sudden they're the biggest group in the world and suddenly – "fucking hell, maybe I should have been nice to them".' (U2 featured a version of 'Love Will Tear Us Apart' in their early live set, the first of the now myriad acts to have thrown their own talents at the song.)

One final thought – what exactly is the correct pronunciation of that title? Is it 'closer,' as in come nearer? Or 'closer,' as in – the end?

(SINGLE) Komakino
8047 Komakino
8048 Incubation
8049 As You Said
ORIGINAL RELEASE: Factory flexidisc – FAC 28 – April 1980
COMMENTS: Three outtakes from the *Closer* album sessions appeared as a limited edition (10,000 copies) flexidisc just ahead of the LP's own release, and quickly ascended to collector/anorak legend. 'Komakino' itself merits all of the attention it has received – the opening line alone, 'this is the hour when the mysteries emerge,' is among Curtis' most potent, even if the track itself seems otherwise unfinished.

The two instrumentals that follow ('As You Said' is untitled on the original disc, hence some confusion over its title) are electrifying too, the first a wired wasp attack that simply never relents, the second a mesmeric drum beat, around which cascade waves of sounds and splinters – including a keyboard overture that certainly gave the Human League something to think about.

(LIVE) Moonlight Club, West Hampstead, London, 2 April 1980
8050 Sister Ray
UNR Dead Souls
UNR Sound Of Music
UNR Wilderness
UNR Colony
UNR Love Will Tear Us Apart
UNR A Means To An End
UNR Transmission

ORIGINAL RELEASE: Compilation *Still*. Remainder on bootleg *Atrocity Exhibition* (FACT 600)

COMMENTS: Savagely mesmeric, the most easily-available rendering of the Velvets classic was recorded at the first of three successive nights at the Moonlight Club, the launch of their latest UK tour and a residency that history now marks out as the beginning of the end of Joy Division.

By the spring of 1980, it was as if the entire nation was awaiting their second album, *Closer*, and, with it, a new single, 'Love Will Tear Us Apart.' The group's first American tour was imminent, and a European one after that. Had Joy Division only wanted to, they could have started filling up their diaries well into the next year.

To friends and family, however, it was also apparent that there was a chilling finality creeping into Curtis' life.

Joy Division were scheduled to play two shows on the night of 4 April 1980. The first saw them opening for the Stranglers at the Finsbury Park Rainbow; the second, the last of their three night residency at the Moonlight Club, placed them top of the bill at a record company showcase. Looking back, everybody concerned agreed that they shouldn't have played either concert. Instead, they did them both.

Curtis suffered his first epileptic fit onstage at the Rainbow, spinning uncontrollably around until he slammed into the drum kit. The other musicians carried him offstage, still convulsing, and locked themselves away with him until the seizure was over. Then they drove to the Moonlight Club. Five songs into the set, as 'Insight' came to an end, Curtis suffered a second episode.

Hook took over vocals for one more song, 'Interzone,' while Curtis was led off stage. But clearly, the show could not continue. Two decades later, Hook outlined the most crippling facet of the singer's dilemma. 'The thing was, it was very sad to look at somebody who was a friend of yours', going through what Ian was going through. He desperately, desperately wanted to do the things he wasn't meant to do. He wanted to play in a group, he wanted to push himself that much, and that made him ill, the exertion. The flashing lights made him ill. He liked the touring around – that made him ill, because he was always tired. He wasn't supposed to drink, he wasn't supposed to stay up late. He wanted that life, and his illness wouldn't allow him to do it. It was obvious, really, that something had to give.'

Incredibly, the band was back on the road the following day. Malvern, where bootlegs capture an inspired onstage jam with the opening act, Section 25, passed off without incident. But the seizures were coming faster, all the same, and the group was collapsing around an illness which medical science could not control, and which was pushing Curtis to the edge of despair. The night before the group's next concert, in Bury, he attempted suicide, overdosing on Phenobarbitone, one of the drugs that was doing such a poor job of controlling his seizures. But he told wife Deborah what he had done; she called an ambulance, and he was rushed to hospital to have his stomach pumped.

Astonishingly, the Bury concert went ahead – or, at least, it tried to. Just three numbers in, however, it was clear that Curtis was not going to complete the show. The singer left the stage, and Alan Hempsall of Crispy Ambulance stepped in to try and replace him. The audience, however, was having none of it. The evening ended in riot and Curtis, watching as the bottles flew and the blood ran, took another psychic blow.

On April 11, Joy Division played the Factory and, indeed, Manchester for the final time, a show that 24 years later, found itself remembered in *Q* magazine's 100 Greatest Gigs feature. 'The atmosphere before the band took the stage was bad and there had been some aggro in the crowd, but Joy Division matched them in aggression and intensity. At the end of their set manager Rob Gretton announced there was to be no encore and got pelted with bottles. The band then reappeared to perform "Atrocity Exhibition".'

A London showcase at the Scala Cinema on 25 April was cancelled because of Curtis' health, along with the following night's gig in Middlesbrough. And, while he recuperated, Curtis tried to explain to Sumner what was happening to him; what had happened before the Bury concert.

The guitarist thought he understood. Echoing one of Curtis' own recent lyrics, the opening line of the new album's 'Colony,' Sumner suggested that the suicide bid was a cry for help. Curtis' response would remain with him always. 'No it wasn't. It wasn't a cry for help. I knew exactly what I was doing when I took the tablets. But when I'd taken them, I realised that I didn't have as many as I thought.' He'd summoned help because he didn't want to risk brain damage. But he never explained why he tried to kill himself, and Sumner admitted that they never really found out why he did it again, six weeks later.

(LIVE) High Hall, Birmingham, 2 May 1980
8051 Ceremony
8052 Shadowplay
8053 A Means To An End
8054 Passover
8055 New Dawn Fades
8056 Twenty-Four Hours
8057 Transmission

8058 Disorder
8059 Isolation
8060 Decades
8061 Digital
ORIGINAL RELEASE: Compilation *Still*
COMMENTS: Joy Division returned to the road a week later, but when the tapes rolled at Birmingham on 2 May, nobody could have known it would be the last live show Joy Division would ever play. It was, however, their last scheduled outing before embarking upon their first ever US tour, and maybe that is why there seems an added fission of excitement to the performance.

A deliciously high-energy set opened with a new song, 'Ceremony' (edited on *Still*, but complete on sundry bootlegs) and, just as they had after *Unknown Pleasures*, it was immediately apparent that Joy Division had no intention of resting on whichever laurels *Closer* might lay in their path – the album itself was still awaiting release, but it was already old news to Joy Division. Days after the Birmingham concert, and days before they were due to fly to New York, the band retired to the studio to capture the first of their new songs on tape.

(STUDIO) Graveyard Studio, Prestwich, May 1980
8062 Ceremony
8063 In A Lonely Place
ORIGINAL RELEASE: Box set *Heart And Soul*
COMMENTS: Joy Division's last ever session took place two weeks before Curtis' death. According to the booklet accompanying *Heart And Soul*, they ensconced themselves with Martin Hannett, within the so-ironically named Graveyard Studios in Prestwich; other sources claim they were at TJ Davidson's Rehearsal Studios.

Wherever it took place, the band laid down the two most recent songs they'd written, a powerful 'Ceremony' showcasing Morris' so-precise percussion; and 'In A Lonely Place,' a melancholy piece inspired, at least in part, by the group's exposure to Nico's latest album, *Drama Of Exile*, but rendered even more foreboding than usual, as Curtis ad-libbed one of the most haunting lyrics he would ever create, one which would certainly haunt his colleagues as they faced a new life without him. It depicted a waiting hangman, and the moment of death as the cord pulls tight.

The quality of the tape is rough – Curtis' voice, in particular, is horribly distorted, while 'In A Lonely Place' abruptly cuts out less than two-and-one-half minutes in. But still it was the rediscovery of these recordings, Peter Hook revealed, that proved the impetus behind the Joy Division box set *Heart And Soul*. 'The only thing, to my mind, that made the Joy Division box worthwhile was putting on "In A Lonely Place" and "Ceremony." I found them on a cassette; it had nothing written on it and I was playing through a few of them to see if I should throw them away, and I put it on and it was Ian singing "In A Lonely Place." We'd completely forgotten we'd done it; and we had to [master the CD] off the cassette.'

Curtis died on 18 May 1980, the day before the band flew out to New York. It was Deborah who discovered his body the following day, when she arrived at the house and saw a note on the mantelpiece. Her first thought was that he'd just scribbled something to her before heading off. Then, out of the corner of one eye, she saw him still in the kitchen.

'What are you doing now?' she snapped, but something about Curtis' stance made her uneasy, even before she'd completed her sentence. 'His head was bowed, his hands resting on the washing machine. I stared at him, he was so still. Then the rope – I hadn't noticed the rope. The rope from the clothes rack was around his neck.' Behind her on the turntable, Curtis' copy of Iggy Pop's *The Idiot* album was still spinning around.

As the days passed, so further details began to emerge. The night before his death, Curtis had telephoned Genesis P-Orridge, leaving his friend seriously concerned about his state of mind. 'I phoned various people in Manchester and told them I really thought Ian was planning to kill himself,' P-Orridge later said. 'They basically ridiculed me and said "Ian's always depressed and suicidal, that's how he is." They persuaded me everything would be fine... that I was just panicking.' (After a decade of silence on the subject, P-Orridge finally wrote Psychic TV's 'I.C. Water' about Curtis' death.)

Bernard Sumner, too, has been haunted by the might-have-beens. 'I've thought about Ian's death countless times. It could have been his epilepsy, that he didn't want to go on with it. It could have been that he couldn't face his relationships crumbling. It could be that the tablets he was on for epilepsy affected his moods so much – and they really did. It could be the fact... that he was a suicidal personality.

'But I tend to think it was a combination of those things coming together at the same time. The one thing I would say about Ian Curtis is that his ambition wasn't – as many singers' ambition is today – to get on *Top Of The Pops* and be famous. That wasn't it. He had something to express. It wasn't a show, it wasn't an act. He wasn't seeking attention. Ian Curtis was the real thing.'

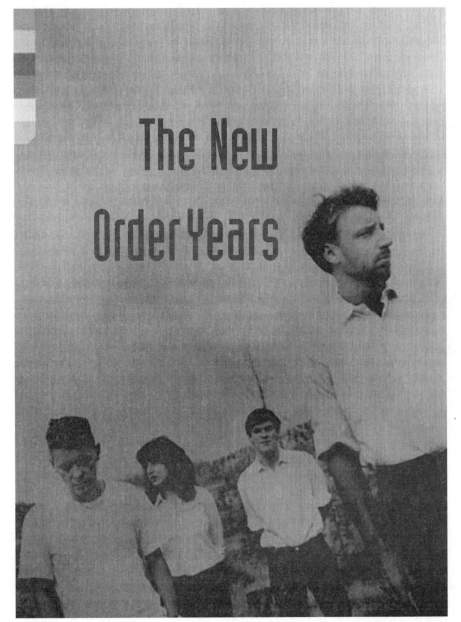

The New
Order Years

1980

The deification of Joy Division commenced immediately – indeed, in many ways it simply picked up where it had left off, as though Curtis' death was simply the awful, inevitable fulfilment of a prophecy he'd been singing all along. And today, more than 25 years later, the group's memory remains as vivid as it ever was.

'I think that sort of thing has always gone on,' reasons Peter Hook; 'it's like one of those records that people play for each other. The thing is, it's quite sad in Britain because most young bands these days seem to be immediately likened to Joy Division, especially guitar bands, everybody always seems to get a reference in some way or another.'

Beginning, of course, with the band that Joy Division left behind. Nobody truly expected Curtis' bandmates to ever recover from the blow, nor to make more than a token stab at continuing. Yet, within days of Curtis' death, Hook, Sumner and Morris were vowing to continue, with Tony Wilson engineering their first steps back into circulation in early July.

(ALBUM) various artists *FROM BRUSSELS WITH LOVE*
8001 Haystack
UNR A Piece Of Fate
ORIGINAL RELEASE: Crepuscule TWI 007 – 1980; reissued on the Hewick compilation *Tender Bruises and Scars: The complete Factory and Cherry Red studio recordings 1980-83* – June 2003
COMMENTS: Ian Curtis had been dead little more than a month when the surviving band members reconvened in the studio for the first time. Factory labelmate Kevin Hewick was recording five songs for inclusion on the *Factory Quartet* EP; the night before the session, label head Tony Wilson suggested Sumner, Morris and Hook should accompany him on at least a couple of numbers, to help ease their own transition back into operation.

Moving into Graveyard Studios with producer Martin Hannett, one track, 'Haystack,' was completed; a second, 'A Piece Of Fate,' was started but would not see the light of day until 1993, when Hewick reworked it as 'No Miracle.'

(LIVE) Beach Club, Manchester, 29 July 1980
With the trio still undecided who would take over lead vocals, the band rejected early names Khmer Rouge and The Witchdoctors of Zimbabwe, and played their first post-Joy Division concert mysteriously billed as the No-Names, and introduced onstage as 'the remnants of Crawling Chaos.' It was a comment that few in the audience seemed to understand ('shit, I didn't know Crawling Chaos had even broken up!'), but it was not an entirely throwaway remark. (Just weeks earlier, Factory released the latest single by that band, 'Sex Machine,' and were (perhaps) astonished when the rumour went around that the spoken-word vocals on the b-side, 'Berlin,' were provided by Ian Curtis. (Factory FAC 17). They weren't, but at least one bootleg, the rather shameful *House Of Dolls*, has perpetrated the legend for fun

and profit.)

Hook mused, 'after Ian died... we were all enjoying what we were doing and, when he died, it was like "God, this has become our life, we're really enjoying it," and it seemed the most natural thing in the world to carry on, so that's what we did. We didn't know how or what we were going to do, we just knew we were going to do it.'

The ensuing all-instrumental set was witnessed by the short-lived *New Music News* magazine (a weekly tabloid born to fill the gap left when the traditional inkies went on strike), who opined, 'no-one could agree as to whether the material was modified instrumental versions of familiar material, or new compositions in the established vein, but we were all agreed that the intensity and novelty of the performance conspired to produce an overall effect rarely equalled. If the band can maintain this level, then their future is assured whatever their name.'

In fact, 'Ceremony' and 'In A Lonely Place' would be the only Joy Division-era songs in the live set. Sumner recalled, 'We felt, after Ian died, we wanted to make it on our own feet and not use the Joy Division songs to propel our career in any way, which was probably a bit naive really. We wanted to start off on our own bat and write our own songs, but it is a bit silly because they were our own songs. I think one of the reasons we didn't play the Joy Division songs after Ian died was that it was so painfully emotional to do it, to play it so close to Ian's death.'

Talking to *Melody Maker* the following year, he conceded, 'it is difficult not to play Joy Division songs... but it is upsetting. It is upsetting to play them after all the work we put into Joy Division with Ian. Without Ian they are not the same.'

The group's new name, New Order, was revealed during this first ever show, and the response was as predictably outraged as that which greeted the emergence of 'Joy Division.' Suggested by Rob Gretton, after he watched a TV documentary on Cambodian dictator Pol Pot, the New Order, among other things, was Adolf Hitler's term for the political and social system he intended imposing upon the world.

No matter that the band themselves insisted they chose it because 'it seemed neutral'; no matter that at least one past band, former Stooges guitarist Ron Asheton's late 1970s hard rock outfit, had used the same name. Critics were quick to seize upon the nasty Nazi connotations and brickbat the band once again, with *NME*'s Chris Bohn asserting, 'it is a stupid name for a group previously steeped in gloomy, magnificent Gothic romanticism.' Three years later, the controversy was still capable of raising its head, as *Private Eye* responded to New Order's *Top Of The Pops* debut by terming New Order 'the unpleasant new name of an even more unpleasant band called Joy Division,' and growling, 'in terms of the rise of fascism in the rock scene, the increasing popularity of Manchester's Factory Records is some cause for concern.'

Journalist Paul Rambali, in *The Face*, suggested, 'Calling themselves New Order was more likely an act of sullen antagonism, part of a wider action to preserve themselves from the morbid fixations of the London media on the group, their late singer, their music and what it certainly represented in the dark, looming depression of 1979/80.' But the group, once again, shrugged off both the speculation and criticism. 'The press draw a picture of us having a load of Nazis following us around in their jack-boots, marching up and down, doing the goose step,' Hook snarled. 'What do we have to do? Apply to the *NME* book of names?'

Besides, as Sumner later remarked, 'They used [the same expression] in *Tron*,' he reasoned. 'But no one calls Walt Disney a Nazi!'

(STUDIO) Western Works Demos
UNR Truth
UNR Dreams Never End
UNR Homage
UNR Ceremony
COMMENTS: Recorded at Sheffield's Western Works studios in July 1980, New Order's first studio recording finds them as uncertain as one would expect, still unsure about who the singer would be (hiding the vocals beneath tons of effects), unwilling to seek out any kind of direction. The academic interest that naturally applies to this historic recording is, therefore, readily out-weighed by the sheer inconclusiveness of it all.

(LIVE) Scamps, Blackpool, 5 September 1980
UNR Dreams Never End
UNR Trust
UNR Mesh
UNR Homage
UNR Sister Ray
UNR Cries And Whispers
UNR Ceremony
COMMENTS: The three-piece New Order played two further low-key UK shows in September (Preston and Blackpool) before undertaking their first US tour, four dates in Hoboken, New York and Boston, by way of replacements for the cancelled Joy Division trip. Blackpool is the earliest-known live New Order recording, most notable for the retention of 'Sister Ray' in the set, though it was a loose instrumental version, and for Morris and Hook sharing lead vocals with Sumner on the closing 'Ceremony.'

(LIVE) Hurrah's, New York, 27 September 1980
UNR In A Lonely Place
UNR Dreams Never End
UNR Cries And Whispers
UNR Truth
UNR Mesh
UNR Homage
UNR Ceremony
COMMENTS: Opening for A Certain Ratio, New Order were welcomed by a club that seemed to include as many journalists as fans and curious onlookers, and a stream of reviews appeared to fall over themselves in a bid to prove their sensitivity towards the new band's recent past. Even without catching the title (or

realising its vintage), the *NME*'s scribe pinpointed the opening 'In A Lonely Place' as 'clearly about loss and memory. My heart goes out; whether it is final, fatal or temporary, lack is lack, you want someone back. Someone whose absence hurts worse than words can prove. I liked this unfamiliar song a lot.'

The return from America saw the band actively searching for a fourth, keyboard-playing member. Keyboards had been growing increasingly important to Joy Division's own sound, as Hook pointed out – 'we started messing about with electronics and synthesizers while Ian was alive; it was quite a natural thing to go on with.' In the past, however, the instrument had been largely confined to the studio. Now the band was looking to prolong the musical vision they had already formulated, and Hook confirmed that particular direction when he affirmed, several years later, 'I think Joy Division would have gone exactly the way of New Order. It's just a feeling you have. I don't think we'd have been that different.'

A number of outside musicians were considered for the vacant position, before Rob Gretton – maintaining the role as a voice of mediating common sense that he acquired during the Joy Division days – suggested they look a little closer to home, and try out Morris' girlfriend (and, of course, future wife), Gillian Gilbert. A former member of the all-girl punk band The Inadequates, Gilbert was now studying graphic design at Stockport Tech, although she readily confesses, 'I didn't want to be a graphic artist. It was just something to do. I didn't really have any ambitions. I didn't want to be in a group [either] – it was just a dream. They approached me.' Gilbert made her live debut with New Order at the Squat on 25 October and, in December, the band went into Strawberry Studios with Martin Hannett, to commence recording what would become *Movement*.

1981

(BBC SESSION) *John Peel Show*: recorded Jan 26 1981; broadcast 16 Feb 1981
8101 Truth
8102 Senses
8103 ICB
8104 Dreams Never End
ORIGINAL RELEASE: Strange Fruit SFPS 039 – July 1987
COMMENTS: In terms of all that New Order would go on to create, their debut Peel session is educational, as opposed to exciting. Sumner – like Curtis at a similar stage of his development as a vocalist – is still seeking his own voice, and sounds just a shade strangled.

All four songs are certainly already well on the way to their *Movement* shaped destiny, however (the percussive 'Senses' might even be better) and the sound, though close enough to the percolating density of the past for comfort, was moving fast enough away from it to ensure that the new group wasn't simply the Old Mark Two, a point that *Sounds* reinforced during a review of one of the band's January live shows.

'The structure of the songs [was] simplified and very strong, the instruments merging into a fluid tide of sound with the formidable arrhythmic backbone of drumming. The songs were distinctive in style but constantly moving and changing within it, the material was far more tenuous than the material they performed long ago, but it was so immediate and so deeply trenchant. New Order have the spirit and the feeling, but we have to be careful not to push them too hard.'

(SINGLE) Ceremony
8105 Ceremony
8106 In A Lonely Place
ORIGINAL RELEASE: Factory FAC 33, January 1981

UK CHART POSITION: 14 March 1981 – #34 (5 weeks)
COMMENTS: Recorded at Eastern Artists Recordings in East Orange, New Jersey, during the US visit the previous September, New Order's first single might, in an alternate universe, have been Joy Division's next. The etchings in the run-off groove of the 7-inch single (the 12-inch followed in March), however, remind us why that could not be, as the so-fitting refrain from 'In A Lonely Place,' 'How I wish you were here with me now,' is joined by 'watching forever.'

Despite the *NME*'s description of the single as 'a brave new beginning... that acknowledges the past without milking it for the myths with which others ungraciously embroidered it,' both 'Ceremony' and 'In A Lonely Place' utilise the Graveyard Studio demos as an almost unerring template. Still the band turned in as dark and moody a vision as their predecessors could ever have, with the record's mysterious edge only amplified by the Peter Saville-designed sleeve's reluctance to feature any personal information anywhere within its design.

'What we want to do is present music without any of the peripheral rubbish around it,' Sumner told *The Face*. 'It doesn't matter who played what solo or what instruments we used or even who we are. If people like the music, that's what's important; that's what they're buying.' The A-side was re-recorded and issued on a second 12" later in 1981.

(LIVE) Heaven, London, 9 February 1981
UNR In A Lonely Place
UNR Dreams Never End
UNR ICB
UNR Truth
UNR Procession
UNR The Him
UNR Senses

UNR Ceremony

COMMENTS: New Order's first London show was a supposedly-secret appearance at Heaven, with all 1,000 tickets selling out instantly. It was not, according to *Alternative Press* magazine 12 years later, an auspicious occasion:

'The room wavers, *Wayne's World* dream-sequence style, and I catapult New Order into my personal flashback hell – the gay Heaven nightclub beneath London's Charing Cross railway station. The club was burning with anticipation... so what did New Order do? They came out and played 40 minutes of electric soup. The songs you should have known were unrecognisable, the ones you recognised turned out to be something else entirely. They didn't speak to the audience once all evening, and I don't think they looked at it either. And, as we left... "Hey, that was fun. Let's go home and watch some *more* paint dry." Hook remembers the show and has his excuses ready. "The sound," he growls, "was awful that night." It wouldn't have mattered, I counter.'

Primal Scream's Bobby Gillespie offers an alternate view on the early live experience; he caught the band for the first time at the Plaza in Glasgow, just three weeks before the Heaven showcase, and recalls, 'it was a weird gig because there was a huge expectancy about it. I'd seen Joy Division supporting the Buzzcocks and that was fucking good. But then you had the whole drama of Ian Curtis killing himself... *Closer* and "Love Will Tear Us Apart," and you thought "how the fuck do these guys follow this up?" So there was this whole mystery surrounding the gig – and the equipment kept breaking down, which was quite frustrating for Bernard. A crazy gig, really unusual, really weird, spooky. Dramatic.'

Heaven was the last in this initial burst of gigging. New Order would be back on the road at the end of March, however, and also submitted to their first ever interview with the national press, with *Melody Maker* on 23 May. 'New Order are *not* the remains of Joy Division,' began writer Neil Rowland. 'They're a whole new entity, struggling with a legend thrust upon them at an altogether pubescent stage, intensified to bursting point by Ian Curtis' ultimate gesture/sacrifice/defeat/fantasy – use whichever word you prefer, for legends are made of mystery....'

With what would soon become wearisome predictability, Curtis – or, rather, Curtis' demise – then began to dominate the proceedings, a spectre that the band themselves did their best to brush off. Asked whether Curtis' intensity affected him, Hook simply shrugged, 'Well, I was just playing. He would write and sing. I didn't really take a lot of notice of him. I couldn't really, you have to concentrate on your own contribution.'

(SESSION) *Celebration* Granada TV, recorded April 1981, broadcast 18 June 1981

UNR Dreams Never End
UNR ICB
UNR Chosen Time
UNR Little Dead *aka* Denial
UNR Ceremony
UNR Truth

COMMENTS: A half-hour television special capturing the band silent and stoney-faced in the studio, working on *Movement*. Scarcely the most exciting New Order footage ever broadcast, *Celebration* does not seem to have resurfaced in any guise beyond an appalling, near-black and white, video dub.

(LIVE) Glastonbury Festival, 20 June 1981
8107 In A Lonely Place
UNR Dreams Never End
UNR Truth
UNR The Him
UNR Procession
UNR Denial
UNR Everything's Gone Green
ORIGINAL RELEASE: Box set *Retro*; 4 tracks on bootleg *Brand New Monotones* (Rentner RR005)
COMMENTS: A handful of now-legendary, hippy-orientated Glastonbury Fayres had already established the event in rock iconography, long before 1979 saw the official birth of the modern festival, with a show headlined by Peter Gabriel. Two years later, Hawkwind and New Order headlined the event, as a benefit for the Campaign for Nuclear Disarmament (CND).

New Order's performance, late on the second (Saturday) evening, was the ideal conclusion to a day of differing musical fortunes – most of which, sadly, have since merged into one long weekend of impatience, tempered by occasional moments of passing joy.

Judy Tzuke and Aswad both turned in memorable performances, but New Order so transcended all that the absence of an official Glastonbury 81 live album is one of the most galling discographical flaws in the entire catalogue. Just one track from the event, a deeply atmospheric 'In A Lonely Place,' has surfaced (on *Retro*), riddled with freakish Eno-esque electronics and an insistent heart attack drum line and, Sumner's occasionally uncertain vocals notwithstanding, it catapults the listener straight back to the third muddy puddle on the left, with a barrage of bikers standing immediately behind you, already chanting for Hawkwind to come on.

(LIVE)
8108 Everything's Gone Green – Brussels 15 May 1981
8109 Truth – Brussels 15 May 1981
8110 Ceremony – CoMANche, Manchester 6 Feb 1981
8111 In a Lonely Place – uncertain date and location (early '82)
ORIGINAL RELEASE: 8108-09 on VHS *A Factory Complication* Ikon IKON1 – Aug 1981; 8110-11 on VHS *A Factory Video* Ikon IKON 3 – Aug 1982
COMMENTS: Appearing on tape alongside fellow Factory stars A Certain Ratio, Crispy Ambulance, OMD and Section 25 (among others), this clear, but clearly uncomfortable live footage only amplifies Hook's own opinions on New Order's live prowess. 'We were very unpredictable live, which is what kept it exciting. When you're in a group with three people who don't want to play live, you

have to make concessions, and take what you're offered.

'But it was exciting; we didn't practice that much; we never played the same set twice; we'd do songs we hadn't played for three years. It kept things very fresh. I know in many ways we shouldn't have done that, because you've paid to come in and we haven't, and there was always the risk we'd make a complete balls of it, which we did on many occasions. But I like to think that even when we were shit, we were special. We were special shit.'

(SINGLE) Procession
8112 Procession
8113 Everything's Gone Green
ORIGINAL RELEASE: Factory FAC 53 – September 1981

UK CHART POSITION: 3 October 1981 – #38 (5 weeks)

COMMENTS: Recorded during the sessions for the forthcoming *Movement* album, New Order's deliciously breezy second single is remarkable, among a clutch of other qualities, for its clear status among the songs that influenced Nirvana *circa* 'Teen Spirit,' that were *not* gleefully seized upon by those who would decry the grungesters' accomplishments. Or maybe everyone wanders around singing 'Hullo, hullo' to themselves. *Sounds*, meanwhile, pinpointed an unexpected point of reference for New Order themselves, as reviewer Gary Bushell described 'Procession' as the sound of 'Pink Floyd ten years on. Just put on those headphones and ride a magic carpet to a purer world. Man.'

The flipside 'Everything's Gone Green,' meanwhile, both deserved and, eventually received, better treatment than most mere b-sides generally do, a compulsive military tattoo that drifts across the ears with mantric purposefulness. 'This was probably the first track we used electronics on,' Sumner later revealed. 'I found an old synthesizer with an oscillator and I wanted to sync it up with the drums. [But] it would drop back out of time… after about eight bars.'

For the collectors among us, nine different coloured picture sleeves (black, red, blue, brown, yellow, orange, green, aqua and purple) emerged to tease out nine times the investment.

(ALBUM) *MOVEMENT*
8114 Dreams Never End
8115 Truth
8116 Senses

8117 Chosen Time
8118 ICB
8119 The Him
8120 Doubts Even Here
8121 Denial

ORIGINAL RELEASE: Factory FACT 50 – November 1981
UK CHART POSITION: 28 November 1981 – #30 (10 weeks)
COMMENTS: Recorded in two weeks at Strawberry, with Martin Hannett in inevitable attendance, *Movement* found the group 'focused on the rhythms, snaking and flowing like a fast moving current, building and ebbing like the tide. In under 40 minutes,' journalist Jo-Ann Greene mused, 'New Order laid out their blueprint for the future, while still providing a link with their Joy Division past.'

'We always know how we want... to sound,' Sumner told *The Face*. 'The way we write a song is usually to start off by improvising in the rehearsal room. Then we take it out live. Sometimes you haven't got any lyrics, so you just make up some garbage. Then you listen to the live tapes, write some more words, and go back and rehearse some more. By the time we record it, we pretty well know how it should be.'

Nevertheless, the album would prove a major disappointment to the band. Sumner told *Melody Maker*, 'I absolutely hated *Movement*. I've hated it since I first heard it. Never played it since. I was so angry with *Movement*, having to put out a record I didn't like.'

The peculiar thing is, he was not being overly harsh. Endured dispassionately, shorn of the time-and-place romanticism with which we traditionally imbue our 'favourite albums,' *Movement* is all mood and very little magic. Peter Hook's vocal showcase 'Dreams Never End' can never lose its appeal, of course – the first chords of the first song of the first New Order album are as powerful as anything the band has done since, and the number rattles along like an express train thereafter.

The throbbing 'ICB,' reflective (whether deliberately or otherwise) of the anti-nuclear sentiments that were then galloping across the European music scene, is remarkable as well, standing alongside 'Senses' in a land where rocketing sound effects and ballistic percussion can be evocative as the lyrics are (of course) non-committal. But too much of *Movement* stands nakedly around in search of either a tune to match its rhythms, or an idea to marry its inspirations, as reviews of the time were mercilessly swift to point out.

'It's terrifically dull,' complained *NME*, 'cornering the market in tender tonal bass harmonics brooding across rumbling drums that wash from speaker to speaker in epic style.' *Sounds* went even further, pegging *Movement* as 'utterly disastrous.' It wasn't, of course, but Sumner, at least, did not find such complaints to be cruel.

The very nature of the band at the time, he complained, was 'a situation of complete turmoil....It was a real learning process. Like the first time you get in a car. You've never driven before, and you feel like you're in a huge metal box which is out of control. The corners are too big and you feel that you're definitely going to bang the car into something. Then, ten times later, you think, "fuckin' hell, what was I so worried about?" It was just like that.

'Personally I lost confidence. We were all wondering what to do next. We feared that we weren't going to be so successful with New Order. When you don't believe in yourself, it reflects on your outlook. We did believe in ourselves. We just didn't know what we were going to write songs about…. so I'm not surprised [the album] happened like that. The first Joy Division songs had been equally awful.'

(SINGLE) Dreams Never End
8114 Dreams Never End
8115 Truth
ORIGINAL RELEASE: Scheduled for October 1981 US release
COMMENTS: The smartest choice for a single from *Movement* ultimately didn't make it out.

(LIVE) Ukrainian National Home, New York, 11 November 1981.
8122 Chosen Time
8123 Dreams Never End
8124 Everything's Gone Green
8125 Truth
8126 Senses
8127 Procession
8128 Ceremony
8129 Denial
8130 Temptation
ORIGINAL RELEASE: VHS *Taras Shevchenko* Ikon IKON 4 – August 1983
COMMENTS: The gig – the sixth of eight dates on New Order's latest American tour – itself received the Factory America catalogue number FA 1, and caught the group headlining a venue better-known for art events than rock shows. It was a dichotomy that *Sounds* noted with dry relish: 'the place is full of the cream of New York's pseudo-continentals, the transparent and ridiculous 80s would-be Bohemians in their long dark coats, scarves and faces. …very much the crowd you would expect for New Order.'

The soundtrack to the show reveals little in defense of this much-maligned audience – studiously cool and, therefore, utterly unlikely to make more than a token cough or two by way of applause, the lack of crowd participation renders *Taras Shevchenko* (the VHS was named for Taras Hryhorovich Shevchenko, the 19th century Ukrainian poet) akin to listening to a studio rehearsal or, at best, a soundcheck. The lack of participation does not, however, hold New Order back. Indeed, this emerges one of the most powerful of all early live performances, as highlights from *Movement* are merged with two past singles and, surprisingly, two forthcoming ones, the Europe-only 'Everything's Gone Green,' and a very tentative 'Temptation,' the lyrics still in a state of semi-completion, but with close to 11 minutes worth of rhythms and beats already firmly established.

(SINGLE) Everything's Gone Green
8113 Everything's Gone Green
8131 Mesh
8132 Cries and Whispers
ORIGINAL RELEASE: 12" Factory Benelux FBNL 8 – December 1981

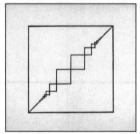

COMMENTS: Confounding discographers and even compilers ever since it was repressed in 1987, the titles are reversed on the flip of this single – the song titled 'Mesh' is actually 'Cries And Whispers,' and *vice versa*.

Reprised from the b-side of the UK 'Procession' 45, 'Everything's Gone Green' is notable as the last record upon which Martin Hannett would work with his most familiar charges. '[Hannett] taught us what to do very early on,' Hook explained. 'We learnt the actual physics of recording from him, although we could have learnt it from anybody. But in the end, there was too much compromise from both sides.'

(STUDIO) uncertain date/location
8133 Video 586 *aka* Haçienda Construction Footage
ORIGINAL RELEASE: VHS *A Factory Outing* FACT 71 – Oct 1983
COMMENTS: An early version of Morris' 'Video 586' (see below) was used to accompany a filmed sequence showing the construction of the Haçienda, the band and Factory's own nightclub and, arguably, the first 'super club' to open in the UK. Modelled on the stylish nightclubs the band had visited in New York, the Haçienda would come to epitomise the dance scene in the UK throughout the 80s and early 90s – indeed, even this early on in its career, it had drawn the withering scorn of at least one observer, as punkish poet Attila The Stockbroker sneeringly 'dedicated' his *Cocktails* debut EP to 'nightclub liggers everywhere. Especially the *NME* Barracuda/Haçienda set.'

Neil Rushton, whose Kool Kat label (in Birmingham) was among the foremost British techno pioneers, recalls the Haçienda as the jumping-off point for a string of classic dance records as the 1980s wore on. It was there, at the hands of DJ Mike Pickering, that British dancers first experienced such seminal tracks as 'Rock To The Beat,' 'Groovin' Without A Doubt,' 'Triangle Of Love' and more (and Pickering himself who, as the M in M People, strung a host of early 90s hits together).

If the Haçienda stands as a crucial factor in the development of the techno and acid scenes, however, it was also in at the birth of what the UK media would swiftly term the 'Madchester' scene – the likes of the Stone Roses and the Happy Mondays coalesced within the Haçienda, long before they actually became bands.

According to A Certain Ratio's Martin Moscrop, 'it was a very important gig for bands at one point. A lot of bands used to gig there. Things like *The Tube* were recorded there. Madonna's first UK gig. It was nice to see the dance music thing go, because it was the first time it made any money. Unfortunately, it starting making money just as Factory started losing money, when the Happy Mondays were at their most expensive. When the Haçienda went down again after the Acid House thing, Factory went down with it, which gave us all our problems really. We were very lucky to get out of it.'

Sumner continued, 'You need a hard nose businessman to run a club. We had violence there. It all went really bad at one point, but a lot of those gangsters – yardies from Jamaica – aren't around, they've all shot each other. We had to close the Haçienda down because someone who got turned away by a bouncer went back and got a machine gun. He chased the bouncer through the club, cornered him at one of the fire escapes and pulled the trigger, but the gun jammed. That cost us a lot.'

Today, a block of flats stands on the club's old site. It is named The Haçienda.

1982

New Order remained relatively quiet through 1982, releasing just one single ('Temptation') and playing a mere handful of live shows – these included a near-riot at a gig in Rotterdam, and a well-received Italian mini-tour.

Behind the scenes, however, New Order were plotting a musical revolution, both in physical terms (the Haçienda Club opened for business on 21 May); and musically. Cultish perfection and dance floor success seldom walked hand in hand through the Eighties – there were too many cooks serving too many broths, and the tyranny of the Beats-per-Minute ensured that even the best ideas would be syn-drummed to death before they left the studio. But, with 'Temptation,' and the myriad ideas that welled up behind it, New Order were preparing to blueprint one of the decade's most forthright musical fashions.

Discussing the vast impact and influence that this shift would come to have, Hook told *Top Of The Pops* magazine 'there is only one thing we have ever done, which is to try and do everything we have done well. And I think that by doing that, and by being a little off the wall – especially with Stephen and Bernard's interest in technology – we were right at the cutting edge then, [although] "cutting edge" sounds too good for it, because it was very rough edge. It was interesting that, by pushing them and by marrying that with the rock thing, we did create something different. And you can hear that in every U2 record.

'I think we borrowed a bit from Detroit ourselves to be honest, especially [after] working with Arthur Baker. The thing is, when you look back at the way Factory was, they were quite good at letting you take chances. Whereas people don't take many chances these days.'

Over the next two years, New Order would be all about taking chances. Gilbert continued, 'When computers first came out, you wouldn't dream of taking them anywhere! But we did. So, it was like a really big hassle every night, and we used to check all of the leads, because it was just like plugs and wires then, and I used to go on and soundcheck all the gear before we actually played the concert, which is stupid. You just don't do that now, but we had to. The gear kept breaking down, so we got like second stand-ins and we ended up with four lots of stand-ins on the stage because they were so unreliable.'

'I remember once playing in Toronto,' Sumner continued, 'and 17 pieces of equipment let me down.'

(TV) *Riverside* BBC2 January 4 1982
Temptation – released on NewOrder Story video
UNR Death Rattle *aka* Chosen Time
ORIGINAL RELEASE:
COMMENTS: The premier edition of BBC2's new flagship live rock show, named for the Hammersmith studios at which it was filmed. Two new songs were introduced, 'Temptation' still rough around the edges but certainly zeroing in on its eventual form.

(MISC) Factory FAC 61 was the catalogue number assigned to the lawsuit initiated by Martin Hannett's solicitor in April 1982 following his departure from Factory, and centred on his earnings from his Joy Division and New Order productions.

(SINGLE) Temptation
8201 Temptation
8202 Hurt
ORIGINAL RELEASE: Factory FAC 63 – May 1982

UK CHART POSITION: 22 May 1982 – #29 (7 weeks)
COMMENTS: For many listeners, 'Temptation' is the moment when New

Order, in the words of *The Guardian*, finally stepped 'out of Joy Division's imposing art-rock shadow and head[ed] optimistically towards the dancefloor instead.' It was also their first self-produced number, although Peter Hook alone had already ventured into those waters with his handling of the Stockholm Monsters' 'Death Is Slowly Coming,' the b-side to February 1982's 'Fairy Tales' 45 (Factory FACT 41).

Although the song itself was already familiar from the live show, 'Temptation' was dramatically reworked once it arrived in the studio, gaining a full lyric, and further tightening its already distinctly dance-oriented purpose. Play the b-side first, and you'd never guess what was about to be unleashed – the so-resolute percussion notwithstanding, 'Hurt' was the last of the 'old-style' New Order songs to be released, and it rattles around as purposefully as any of them. But 'Temptation' is an absolute revelation by anybody's standards, seven clattering minutes that seem to start halfway through a song already in-progress, and end a tantalisingly few minutes before it reaches its conclusion.

If you want to be technical about it, there are all manner of things *wrong* with the record. Sumner can neither find, nor decide upon, which key to sing in; the 'ooo-ooo' harmonies sound thin and unfinished; and the mix is so disheveled that, no sooner are you concentrating upon one tone or texture, than another wades in to slash it out of sight.

But though it might have been the first time, it certainly wasn't the last on which New Order purposefully pursued 'mistakes' in search of their own brand of perfection. Sumner explained, 'at that time, I was really influenced by Italian disco records. There were two scenes at that time: American dance music, which was very slick and dead professional. That didn't appeal to me, because it was so polished, it was boring. The Italian stuff was funny because you'd hear the bad mistakes and that gave the songs character.'

Of all the 'mistakes' left in place, perhaps the most charming was uncovered by *The Guardian*, a full twenty years later. 'His mind bent slightly out of shape by the effects of a mild dose of LSD, [Sumner] is about to put the finishing vocal touches to "Temptation." Just as he's about to start singing, Hook rushes in from the snow storm outside and stuffs a snowball down his singer's shirt. Listen carefully and you can pick out Sumner's startled yelp during the song's intro.'

(BBC SESSION) recorded unknown date; broadcast 1 June 1982
8203 Turn The Heater On
8204 We All Stand
8205 Too Late
8206 5-8-6
ORIGINAL RELEASE: Strange Fruit SFPS 001 – September 1986
UK CHART POSITION: 27 September 1986 – #54 (1 week)
COMMENTS: Although the vast majority of sessions aired by Peel were recorded at the BBC's own studios, New Order's second appearance was taped privately in Manchester, then delivered to the station for broadcast. From all appearances, however, it adheres rigidly to the BBC's own policy of 'get in, lay it

down, then get out,' and the ensuing four songs rank among New Order's most captivating performances yet.

The moodily shifting '5-8-6' with (let hindsight be our guide) the spirit of 'Blue Monday' already rumbling round its rhythms, broods with deliberate incisiveness, a temperament that both 'Too Late' and 'We All Stand' readily echo. But it is the final track, a supremely Spartan rendition of reggae artist Keith Hudson's 'Turn The Heater On' that truly marks this out as a classic Peel Session. Beautifully understated, supremely sinister and irresistibly danceable, the performance makes one wonder why New Order never took the song any further than a one-off radio session.

(SINGLE) Christmas Flexidisc
8207 Rocking Carol
8208 Ode to Joy
ORIGINAL RELEASE: Factory FAC 51b – limited edition of 4,400 given away at the Haçienda, Christmas Eve 1982.

COMMENTS: Recorded in December 1981 for a Granada TV special, this improbably rare little flexi was sleeved in a brown bag stamped FAC51 HAÇIENDA. The bag also contained a party hat, a whistle, a coiled streamer, and a yellow-and-blue rock-shaped sweetie.

Eschewing any identifiable artist name, the flexi was instead credited to Be Music, a title that New Order had adopted earlier in the year for, first, their own music publishing company; then as an umbrella term for their slowly-burgeoning outside production duties.

Hook was responsible for the first of these, when he oversaw the Stockholm Monsters b-side 'Death Is Slowly Coming' (see 'Temptation' above) at the end of 1981. Over the next two years, members of New Order, as Be Music, would produce a string of singles both for sundry fellow Factory artists, and a handful of other acts: Nyam Nyam, Lavolta Lakota, Royal Family and the Poor and Ad Infinitum (Peter Hook), 52nd Street, Quando Quango, Section 25, Marcel King, Paul Haig (Bernard Sumner) and Red Turns To, Thick Pigeon and Life (Morris and Gilbert). Factory's own in-house producer Donald "Dojo" Johnson frequently co-produced.

Few of these records will actively surprise the seasoned New Order listener, adhering as they do to the dance-oriented templates that the group itself was already beginning to explore. Neither were they granted much attention by the UK music press, despite proving major successes on the club circuit both at home and abroad. (Naturally, they were huge at the Haçienda.) But both proven sonic notions, and speculative ideas surface across the catalogue, to provide an alternative soundtrack to much that New Order themselves would wreak during the same 1983-85 period. It may also be of note that Quando Quango's 'Atom Rock' single (Factory FAC 102), from spring 1984, marks the first collaboration between Bernard Sumner, as producer, and Johnny Marr, as guest guitarist.

No less than 11 of the best Be Music/Factory productions were subsequently (2004) compiled onto the CD *Cool As Ice: The Be Music Productions* (LTMCD 2377).

(ALBUM) various artists *FEATUREMIST*
8209a Video 586 (part 1)
8209c Video 586 (part 2 – actually Part 3)
ORIGINAL RELEASE: Cassette only Touch T01 – December 1982

(ALBUM) *TOUCH SAMPLER 2*
8209b Video 586 (missing second segment)
ORIGINAL RELEASE: Touch T ZERO 2 – 1996

(SINGLE) Video 586
8209 Video 586
ORIGINAL RELEASE: Touch TONE 7 – 1997
COMMENTS: 'The [22 minute] track begins with the stomping beat from Gary Glitter's "Rock'n'Roll" (!!!), the bass begins to follow, the keyboard tentatively joins in...and, slowly, the melody and beat are cobbled together into "Blue Monday." This doesn't appear to be a demo, but a rehearsal tape, reportedly recorded on a four track back in February, 1982, and so what you're hearing is creative genius at work, and history in the making.' *Goldmine* magazine, 1998.

'"Video 586" was something we did for *Featuremist* magazine, years and years and years ago,' Peter Hook recalls. 'It was meant to be a soundtrack for the magazine; you put it on while you're reading it, a good idea and obviously, it wasn't like songy, it was meant to be a bit of a downer. They just re-released it; they didn't even remix it. They just put it out. Everyone was calling me up saying "what's this about New Order having a new single out?" and I was, "the bastards, they've gone in and done a new single without me"; double-paranoid! But, as it turned out, it was just this rerelease.'

1983

Although New Order would release three singles and a great album over the next twelve months, 1983 was destined to be dominated by just one track. 'Blue Monday' not only made a mockery of received dance-floor wisdom, it also hauled an entire musical genre out of the shadows of cult (dis-) respectability, and into the Top 40 mainstream.

Recorded during the sessions for the band's second album, *Power, Corruption And Lies*, a dance heavy and synth dominated set which proved, too, that the band's songwriting had suddenly emerged as an incontestable indication of their commercial intentions, 'Blue Monday' took everybody by surprise.

It shocked the band's fans, who had long grown accustomed to blank looks and vague nods from anyone they mentioned them to. It shocked radio DJs, who simply couldn't perceive how a seven minute song slipped so effortlessly into three minute programming slots (the band refused to allow the song to be edited; refused, too, to release it on 7-inch vinyl. It existed exclusively as a 12-inch). And it shocked New Order themselves, as it catapulted four anonymous faces into the national headlines and ensured they would never return to normalcy again.

Yet even at the height of their success – a period that extended over the next seven years, and has re-emerged with every (albeit sporadic) reappearance since then – the group managed to retain their own cult status; were never reduced to the simple superstar figureheads that others of their ilk would be forced to conform to.

'I think that's down to the way you act,' Peter Hook reasoned. 'If you don't play the game like other people, and seem a little different, it's quite easy for people to discern you are different. Even with people like my peers, people like U2, who we started with, and who are obviously much richer than we are, you can still hold your head up and they still show you the same respect. You gained respect by the way you acted, the way Factory records acted, it actually made an impact on the way people did business. To me, it's all about being true to yourself.'

New Order's refusal to 'play the game' was not restricted to their continued refusal to place personal credits on their record sleeves. Although they had granted a handful of interviews over the past two years, and would continue to do so, still the group garnered a reputation for being both difficult and reluctant interviewees, a policy that Hook (presumably unwillingly) reviewed for *Melody Maker*, on the eve of the release of *Power, Corruption and Lies*.

'It's never been a ploy. We just don't like sitting down in front of somebody who's got a prepared list of questions. It's so artificial that it doesn't seem worth wasting time on. And any answers we give will never come out that well in print, anyway.'

He elaborated in conversation with writer Mick Middles. 'We don't like doing interviews, simply because the questions asked have already been answered a thousand times and can be looked up so easily. There is really no point in going over all that groundwork again. But we will talk to anybody, really. We don't strive to be aloof and we DO in fact quite often politely answer the same questions. We only become angry when we're tired and bored.'

(**LIVE**) The Haçienda – Manchester, England, January 26 1983
8301 Your Silent Face
UNR Temptation
UNR Ceremony
UNR Leave Me Alone
UNR Denial
UNR 586
UNR Age Of Consent
UNR Blue Monday

ORIGINAL RELEASE: VHS *A Factory Outing* FACT 71 – Oct 1983. Entire concert as above on bootleg *Radio Pictures* (FACT Records 05)

COMMENTS: Material destined for the new album was slowly inching into the live set, with early airings for 'Age Of Consent' and, though it still sounds unformed, 'Blue Monday,' both joining 'Temptation' in demonstrating the speed with which New Order – like Joy Division, at a similar stage of *their* existence – were now moving. Suddenly, Sumner's insistence that *Movement* was unfocussed and directionless was borne out with harsh clarity. The older material already sounds out-of-place and, the occasional rearrangement notwithstanding, would continue to do so as the year passed.

(ALBUM) various artists *THE QUICK NEAT JOB*
8302 Be Music Theme (Homage a MGM)
ORIGINAL RELEASE: Various artists collection Crepuscule TWI 643 –
January 1986
COMMENTS: Peter Hook alone assumed the Be Music alter-ego to record this
theme to an imaginary movie soundtrack overlaid with random monster noises, for
use as a live intro tape for the band Lavolta Lakota (whom he produced and did the
live sound for). Percussive and dramatic, it long deserved a wider hearing, but
waited three years before it finally received one. It was subsequently reissued on the
compilation *Cool As Ice: The Be Music Productions* (LTMCD 2377).

(LIVE) Tolworth Rec Centre, Kingston, 12 March 1983
UNR Blue Monday
UNR In A Lonely Place
UNR Chosen Time
UNR Dreams Never End
UNR We All Stand
UNR Leave Me Alone
UNR Age Of Consent
UNR Temptation
UNR 586
8303 Everything's Gone Green
ORIGINAL RELEASE: Box set *Retro*
COMMENTS: New Order gigged sporadically in the UK and Scandinavia
across the first months of the year, before launching their latest UK tour in mid-
March, to coincide with the release of the 'Blue Monday' single. A set heavy on the
new material also featured some subtle, but nonetheless stunning rearrangements,
with this jangling revision of 'Everything's Gone Green' readily lending itself to the
new dance sensibilities. One exception to the group's penchant for the unfamiliar
was made in Blackpool on May 9, the anniversary of Ian Curtis' death, when the
band opened with an (admittedly over-fast) 'Love Will Tear Us Apart' – and must
have been astonished to hear the entire audience bellowing the chorus back at them.

Peter Hook recalled, 'That Tolworth gig was the one where the T-shirt tout guy
tried to give us some money because we didn't have any, and he felt guilty 'cos he
was selling so many bootleg T-shirts. But we threw him out because we were very
anti-merchandise, being poncey and exploiting your image and all that crap. And
then Bernard ran down the road after him going "come back, come back! I'll have
it!"' (The notes for *Retro* misdate this show to 6 December 1985).

(SINGLE) Blue Monday
8304 Blue Monday
8305 The Beach
ORIGINAL RELEASE: Factory FAC 73 – March 1983

UK CHART POSITION: 19 March 1983 – #12 (17 weeks); reissue 13 August 1983 – #9 (17 weeks); reissue 7 January 1984 – #52 (4 weeks)

COMMENTS: Although its genesis lay in the 'Video 586' creation, 'Blue Monday' was born from a remarkable studio-bound collision between a clutch of favourite records. Bernard Sumner revealed, 'the arrangement came from "Dirty Talk" by Klein & MBO, the beat came from a track off a Donna Summer LP, there was a sample from "Radioactivity" by Kraftwerk, and the general influence on the style of the song was Sylvester's "(You Make Me Feel) Mighty Real".'

Yet the hybrid was so deftly constructed that, within weeks, 'Blue Monday' itself was as much a template for future reference as any of its own components – as the Cure discovered as they readied their own next single, 'The Walk,' for release. Although similarities between the two songs owed as much to the technology of the time, as to any musical magpie-ing, still Robert Smith briefly considered canceling the release of 'The Walk,' to avoid any untoward comparisons. Ultimately he went ahead with it, critics be damned, and was rewarded with the Cure's biggest hit (#12) yet. New Order themselves acknowledged the two songs' shared lineage when they borrowed the 'descending doll' sequence from the accompanying Cure video, for inclusion in their own 'Blue Monday 88' remake video.

Recorded during the sessions for the band's forthcoming second album, 'Blue Monday' was never destined for inclusion on the long-player, as the group adhered to their long-held belief that singles and LPs should be kept very separate. (Both 'Blue Monday' and its instrumental doppelganger b-side, 'The Beach,' were subsequently added to the album's CD version in the US). It was, manager Rob Gretton remarked in 1993, 'one of the smartest moves they ever made.'

For all its magnificence, 'Blue Monday,' like 'Temptation,' was not a *perfect* record – and neither was it intended to be. 'There was definitely an awkwardness about "Blue Monday",' Sumner admitted. 'But that's what made it so strong.' Indeed.

An immediate critical success, 'Blue Monday' was released *only* on 12-inch single, an unprecedented move at a time when British radio was still obsessed with three minute quickies. But history was riddled with exceptions to that rule – the Beatles' 'Hey Jude' and Queen's 'Bohemian Rhapsody' had both broken through that barrier by virtue of their length, and 'Blue Monday' was quick to ascend into a similarly rarified strata. Its first chart run, in March, took it to #12; it fell from the charts, then promptly turned around and rose back up to #9, selling over 600,000 copies in the process – again, unheard of for a 12-inch single. Musing on precisely how much money the band was making, *The Face* revealed that the band members 'pay themselves a wage of £72 a week each [rising to £103.50 in the wake of the hit]. But they all drive late-model cars: Bernard Sumner has a W-reg Mercedes 200; Stephen Morris owns a Volvo Estate; Peter Hook has an Audi Coupe. [But] the rest of their earnings — in fact the bulk — is spent on equipment.'

'Blue Monday' marked any number of firsts for the group, including their first ever use of a sequencer – made from an electronic kit by Sumner. 'Only the Roland MC4 was available at the time and it was out of our budget.'

It was also their first concession to a live audience's need for an encore, an extravagance that New Order rarely felt like delivering. With a grandiose nod towards Kraftwerk, who made a similar gesture in the late 1970s, Sumner explained, 'with all this technology coming out, [we thought] it possible that the machines could play a song.' The band would return to the stage, press a button, then leave, and so everybody would be happy. 'We wouldn't have to do an encore, but the audience would get one, and that'll confuse them and they'll all fuck off.' The experiment went as far as recording a robot vocal for the track (handled by Morris), before an engineer accidentally wiped it, and no-one could be bothered to do all that work again.

The song then brought the group their first ever appearance on *Top Of The Pops*, a ghastly live-in-the-studio performance in which the thin sound was matched only by Sumner's even thinner vocal. 'We are the only band that appear on *TOTP* and then watch our record sales go down,' Hook admitted. '[Someone] said to us: "It's amazing, you play live and your record goes down every time. Every other band it goes up." The great thing about *TOTP* was that your mum got to see it. It was one of those things. We fought for ages to get on live and, when we came to do it, we realised why people didn't do it. But we were punks and you had to have your punk credentials, didn't you.'

Another break with tradition came with the employment of an instrumental mix on the b-side. Hitherto, explained Morris, 'at the time, we would never put something as tawdry as a dub version or an instrumental as a b-side, we thought value for money was giving people two songs, irrespective of the fact that nobody ever plays them.' They would not make that mistake again.

The song's subject matter proved as intriguing as its sound. Although Sumner insisted 'it's about nowt,' other sources have defined it as everything from (somehow) a commentary on the previous year's Falklands War, to another lament for Ian Curtis. It was Rob Gretton who composed the most piquant explanation, however, when he described the song as an account of a string of student suicides that swept Sweden during the late 1950s, all of which were apparently triggered by listening to the latest Fats Domino single – 'Blue Monday.'

The record's sleeve was also fascinating. Designer Peter Saville based it upon the flexi-disc that Morris used to store the sequencer information on, but it was so expensive to produce that legend swiftly insisted that Factory (and, therefore, the group) actually lost money on every copy sold. In fact they didn't, but the myth has persisted through countless retellings.

(ALBUM) *POWER, CORRUPTION AND LIES*
8306 Age of Consent
8307 We All Stand
8308 The Village
8309 5 8 6
8310 Your Silent Face
8311 Ultraviolence
8312 Ecstasy
8313 Leave Me Alone
ORIGINAL RELEASE: Factory FACT 75 – May 1983

UK CHART POSITION: 14 May 1983 – #4 (29 weeks)

COMMENTS: New Order's second album was released two months into 'Blue Monday's lifespan and, suddenly, a record that might otherwise have been left to mosey around the cult confines of the group's traditional manor suddenly found itself feted among the most heavily anticipated records of the year.

Of course the single was always going to be a hard act to follow, but the bulk of *Power, Corruption And Lies* was up for the challenge. The opening 'Age Of Consent' was especially startling; a second-cousin to 'Temptation' in that it feels you've joined the fun someway into the story, it also offers clues as to one of New Order's most adventurous future courses, that which led them onto such epics as 'Love Vigilantes,' 'True Faith' and 'Regret.' 'Proper songs,' as one American critic put it a few years later.

Faced with their biggest self-production project yet, New Order undertook considerable preparation for the album sessions. 'We put together maybe 30 percent [of the album] in the studio,' Sumner said. 'The rest we had when we went in.' Only the lyrics remained to be completed as the sessions began. 'Some, like "Blue Monday," we had written when we went in, but most of them were made up on the spot, or taken from live tapes. If we haven't got enough songs when we play live, we make them up as we go along and we take the best bits from these and condense them all into one song.'

One such condensing forged '5-8-6,' a child, of course, of the lengthy 'Video 5-8-6,' and possibly more satisfying in its abbreviated form than the full feast could ever be. Another resulted in 'Ecstasy,' an electronic overture that had hitherto done duty as 'Only The Lonely,' and whose vocal effects were delivered in a vocoder-style very similar to that employed by Neil Young on his most recent album, the brutally-pulsing *Trans*.

Elsewhere, the sweeping 'Your Silent Face' was all the justification *Rolling Stone* apparently required before labeling New Order 'as the thinking man's Human League' – three years on from 'Don't You Want me' *et al.*, Sheffield's finest were still regarded as the founding king-pins of the synthpop scene that, the absence of too much pop notwithstanding, New Order's own interest in electronics could have been seen to combine them with.

Elsewhere across the album, 'The Village' was one of several songs that might have dignified *Movement*, while 'We All Stand' remains one of New Order's most utterly haunting ever. Everywhere, then, the overall sense was one of inexorable progress, with the aptly-titled 'Ultraviolence' anticipating the group's next single, 'Confusion,' with its high beats, repetition, and a lyric that borders upon homily: 'everyone makes mistakes... even me.'

Not here, they didn't.

(LIVE) Paradise Garage, New York, 7 July 1983
UNR Your Silent Face
UNR Hurt
UNR Confusion
UNR Leave Me Alone
UNR Dreams Never End
UNR Thieves Like Us
UNR Everything's Gone Green
UNR Ceremony
UNR Blue Monday
UNR Temptation
ORIGINAL RELEASE: On bootleg *Live New York 1983* (HE 006)
COMMENTS: With the end of New Order's longest (four weeks) American tour yet now in sight, tapes of the Paradise Garage show indicate just how tight the band had become in a relatively short period of time. Still prone to wander off on flights of distracted musical fancy, the quartet had nevertheless reigned in some of their more experimental instincts, as *Sounds'* review made clear: 'without doubt, and for a change, everything runs perfectly.... It's a highly danceable set... The music is compelling, indicating perfectly the class difference between New Order and would-be similar outfits.'

That said, the audience's apparent unfamiliarity with a handful of songs does rankle with the band. 'Just about the most unresponsive crowd we've ever played to. Yank bastards!' complains Sumner as the intro to 'Age Of Consent' fails to garner more than a scant cheer or two; later, during 'Blue Monday,' he amends the opening lyric to ask, 'How does it feel – to stand in front of bastards like you?' It was with some glee, therefore, that the band included a rare performance of the newest song in their arsenal, 'Thieves Like Us,' an 11 minute opus that didn't even boast a vocal until one-third of the way in.

Pre-show, the soundcheck was given over to shooting footage for the group's next single (and first video), 'Confusion';

(SINGLE) Confusion
8314 Confusion
8314a Confused Beats
8314b Confusion Instrumental
8314c Confusion Rough Mix
ORIGINAL RELEASE: Factory FAC 93 – August 1983

UK CHART POSITION: 3 September 1983 – #12 (7 weeks)

COMMENTS: The notion of pairing New Order with Arthur Baker, the undisputed king of the New York dance/remix scene came about through Michael Schamberg, head of Factory's New York office. Hook explained, 'We heard a few of Arthur Baker's records, because there was a Factory New York division at that point, and [Michael] kept [us] abreast of everything that was happening there. We'd done "Everything's Gone Green," "Temptation" and *Power, Corruption and Lies*, and he suggested that we work with Arthur Baker because Arthur was really happening with "Walking on Sunshine" and "I.O.U".'

Sumner recalled, 'we went into that studio [with Baker] in New York with no song whatsoever. We've never done that before, so it was, in fact, a completely experimental thing with a producer we didn't know'... so experimental that, with the session over, the entire band left the room, refusing to sit through any playbacks of the finished track. 'I'm scared to hear it,' Sumner confessed. 'I really am. It seems, if we all agree, that it will be the next single and that's why we are scared to listen.'

Baker was working with Freez at the time, putting the finishing touches to the forthcoming 'IOU,' and early reviews of 'Confusion' were quick to point out similarities between the two groups' sound – a coincidence that Sumner, perhaps surprisingly, agreed with. 'It sounds similar, although the songs are very different really. There is, I believe, a mix [that's] already been made of the two songs together, which is interesting.'

Baker himself was fascinated by New Order's distance from the kind of artists he customarily worked with. 'The fact that they make depressing-sounding records isn't what attracted me to them. But, once we got in the studio, I used that the way I would use it in one of my own songs. I really do not write happy music myself. My songs are based in reality, on human situations. And that's what I liked about their stuff.'

'We thought that Arthur Baker was going to be this technological genius creating these dance records,' Hook recalled almost 20 years later. 'And, really, he was just a punk let loose in a recording studio, who didn't know what the fucking hell he was doing – he was just pushing sliders up and down. We were terrified of going over there to meet him, but when we got there we realised he was just like us. We thought he was the bee's knees, and he thought we were! He's still a great friend, he's a great guy.'

The session itself was not, however, painless. Not only had Sumner contracted a debilitating flu, but the instrumental recording took so long that the vocal needed to be simply 'slung down' right at the end: 'we had a flight at 4pm and I started singing at [noon].' When the opportunity came to rerecord the song in 1987, Sumner's dissatisfaction with his vocals would prove one of the key incentives.

Setting the pace not only for New Order's own future, but also for the British dance scene in general, the ensuing 12-inch single boasted four separate mixes of 'Confusion', all manipulated by Baker himself with the help of John "Jellybean" Benitez. And, two decades later, in the liner notes to the *Retro* box set, Morris admitted that New Order had still to encounter a remixer whose ear was closer to their own wavelength than Baker. 'That's why we [still] work with [him]. Or maybe it's because we like buying him drinks. No, it's because he likes a lot of the stuff that we like. Arthur's DJ-ing clears the floor, and so does mine.'

New Order played just two live shows to mark the release of this groundbreaking new single, at the Haçienda in July, and New York in August. Aside from a handful of shows around the UK in December 1983, the band then remained out of sight for the remainder of the year.

1984

(TV) *The Tube*, 27 January 1984
UNR Cool As Ice
UNR Confusion
UNR Shack Up
UNR Love Will Tear Us Apart
ORIGINAL RELEASE: T-shirts, posters and booklets commemorating the show were assigned the catalogue number FAC 104. As was the show itself.

COMMENTS: Celebrating the new year with the cast and crew of Channel Four's then revolutionary Friday night rock show, itself abandoning its customary studios in Newcastle for the Haçienda instead, New Order appeared as members of the Factory All-Stars, alongside members of A Certain Ratio and 52nd Street (among others). Each of the three main bands had one of their own numbers incorporated into the set, before the broadcast played out with a *tout ensemble* rendition of 'Love Will Tear Us Apart.'

The Smiths were numbered among the show's other guests.

(SINGLE) Thieves Like Us
8401 Thieves Like Us
8402 Lonesome Tonight
ORIGINAL RELEASE: Factory FAC 103 – April 1984

UK CHART POSITION: 28 April 1984 – #18 (5 weeks)

COMMENTS: Refined by close to a year of explorative live performance, 'Thieves Like Us' had developed into a remarkably compulsive little dance number by the time New Order finally took it into the studio. Critics did, with some accuracy, point out a passing resemblance to the Human League's 'Love Action,' but the hallmarks of New Order were all over it as well, beginning with the protracted instrumental intro that spread across the 12-inch single, driving through one of Hook's most addictive bass lines, and onto a refrain ('it's called love') that, typically, had nothing whatsoever to do with the title.

On the flip, 'Lonesome Tonight' contrasted a muffled vocal with some supremely chunky, delightfully choppy, guitar across a number that, with a more dynamic mix, might well have made it as a single in its own right.

(SINGLE) Murder
8403 Murder
8401a Thieves Like Us (instrumental)
ORIGINAL RELEASE: Factory Benelux FBN 22 – May 1984

COMMENTS: Recorded at the same time as 'Thieves Like us' but, for whatever reason, preferred over that song for New Order's European single, 'Murder' is one of those songs that could, were one feeling mischievous, be considered New Order's response to the Cure's recent hijinks on the fringe of their territory. A brutal, percussive instrumental, clattering through raw noise and dark cries, 'Murder' emerges close enough to Robert Smith and co's 'Splintered In Her Head' that any perceived past slights are surely remedied.

Or are they? Weeks later, as the Cure's 'In Between Days' single weighed into the UK chart, Peter Hook was prompted to admit, 'even my mother got upset. Phoned me up, she'd just heard their "In Between Days", she was like "You've got to sort this out, our Peter!'"

Over on the b-side, the instrumental take on 'Thieves Like Us' is just that, a vocal-less rendering that runs out some 20 seconds longer than the regular version. And there really isn't much else to say about it.

(LIVE) Paradiso, Amsterdam, May 17 1984
UNR Skullcrusher
UNR Procession
UNR Dreams Never End
UNR Lonesome Tonight
UNR Thieves Like Us
UNR The Village
UNR Ceremony
UNR Confusion
UNR 586
UNR Blue Monday
UNR Decades
UNR Love Will Tear Us Apart
ORIGINAL RELEASE: On bootleg *441* (Hawkeye HK 007)
COMMENTS: With New Order having been on the road almost constantly since mid-March, one thing is certain from the bootleg. This gig was *not* played for the fans. Rather, its proximity to the anniversary of Ian Curtis' death seemed to place the band at distinct odds with the audience, even if they only admitted it for the encores – 'Decades' and 'Love Will Tear Us Apart' of course – which they dedicated to 'a friend who died some years ago.'

(LIVE) Studio 54, Barcelona, Spain, 7 July 1984
8404 Ceremony
UNR Your Silent Face
UNR The Village
UNR Skullcrusher
UNR We All Stand
UNR Lonesome Tonight
UNR Confusion
UNR Hurt
UNR Age Of Consent
UNR Blue Monday
ORIGINAL RELEASE: Box set *Retro*
COMMENTS: Speaking for the *Retro* liners, Sumner admitted that he was rarely happy with the group's earliest live recordings (or the studio ones for that matter), 'because I'm struggling with my voice on them. I didn't know how to sing.' Morris, on the other hand, confessed that he had always enjoyed playing 'Ceremony.' 'You can fall asleep doing that one, or think about your shopping.'

(RADIO/TV) *Saturday Live*, 25 August 1984.

UNR Sooner Than You Think
UNR Age Of Consent
UNR Blue Monday
UNR In A Lonely Place
UNR Temptation

COMMENTS: Among the myriad of BBC recordings that have been released, the continued unavailability of this performance is baffling, all the more since it is at least the equal of those sets that have seen the light of day.

Four nights earlier (21 August), New Order appeared within Channel 4's *Play At Home*, a documentary on Factory Records that featured the band members decidedly not being a band... or, at least, not the band we thought they were. And so Hook rides a motor bike, Morris plays photographer and Gilbert sits in the bath with Tony Wilson. Bizarre, but amusing.

It was back to business on the Saturday, however. To celebrate the 30th anniversary of the record that, historically, launched Rock'n'Roll, BBC 2 was devoting a full 24 hours to rock programming, in a weekend slot titled (what else?) *Rock Around The Clock*. Broadcast live, footage of New Order's *Saturday Live* performance was included within that marathon and, once it was all over, their five song set ranked among the highlights of the entire bash.

It was a close-run thing, however. As their latest British tour ran down (two further gigs remained, in Portsmouth and London's Heaven), New Order were playing in St Austell, Cornwall, the evening before the broadcast, intending to return to London in a leisurely fashion the following day. But they reckoned without the August weekend traffic, which snarled them in automotive molasses for two hours, before they'd even escaped the county. 'We had to drive at 120 miles an hour for the last three hours,' Sumner shuddered later. 'And we [still] got there only 25 minutes before the programme went out.'

Worse was awaiting them at the studio. 'A piece of equipment had broken down, which meant we couldn't play the songs we wanted,' and the gear they did have to hand did not improve the group's demeanour. Sumner continued, 'the whole thing was daft because we don't record in a studio like that, and we never wear headphones. We had four synthesisers, an Emulator, guitar, bass, electronic drums, drum machine, acoustic drums and vocals and trying to put that lot through a pair of headphones with two inch speakers is completely and utterly stupid.'

But it was also remarkably effective. A duel between percussive regimentation and wild sound effects, 'Blue Monday' was an absolute treat. And so, once past the hideously flubbed intro, was 'Age Of Consent.' An utterly unexpected pounding through 'In A Lonely Place' is lightened by Sumner's demand that Morris 'speed things up a little,' and his own apparent inability to remember the words. But still it's a stately rendering, as electrifying as the hyper-active 'Temptation' and the haunted 'Sooner.'

So far as Sumner was concerned, the entire experience 'was awful, a total fuck up.' For anybody listening from the other side of the broadcast, however, it was a night of magic.

(STUDIO) out-take
8405 Elegia (full length version)
ORIGINAL RELEASE: box set *Retro* (limited edition 5-disc version only)
COMMENTS: According to Morris, a 20 minute version of 'Elegia' was recorded during an impromptu 24 hour session, which itself kicked off immediately after the after-show party following the band's August 27 gig at Heaven. This same take was then savagely edited (to under five minutes) for inclusion on the group's next album.

1985

Having spent the autumn recording, the New Year began with news that New Order had become one of the first acts signed to Quincy Jones' new Qwest label, an indisputable indication of the group's growing pre-eminence on the US dance scene. A subsidiary of Warner Brothers, Qwest would henceforth handle all of New Order's American releases, replacing Rough Trade, whose own inroads into the market remained distinctly cultish.

They were actually signed by former MCA/Backstreets supreme Tom Attencio. 'Backstreet... ended in '83. After that, Quincy Jones called me and said they really liked what I did there – I was just starting to work with dance acts and they wanted to know if I was interested in working with Qwest. At the time, it was all black – Sarah Vaughan, classic blues and jazz performers. And I thought, how can I possibly burnish Quincy Jones' star and I thought about New Order. And I thought how much I loved them and how they'd never done a deal in America. This was after "Blue Monday." I knew that every record company had offered them everything. Bob Krasnow [at Elektra] had offered them a blank check – a nice American style, isn't it? David Geffen [Geffen], Mo Ostin [Reprise]...'

The band were initially uncertain, or so it seemed – Attencio admitted that the first time he spoke to Rob Gretton on the phone, 'I probably only understood every fourth word.' The American industry, too, was shocked – once the news broke, Attencio laughed, the biggest question was, '"What the hell is New Order doing on basically a black musician's semi-obscure label? How the hell has that happened?" But I think the idea of being on a black musician's label was really appealing to them.'

The move paid immediate dividends, as the group's next release, the *Low Life* album, became New Order's first ever American chart hit, reaching #94, while 'The Perfect Kiss' went Top 5 on *Billboard* magazine's dance chart.

New Order gigged sporadically around the UK between January and March, then more intensively in April, before celebrating this upsurge of Stateside interest with their longest American tour yet, hot on the heels of their first ever visits to China (one show in Canton), Japan, Australia and New Zealand. There was also a contentious appearance at Peter Gabriel's WOMAD Festival in July, where New Order took the stage two-and-one-half hours late, then proceeded to play a set that sent nobody away feeling satisfied.

(LIVE) Kosei Nekin Kaiken Hall, Tokyo, 1 May 1985

UNR In A Lonely Place
UNR Subculture
UNR This Time Of Night
UNR Denial
UNR Your Silent Face
UNR Leave Me Alone
UNR The Village
UNR 586
UNR Twats Like Us (*aka* Thieves Like Us)
UNR Face Up
UNR Age Of Consent
UNR The Perfect Kiss
UNR Ceremony
ORIGINAL RELEASE: On bootleg *Kohseinenkin Hall* (Hawkeye 010)

(LIVE) Kosei Nekin Kaiken Hall, Tokyo, May 2 1985
8501 Confusion
8502 Love Vigilantes
UNR The Perfect Kiss
8503 We All Stand
8504 As It Is When It Was
8505 Sub-culture
8506 Face Up
UNR Age Of Consent
UNR Temptation
8507 Sunrise
8508 This Time of Night
8509 Blue Monday
ORIGINAL RELEASE: VHS *Pumped Full Of Drugs* Ikon IKON 17 – August 1986

COMMENTS: New Order's Japanese shows were well-documented by the underground tapers, although Factory's official record of the visit, the wryly titled *Pumped Full Of Drugs* VHS, does a more than adequate job of delivering both a representative set list, and an excellent performance. (The title *Pumped Full Of Drugs* itself is taken from Sumner's introduction to 'This Time Of Night'.)

Preparing for this latest bout of touring, New Order had programmed almost their entire repertoire onto computer, enabling them to continue switching the order and/or content of each night's set at will, and permitting them a surprising amount of freedom from the customary tyranny of the machines. (The individual musicians' own instruments, of course, were played live.) The results, as (seen and) heard on *Pumped Full Of Drugs* were frequently exhilarating – although none of the performances here could be described as career-best, and the show itself is strong without being strenuous, New Order retain all the edginess of their earliest performances.

A T-shirt promoting this release was assigned the catalogue number IKON 17G/17W.

(SINGLE) The Perfect Kiss
8510 The Perfect Kiss (edit)
8510a The Perfect Kiss (12-inch version)
8510b The Perfect Dub (same as the Kiss of Death)
8510c Kiss of Death
8510d Perfect Pit
8511 The Perfect Kiss (live version from The Perfect Kiss video)
ORIGINAL RELEASE: Factory FAC 123 – May 1985
UK CHART POSITION: 25 May 1985 – #46 (4 weeks)
COMMENTS: A marvellous song that deserved to achieve far more, chartwise, than it wound up with, 'The Perfect Kiss' previewed the forthcoming *Low Life* album with evidence that New Order's grip on contemporary dance music was tightening at a phenomenal rate, without sacrificing an iota of the melodicism that dictated their best songs.

The group's Far Eastern tour was looming as the session hove into view; according to Sumner, they had just 72 hours in which to complete the single before flying out, and they wound up using every one of them – 'three days without sleep.'

The accompanying video was shot as the band recorded, explaining the somewhat weary expressions on the musicians' faces; a US promo single was released featuring the ensuing unique mix. Of the other mixes released, 'Kiss Of Death' was little more than an unadorned instrumental version.

(ALBUM) various artists – *DISCREET CAMPAIGN*
8512a Sunrise (instrumental rough mix)
ORIGINAL RELEASE: Cassette Rorshack Testing ROR 1 – 1985
COMMENTS: An interesting work-in-progress.

(ALBUM) *LOW LIFE*
8513 Love Vigilantes
8510 The Perfect Kiss
8514 This Time of Night
8512 Sunrise
8405a Elegia
8515 Sooner Than You Think
8516 Sub-culture
8517 Face Up
CASSETTE BONUS TRACKS
8510a The Perfect Kiss (12" version)
8510c The Kiss of Death
8510d Perfect Pit
ORIGINAL RELEASE: Factory FACT 100 – May 1985

UK CHART POSITION: 25 May 1985 – #7 (10 weeks)

COMMENTS: The band's secret so far had been the ability to keep their singles and albums very separate – the inclusion of both 'The Perfect Kiss' and 'Sub-Culture' on *Low Life* certainly contributed to the singles' poor chart showing, but did not harm the album's chances any, as it became New Order's first ever US chart entry.

Early opinions of *Low Life* condemned it as a disappointment when compared to all that New Order had been building up to since *Power, Corruption and Lies* although time quickly revealed the album to be considerably wider-reaching than might ordinarily have been expected. The instrumental 'Elegia' headed the handful of tracks that insisted the group could never be pigeon-holed as just another modern dance act ('Sooner Than You Think' falls into the same category), while 'Love Vigilantes' rises above its occasionally excruciating lyric to rest alongside 'Age Of Consent' and 'The Perfect Kiss' among the band's most memorable melodies. Plus, alongside Godley & Creme's 'Under Your Thumb,' has there ever been a better musical ghost story?

The album was originally intended to be titled for its opening track, 'Love Vigilantes' – the change was made very late in the day, and sleeve designer Peter Saville later acknowledged that his own work was completed long before anyone told him the news. He was not, however, perturbed – in the past, he'd completed designs before the band had even come up with any kind of title, let alone a final one. 'Throughout the 1980s, there was a certain detachment. The feeling was, they were doing the records, I was doing the sleeve, and we'd get together at the end of the day. In some cases, they didn't even see it *at* the end of the day. They'd have to wait until it was printed.'

Saville confessed it was both a frustrating and a gratifying way of working. While he relished the absolute freedom it entailed, he also confessed, 'it is nice to be working with a brief, because you have a direction and you know what you're doing. The problem with New Order was that it would be my responsibility to make a statement. I'd come up with things that I thought were timely, visual statements that I wanted to make. And there would always be some sort of way for it to fit into the music, one of those lovely chance things that happens when the title comes through – and sometimes, a new meaning is created by the combination of the title and the image.'

(SINGLE) Subculture
8516 Sub-culture
8516a Dub-vulture
8516b Sub-culture (remix edit)
8516c Sub-culture (extended version)

8516d Dub-vulture (extended version)
ORIGINAL RELEASE: Factory FAC 133 – November 1985
UK CHART POSITION: 9 November 1985 – #63 (4 weeks)

(SINGLE) *Record Mirror* free 45
8516e Sub-culture (exclusive remix by Joseph Watt)
ORIGINAL RELEASE: Record Mirror RMEP2 – 1986
COMMENTS: Not necessarily the most logical choice for a new single *per se*, and certainly not the ripest follow-up to the group's success on American dance floors, the vaguely downbeat 'Sub-culture' was absolutely reinvigorated by a host of remixes. The 12-inch extension stands as a virtual reinvention of the song, strengthening Sumner's original fragile vocal, adding an impossibly chirpy backing chorus and upping the tempo to an almost unrecognisable pitch. A masterpiece!

The *Record Mirror* EP, incidentally, pairs New Order with Hipsway, Raymonde, and the Adventures.

(LIVE) *Old Grey Whistle Test*, 3 December 1985
UNR As It Is When It Was
UNR Sunrise
COMMENTS: A live broadcast of the opening two songs from the band's concert that night at the Haçienda.

(LIVE) Central London Polytechnic, London, 6 December 1985
UNR Atmosphere
UNR Dreams Never End
8518 Procession
UNR Sunrise
UNR Lonesome Tonight
UNR Weirdo
UNR 586
UNR The Perfect Kiss
UNR Face Up
UNR Age Of Consent
ORIGINAL RELEASE: Box set *Retro*; entire concert on bootleg *More Than Despair* (PCL Records 586)
COMMENTS: The best shows in this latest round came towards the end of the span, as the group began violently experimenting with their live set, a process that reached its peak at the central London Poly.

Audiences were not necessarily convinced. A rare airing for the Joy Division-era 'Atmosphere' is 'rewarded' by the unerring flight of a beer can, making contact with Hook's skull just as he prepares to start singing 'Dreams Never End.' He falters and comes in late, but the song – and the concert – swiftly recover from the shock, as the set divides itself very neatly into a gig of two halves, the first devoted to the group's earliest years, the second moving smartly into the modern age. 'Procession,' as found (superbly remastered) on *Retro*, highlights the first half, a thunderously turbulent version that might be a little too fast, but lacks nothing in terms of bass-bashing power.

1986

(LIVE) Royal Court Theatre, Liverpool, February 8, 1986
ORIGINAL RELEASE: T-shirts for this event, staged in support of Militant tendency, were assigned the catalogue number FAC 152
COMMENTS: New Order opened the year with a short Irish tour, before returning to the UK for the *From Manchester With Love* benefit. There, they joined the Fall, John Cooper Clarke and the Smiths to raise funds for 49 Liverpool Labour councillors, led by Derek Hatton, who were being taken to court by the government as a dispute over a newly imposed system of rates (the predecessor of the Poll Tax) soared to angry heights.

(SINGLE) Shellshock
8601 Shellshock (edit)
8601a Shellshock
8601c Shellcock
ORIGINAL RELEASE: Factory FAC 143 – March 1986
UK CHART POSITION: 29 March 1986 – #28 (5 weeks)
COMMENTS: The band's American profile was given a sizeable forward jolt after they gifted a new song, 'Shellshock,' to the soundtrack of John Hughes' *Pretty In Pink* movie. The Psychedelic Furs' title track might have lodged deepest in the collective memory, but the entire soundtrack bristled with 'alternative' rock gems and the deliberately dislocating 'Shellshock' was one of the most alternative of them all.

It also lent itself ideally to the remix platform, the sparsity of the actual lyric and melody offering producer and co-writer John Robie a boundlessly expansive palette. Two extended versions vie for the 'best of' throne, the seven minute Robie remix most readily located on *Retro*, and the ten minute extended mix featured on the original 12-inch single.

Robie himself later told *Q*, 'I didn't realise how good they are on melodies and the reason I'd never heard the melodies before was because they didn't know what a key was.' He set about showing them, but ran into a most unexpected piece of resistance. 'Hooky was really concerned about the concept of keys. He thought I was trying to change the band or something.'

(LIVE) Spectrum Arena, Warrington, 1 March 1986
UNR State Of The Nation
UNR The Village
UNR Broken Promise
UNR As It Is When It Was
UNR Your Silent Face
UNR Confusion
8602 Age Of Consent
UNR Temptation
UNR Sunrise

UNR Blue Monday
UNR Shellshock
ORIGINAL RELEASE: Box set *Retro*
COMMENTS: The wealth of shows the band played this year was not their own preferred way of spending time, as Sumner confessed. 'We had enormous tax problems so we had to go out and play vast numbers of gigs. Not because we wanted to play live, but purely to pay off all the tax bills we had. That's why I seemed so unhappy... I wasn't happy being Mr Rock'n'Roll. I hate those pressures.

'We can make as much money off a tour like we've just done in America as we can from an LP. So it's quite important but it's very hard work and it can be a bit soul destroying. Especially when I'd wake up spewing up in Chicago after getting drunk the night before and having to get a plane at eight o' clock in the morning in order to go to another gig with another soundcheck before it. I was very upset that I wasn't going to get any of the money I was earning.'

In fact, the band played 51 shows during the year, including a six week American tour in November/December, although the live portion of *Retro* scarcely nods in the direction of this workload – just one 1986 recording is included, a less-than-hi-fi rendering of 'Age Of Consent' which scarcely deviates from the regular studio version.

(LIVE) Festival of the Tenth Summer, Manchester, 16-19 July 1986
UNR Elegia
UNR Shellshock
UNR Paradise
UNR Bizarre Love Triangle
UNR Way Of Life
UNR State Of The Nation
UNR Face Up
UNR The Perfect Kiss
UNR Ceremony
UNR Temptation
ORIGINAL RELEASE: Event assigned the catalogue number FAC 151
COMMENTS: The festival at the Greater Manchester Exhibition Centre (G-Mex) celebrated the tenth anniversary of Punk, with performances by A Certain Ratio, The Smiths, New Order, The Fall, Cabaret Voltaire, the Freshies, Pete Shelley, the reformed Worst, and 60s survivor Wayne Fontana, an exhibition at the City Art Gallery, a clothes show at the Haçienda, a Kevin Cummins photo exhibition, a music seminar, an exhibition of stuff by Malcolm Garrett and Assorted Images, and film & video shows. Factory produced a great deal of merchandise for the festival, including a badge displaying the '10' logo and 'FAC 151' on it (the only item to be so-numbered), T-shirts, a boiler suit, sets of posters and postcards, and a booklet with pieces by Cath Carroll, Linder, Richard Boone, Tony Wilson, Paul Morley, and others.

New Order's set, while concentrating on recent activities, nevertheless found room for one surprise, as Ian McCulloch, of Echo and the Bunnymen, emerged to take lead vocals on the closing 'Ceremony' – bootleg tapes from the event, unfortunately, give a better idea of the audience's excitement and singalong than the performance itself, but still this union of two of the age's most distinctive acts packs a memorable punch.

It was the first of two onstage appearances McCulloch has made alongside New Order – a little over a year later, in Buffalo, New York on 4 September 1987, he joined the group to perform the Velvet Underground's 'Run Run Run.' The two groups' friendship was further proven on 16 June 1989, when New Order dedicated their entire Irvine Meadows set to Pete DeFreitas, the former Bunnymen drummer who was killed in a motorcycle accident that same day.

(SINGLE) State Of The Nation
8603 State Of The Nation
8603a Shame Of The Nation
ORIGINAL RELEASE: Factory FAC 153 – Sept 1986
UK CHART POSITION: 27 September 1986 – #30 (3 weeks)
COMMENTS: Visiting Japan in May 1985, New Order briefly availed themselves of some Tokyo studio time, to lay down this taster for the then barely-gestating next album – albeit one that works better on the dancefloor than it does on the home stereo.

(ALBUM) *BROTHERHOOD*
8604 Paradise
8605 Weirdo
8606 As It Was When It Was
8607 Broken Promise
8608 Way of Life
8609 Bizarre Love Triangle
8610 All Day Long
8611 Angel Dust
8612 Every Little Counts
CD BONUS TRACKS
8603 State of the Nation
8609a Bizarre Love Triangle (Shep Pettibone remix) [Canadian CD only]
ORIGINAL RELEASE: Factory 150 (October 1986)

UK CHART POSITION: 11 October 1986 – #9 (5 weeks)
COMMENTS: With many of the band's latest songs already familiar from live performances over the past year or so, *Brotherhood* was less a 'new' album in some

fans' eyes, than a summary of their most recent activities. 'Weirdo,' 'As It Is When It Was,' had been in the set since spring 1985; 'Broken Promise' and a still-instrumental rendition of 'Bizarre Love Triangle' since the October tour.

Nevertheless, Sumner recalled, 'before *Brotherhood* came out, our American manager came over to listen to some tracks. He wanted to know if we had any lyrics finished. Well, we always leave the lyrics until last. I always sit there in the studio annoyed at having to do it. It's *always* such a chore. I'll just sit there completely bored until a line comes into my head or I get a picture of some scenario. It gets to the last week of the last month in the studio and everyone's saying, "Ahem, have you started any lyrics yet?" I've never got any.

'So the American manager came over and the only track that was finished was "Every Little Counts." He wanted a cassette to take back to the president of Warners in America. So we played him the song and he goes, 'Well... ahem... *that* is great... but when are you going to do the proper vocals?' We said, "Well, that *is* the finished vocal!" So he had to go back and play that to everyone. We could just imagine their faces in the boardrooms!'

Of course the finished album lived up to all expectations, with several tracks leaping out as potential hits – and just as many maintaining the group's stubborn refusal to be locked in any stylistic box. 'Every Little Counts' does indeed pack a shockingly unfinished-sounding vocal, with Sumner seeming to break down into an uncertain laugh as he 'forgets' one line, and a row of 'doo-doo-doo's apparently filling in for a still-absent verse. Yet this so-unconventional approach works, as the song lopes along in distinct emulation of Lou Reed's 'Walk On The Wild Side,' and the fragile voice matches the tongue-tied nervousness of the song's own protagonist.

Elsewhere, the admonitory 'All Day Long,' though it certainly over-works Hook's patented 'New Order bass sound,' is far from the arenas into which the band were regularly placed, while 'As It Is When It Was' takes the group's tempo and mood as close to a gentle ballad as they had ever come. But 'Angel Dust,' 'Paradise' and the remarkable 'Weirdo' serve up all the bpms that the group's dancefloor audience could demand, however, while 'Bizarre Love Triangle' was soon to peel off the parent disc and land New Order another major club hit single.

(SINGLE) Bizarre Love Triangle
8609a Bizarre Love Triangle (Shep Pettibone remix)
8609b Bizarre Dub Triangle
ORIGINAL RELEASE: Factory FAC 163 – November 1986
UK CHART POSITION: 15 November 1986 – #56 (2 weeks)
COMMENTS: With New Order now two weeks into a six week US tour, the release of 'Bizarre Love Triangle' could scarcely have been better timed – or more superbly remixed. Shep Pettibone's percussion-heavy revision received the most play as the club circuit took the song to its soul, but cunning DJs who segued it into the dub mix garnered the most plaudits, as they constructed a 14 minute slab of non-stop drama that remains one of the most pervasive memories of an entire year's worth of dance culture.

1987

(LIVE) Academy, Brixton, London, 4 April 1987
UNR Touched By The Hand Of God
8701 Bizarre Love Triangle
8702 Perfect Kiss
8703 Ceremony
8704 Dreams Never End
8705 Love Vigilantes
8706 Confusion
8707 Age of Consent
8708 Temptation
ORIGINAL RELEASE: VHS *Academy* Palace PVC 3019M
COMMENTS: Home from the American tour in mid-December, the band barely
had time to unpack their luggage before the New Year drew them away again, for a
handful of gigs in Japan and New Zealand, and a major tour of Australia. A month
off then threw them back on the road in April, second-billed to Bronski Beat at an
AIDS benefit. (Sandy Shaw and Buddy Curtis completed the bill.)

They marked the occasion with a near-perfect greatest hits set (albeit lacking
'Blue Monday'); it was, however, one of the few straight-forward performances
they would muster all year. Indeed, 1987 saw New Order perform some of the most
surprising material of their career-so-far, as the sheer weight of scheduled shows
sent them searching far and wide for 'new' material to perform.

Reintroduced from the Joy Division days, the Velvet Underground's 'Sister Ray'
had already been in and out of set since 1982; now it was joined by the same band's
'Run Run Run' and the pre-Velvets Lou Reed novelty dance song 'Do The Ostrich.'
The Sex Pistols' 'Anarchy In The UK' also made a couple of (admittedly chaotic)
appearances during the US tour that autumn.

Other moments to cherish included the utterly whacked version of 'Weirdo' that
was inflicted upon an unsuspecting Byron Bay audience during the Australian tour,
and the band's appearance at the Factory all-day festival in Finsbury Park on 6 June.
Headlining over labelmates A Certain Ratio, the Railway Children and the Happy
Mondays, New Order were introduced onstage (by Rob Gretton) as 'Joy Division
from Macclesfield,' before Sumner ambled up to the mike and announced, 'we'd like
to dedicate this set to Caroline and Peter who should have been here tonight but
Caroline's not here because she's dead.' Then, when someone in the audience
laughed, he continued, 'It's not a joke and it's not funny. But, then again, we never
are.'

(LIVE) Glastonbury Festival, 19 June 1987
8709 Elegia
8710 Touched By The Hand Of God
8711 Temptation
8712 True Faith

8713 Your Silent Face
8714 Every Second Counts
8715 Bizarre Love Triangle
8716 Perfect Kiss
8717 Age Of Consent
8718 Sister Ray
UNR Ceremony
UNR Subculture
UNR Sunrise
ORIGINAL RELEASE: 8709 on box set *Retro*; 8710-18 on *Radio 1 Live In Concert* – Windsong LP 011 – January 1992.
UK CHART POSITION: 22 February 1992 – #33 (2 weeks)
COMMENTS: Though there had been many, so many, live videos, it would be 1992 before New Order finally released a full live *album*, as the BBC pulled their live broadcast of Glastonbury out of the vault.

It was not a decision that Sumner, at least, relished. While the performance is certainly indicative of New Order's then-current sound and state, and includes sharply defined renditions of at lcast half a dozen all-time favourites (including a spellbinding 'Sister Ray'), still the guitarist conceded to *Alternative Press* magazine that he'd have been happier not to have seen *In Concert* released. But it's the journalist, not the bandmate, who gets the rough edge of Hook's tongue. 'So, what you're saying is, we're shit live.'

Morris attempted to outline the group's approach to live work. 'You can go at it really professionally, playing the same standard show every night, with the same songs and the same jokes in the same places....' 'Or,' abetted Hook, 'you can go at it naturally and let things develop as they will, which is the way we approach it.'

'So sometimes,' concluded Gilbert, 'we're good, and sometimes, we're not. We want the spontaneity, and we'd rather trade polish for performance. Which is when we get people like you coming along saying, "Oh God, you're shit live."'

And the writer senses, rather than sees, Hook smirk with satisfaction. Chalk one up for the band.

This disc was subsequently repackaged alongside Joy Division's *Complete BBC Recordings* album as *New Order & Joy Division: Before & After – The BBC Sessions* (Fuel 302 061 213).

(STUDIO) May 1987
8720 Confusion
8720a Confusion (dub)
8721 Temptation
ORIGINAL RELEASE: *Substance*
COMMENTS: Rerecordings of the original singles cut for inclusion within the group's first retrospective, *Substance*. 'I really like the "Confusion" remix because my vocals are a lot better,' Sumner confessed, recalling the dose of flu and super-cramped schedule that had marred the original performance. In addition, four years of regular live performances had honed the song to razor-sharpness.

(SINGLE) True Faith
8722 True Faith
8722a True Faith (remix by Shep Pettibone) *AKA* (the Morning Sun Extended Remix)
8722b True Dub *AKA* (Alternate Faith Dub)
8723 1963
8604a Paradise (Robert Racic remix)
ORIGINAL RELEASE: FAC 183 – July 1987

UK CHART POSITION: 1 August 1987 – #4 (10 weeks)
COMMENTS: Already scheduled as the group's next single (and a taster for the forthcoming *Substance* greatest hits collection), 'True Faith' received its first ever live airing at the Glastonbury Festival, as Sumner announced, 'this is a new song which we've never played before. So bear with us….' In fact, 'True Faith' emerged one of the most dynamic moments of the entire performance, and went onto become one of New Order's best loved, and most successful singles of all time.

According to Sumner, the song was 'about drug dependency. I don't touch smack but, when I wrote that song, I tried to imagine what it's like to be a smackhead and nothing else matters to you except that day's hit. There's a line in the song, "When I was a very young boy, very young boys played with me/Now we've grown up together, they're afraid of what they see." The original was, "Now they're taking drugs with me," but Stephen Hague, our producer, made us change it because he said it wouldn't be a hit if we kept that line in. He was right. It was a very big hit, but we chickened out. I change it back sometimes live.'

Of the b-sides, Australian DJ/producer Robert Racic's remix of 'Paradise' was targeted wholly at the dance floor, but scarcely improves on the original; while '1963' was described by Morris as 'basically a waste of a song.' It was considered as a single in its own right, but was scrapped because they didn't have a suitable b-side for it. But it got reclaimed by Arthur [Baker] and tarted up a bit. And was reissued as an A-side several years later.

Remixes of 'True Faith,' on the other hand, were absolutely dynamic, with the dub version the band's most effective excursion in that direction since 'The Beach,' four years before. And then there's the video, which presupposes almost everything that both the Blue Man Group and the Teletubbies would ever accomplish.

(SINGLE) Touched By The Hand Of God
8724 Touched By The Hand Of God
8724a Touched By The Hand Of God (extended version)

8724b Touched By The Hand Of Dub
8720a Confusion (dub)
8721 Temptation [8721 version used due to a mispressing]
ORIGINAL RELEASE: Factory FAC 193 – December 1987

UK CHART POSITION: 19 December 1987 – #20 (7 weeks)

COMMENTS: A three month American tour through the summer and autumn, followed by a clutch of major shows around the UK and Europe in the run-up to Christmas left New Order little time to prepare anything for their future. The approach to record five songs for the soundtrack to *Salvation!*, then, found them forced to work at record speed, with the creation of 'Touched By The Hand Of God' described by Morris as 'a land speed songwriting attempt.'

After a week in the studio working on their soundtrack contributions, the group had completed just four of the scheduled five songs. 'So it was basically sit down and write it in a day.' The entire performance was then completed in under seven hours – 'it was midnight and we had nothing,' Sumner reflected. 'The courier was coming for the tape at 7am.'

The singer also claims that, 'if you listen hard,' you can hear the Happy Monday's Bez 'snoring away in the background.'

1988

It is a point of pride in Manchester that, though the metropolis has by no means produced as many bona fide chart-toppers as other major cities, those it does throw up tend to be the benchmarks by which all the others are measured. In '77 it was the Buzzcocks, in '79 Joy Division, in '83 the Smiths – and now it was the Stone Roses, a band whose brief apprenticeship on the local scene had already seen them heralded as a second coming of sorts, at least until their similarly-titled sophomore album proved they most certainly weren't.

Peter Hook first encountered the group through Gareth Evans, a friend who hung out at the International nightclub, and who happened to be the Roses' manager. 'He was one weird character. He'd come up behind you with a bottle of Pernod and some cans of beer, then run off. In the end, we got talking.'

Two singles had already threatened, but not quite succeeded, in capturing the unique fusion of acid, rock and art that was the Stone Roses' gestating strength; Evans was convinced that Hook might well be the man who could coax the band's vinyl into taking that final step and, early in the new year, the team entered Revolution Studios in Rochdale to record 'Elephant Stone.'

'They were great players,' Hook reflected. 'We tracked up loads of guitars and I bored the band with anecdotes.' And later, once the Roses' career had stumbled to its bitter end, 'they could have been massive, couldn't they? They really had it. It reminds me of Joy Division, really. We would have been massive in America like they would have been, if we had just got there at the right time. But we lost a singer and the Roses wouldn't go because Gareth told the record label he wanted screaming girls at the airport like the Beatles....'

Produced by Hook, 'Elephant Stone' itself took close to a year to be released, as the Roses sought out a record deal; the first release on the Silvertone label (ORE 1) in late 1988, it finally made the UK chart in March 1990, as the follow-up to the group's top 10 debut, 'What The World Is Waiting For.' Hook, meanwhile, was the group's first choice to produce their debut album. 'But I had to go and record a New Order one instead.'

(ALBUM) original soundtrack *Salvation! Have You Said Your Prayers Today?*
8801 Salvation Theme
8724c Touched by the Hand of God (early version)
8802 Let's Go
8803 Sputnik
8804 Skullcrusher
CD BONUS TRACKS
8724a Touched by the Hand of God (extended version)
8724d Touched by the Hand of God (extended version – exclusive remix)
ORIGINAL RELEASE: Crepuscule TWI 774 – January 1988

COMMENTS: According to *Keyboard Magazine*, all but two of the songs (the long-standing live inclusions 'Let's Go' and 'Skullcrusher') were written specifically for the movie – and it shows. Clocking in at just a shade over two minutes, 'Salvation Theme' is little more than a loping keyboard loop, through which Peter Hook's bass line wanders like a vaguely cute predator, while the similarly brief 'Sputnik' is simply a piece of spacey ambience... which isn't to deny either track's suitability as soundtrack material, just to point out that speed and quality do not necessarily march hand-in-hand. (Neither, it seems, do words. 'Touched By The Hand Of God' is the only track that has any.)

'Touched' itself appears in something midway between demo and finished stage, with the lyrics in place, but the backing somewhat harder, and more laboured than the familiar hit take. But it is relentless across its five minute length, and emerges far and away the best of all New Order's contributions.

Seldom seen or heard since its limited release way-back-when, *Salvation!* was directed by New Yorker Beth B, a leading player within that city's early 80s Cinema of Transgression movement, and revolves around the kidnapping of a demented TV evangelist, played by Stephen McHattie. Dominique Davalos and X vocalist Exene Cervenka co-star, but the film is nowhere near as promising as its soundtrack – and the soundtrack turns out to be not so hot either – Jumpin' Jesus, Cabaret Voltaire, Hood, Dominique and Arthur Baker also contribute.

(SINGLE) Blue Monday 88
8805 Blue Monday 1988 (7" version)
8805a Blue Monday 1988
8805b Beach Buggy
8805c Blue Monday 1988 (dub version)
ORIGINAL RELEASE: Factory 73r – March 1988
UK CHART POSITION: 7 May 1988 – #3 (11 weeks)
COMMENTS: Buoyed by the club success of the 'Confusion' remake, New Order celebrated the fifth anniversary of their biggest hit ever by rerecording it, not only for a single but also for use in an advertisement for Sunkist orange juice. A new lyric was supplied by the advertising agency, and Sumner confessed, 'I kept laughing when I was singing it, so Hooky got a piece of card and wrote "£100,000" [the band's fee] on it, held it up, and I sang it perfectly: "How does it feel/When you're drinking in the sun? Something something something/Sunkist is the one/How does it feel/When you're drinking in the sun/All you've got to believe/Is Sunkist is the one."'

Unfortunately (or otherwise), Rob Gretton quashed this early move into a field that today, is gleefully ridden by artists from across the musical spectrum; at a time when rock's loudest critics were only just getting used to classic oldies (Marvin Gaye, Sam Cooke) being resurrected for TV commercials, it was simply too risky, and too demeaning, for a band of New Order's stature to open that door any further. Two years later, of course, the Clash would barrel through all such objections when they freed up 'Should I Stay Or Should I Go' for use in a Levi's ad, and were rewarded (among other riches) with their first ever UK #1. 'But did you ever forgive them for doing so?' Gretton asked a journalist in 1993. 'I didn't.'

The so-called Sunkist lyrics were subsequently transplanted onto a further remix from the '88' sessions, by house producer Steve "Silk" Hurley; this, too, was suppressed.

As for the released version, the worst thing one can say about it is, it sounds a lot more precise and professional than its predecessor – the much vaunted imperfections that characterised the 1983 version have been wrung out of sight, granting the new performance an almost robotic air. Would it have succeeded so well had it originally been issued in this form? Maybe… but probably not. A lot of people liked the old mistakes.

(MISC) Factory Blue Monday 1988 Flicker Book.

ORIGINAL RELEASE: This promotional item seen in the 'Blue Monday 1988' video was assigned the catalogue number FAC 235. 300 were manufactured.

(SINGLE) Fine Time
8806 Fine Time
8807 Don't Do It
8806a Fine Line
8806b Fine Time (Steve Silk Hurley Mix)
8806c Fine Time (messed around mix)
ORIGINAL RELEASE: Factory FAC 223 – December 1988

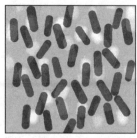

UK CHART POSITION: 10 December 1988 – #11 (8 weeks)

COMMENTS: After the crazed live itinerary of the previous two years, New Order devoted 1988 almost exclusively to the studio, working towards their next album. Incredibly, four months had elapsed before it was complete, two spent in the sun of Ibiza, two more at Peter Gabriel's Real World studios in Bath. Now Factory was demanding a single, but the band was so sick of hearing the songs that not one of them could bring him (or her) self to actually venture a suggestion at what it should be. And so, Sumner laughed, Rob Gretton asked if he could choose, and promised each of the band members £250 if he got it wrong.

He chose 'Fine Time,' a song originally written and recorded in Ibiza with a sexy Donna Summer vocal line. The following day, Sumner admitted, 'it got laughed out of the studio because it didn't sound erotic at all. It sounded like I was stuck on the toilet with constipation.' That vocal would eventually appear on the Steve Hurley remix; for the album and single, a new one was recorded in Bath.

'Virtually every track [on the album] could have made it [as a single],' Sumner mused. 'We thought "Fine Time" was all right, but it was more like a novelty record. I think it's funny. Not like a football record. Like "Every Little Counts" in a way. So Rob says, "I bet you this goes Top 10. And, if it doesn't I'll give you £250 each." So that was that. I couldn't care less if it goes Top 10. I just want the money!'

He got it as well, as the single slid no higher than #11 but, not only was it a close run thing, Gretton was also very unlucky – 'Fine Time' might not be 'classic' New Order in the way that 'True Faith' or 'Blue Monday' are classics, but it was a punchy track all the same, a hyper-active rhythm that certainly owed (or showed) the Happy Mondays something, on its way around the acid house, and came to even more startling life once Steve Hurley got his hands on it.

But chart competition that included Petula Clark's 'Downtown 88,' U2's 'Angel

Of Harlem,' Inner City's 'Good Life' and Status Quo's 'Burning Bridges' was never going to let New Order crash the Christmas party, while the Top 3 of the season... Cliff Richard, Kylie Minogue and Erasure... was not going to budge for anyone.

Among the b-sides, 'Don't Do It' holds claim to being one of *the* all-time great lost New Order numbers, a stately near-instrumental with a hint of hyper-active *Randall & Hopkirk Deceased*s to it.

(LIVE) Sao Paulo, Brazil, December 1 1988
UNR Ceremony
UNR True Faith
UNR Subculture
UNR Paradise
UNR Thieves Like Us
UNR Mr. Disco
UNR Your Silent Face
UNR Bizarre Love Triangle
UNR Blue Monday
UNR Age Of Consent
UNR Temptation
UNR The Perfect Kiss
UNR Touched By The Hand Of God
8808 Sister Ray
ORIGINAL RELEASE: Compilation *Like A Girl, I Want To Keep You Coming*: US Giornio Poetry Systems GPS 040 – Oct 1989
COMMENTS: Having devoted so much of the year to the studio, it was almost a relief for New Order to finally get out on the road again, as they launched a six shows in eight days tour of Brazil, then retired again with a pre-Christmas show in Manchester, billed alongside the Happy Mondays at the G-MEX. **(LIVE)** A party staged in the Haçienda basement following this latter concert was assigned the catalogue number FAC 208.

(MISC) Factory's accounts for Joy Division and New Order were assigned the catalogue number FAC 233 during 1988.

(MISC) *Here Are The Old Men* was an unrealised New Order video project, assigned the catalogue number FAC 237.

1989
(STUDIO)
8901 The Happy One
ORIGINAL RELEASE: VHS *Substance 89*, Factory/Virgin FACT 225 – September 1989
The quirky 'The Happy One' was recorded during the *Technique* sessions in Ibiza, and won the instant approval of Tony Wilson and Rob Gretton. The band,

however, were less keen, and ultimately approved its use only as interlude music before each of the videos included on *Substance 89*.

(ALBUM) *TECHNIQUE*
8902 Fine Time
8903 All the Way
8904 Love Less
8905 Round & Round
8906 Guilty Partner
8907 Run
8908 Mr. Disco
8909 Vanishing Point
8910 Dream Attack
ORIGINAL RELEASE: Factory FACD 275 – January 1989
UK CHART POSITION: 11 February 1989 – #1 (19 weeks)
COMMENTS: Promotional activities for Technique started early and, in typical Factory style, across some unusual formats. The cherub adorning the cover, designed by Stephen Mason, was assigned the catalogue number FAC 243. The advertising campaign accompanying the album's release was assigned the number FAC 271, while notepaper headed 'Campaign Technique' became FAC 289 – uniquely sharing that number with the singularly-named Wendy's 'The Sun's Going To Shine For Me Soon' single.

The album sessions themselves had been extraordinarily protracted – more than four months were spent in the studio, although the band readily admitted that not all the time had been spent working. According to Hook, the Ibiza set-up, Mediterranean Studios, was 'shit. But it [had] a pool and a bar.' The sessions swiftly became a whirl of social activity, as the group hit the nightclubs, sunbathed and wrote off their rental car, but the studio itself produced little useable music beyond a few drum tracks.

Not until the band relocated to the somewhat less glamorous surroundings of Peter Gabriel's Real World Studios in Bath, could recording begin in earnest – so earnest, in fact, that it was only when the band came to finally editing and programming the tracks ('at six in the morning on the last day,' sighed Sumner) that they realised they didn't have any song titles.

'Usually we have a sheet of paper pinned to the wall and everyone scribbles down words. They might see something in a book or hear a word in a film they like. Then, at the end, everyone puts a tick by the ones they like and the ones with the most ticks go on the album. This time we didn't have any. By seven o'clock, though, we'd got them all.'

The group's first British LP chart topper, *Technique* is unquestionably a child of its time – other New Order records may be dated by their technology, but *Technique* screams 'the end of the 80s' from every pore, as the Madchester sound (which, admittedly, they were so responsible for spawning) takes hold. It's by no means a rave from start to finish ('Fine Time' sews that requirement up all by itself), and there are sufficient tracks ('Guilty Partner' and the lovely 'Loveless' among them) to fly the flag for traditional New Order. But still the album as a whole loses much of its appeal if you should ever tire of the epoch it so evokes.

(SESSION) TV *THE OTHER SIDE OF MIDNIGHT* broadcast February 1989
UNR The Happy One
COMMENTS: Tony Wilson's second major contribution to British rock television culture, *The Other Side Of Midnight* ran through the late 1980s and, though its brief extended across the arts scene, it is best remembered for offering early television exposure to an entire new generation of British bands, the Stone Roses, the La's, the Happy Mondays and Inspiral Carpets among them.

A solo Peter Hook appeared on the show shortly after the release of *Technique*, armed with a vast array of sequencers and computers, and gave the *Technique* out-take 'The Happy One' its only full public airing.

(SINGLE) Round & Round
8905 Round & Round (new single mix)
8905a Round & Round (12-inch version)
8905b Round & Round (Club mix by Kevin Saunderson)
8905c Round & Round (12" remix by Ben Grosse)
8905d Round & Round (Detroit mix)
8909a Vanishing Point (instrumental making out mix)
8911 Best And Marsh
ORIGINAL RELEASE: Factory FAC 263 – February 1989
UK CHART POSITION: 11 March 1989 – #21 (7 weeks)
COMMENTS: An inevitable choice for the album's second single was at least distinguished by Kevin Saunderson's dynamic club mix, and a release for 'Best And Marsh,' a song originally commissioned to accompany a Tony Wilson television series on the footballers George Best and Rodney Marsh, the aptly named *Best & Marsh: The Perfect Match.*

According to Peter Hook, 'a guy at Granada [Television Studios] [was using] instrumental… versions [of our songs] for the football [coverage]...he used to use acoustic versions of "Sunrise," "Your Silent Face," "Dreams Never End"… he used to use loads of things for sports programs. So it came on from there and when Tony Wilson came to do a program on George Best and Rodney Marsh, he asked us to do the music specifically for the programme. So we actually wrote a piece called "Best and Marsh," and used it in the programme.'

Its title notwithstanding, 'Best And Marsh' has very little in common with anything remotely approaching your 'typical' football song – for a start, it's an instrumental, which leaves no room whatsoever for singing, chanting or cries of ''ere we go'; furthermore, it rumbles past at a pace more in keeping with the turpitude of a mid-70s Arsenal side, than either of the maestros for whom it was titled.

(LIVE) Poplar Creek Music Theater, Hoffman Estates, Illinois, 30 June 1989
UNR Ceremony

UNR Touched By The Hand Of God
UNR Dream Attack
UNR True Faith
UNR Mr. Disco
UNR Your Silent Face
UNR 1963
UNR Vanishing Point
UNR Round And Round
UNR Temptation
UNR The Perfect Kiss
UNR Bizarre Love Triangle
8912 Fine Time
ORIGINAL RELEASE: Box set *Retro*
COMMENTS: New Order launched their latest American tour in April, having warmed up with four shows in France and England over the preceding months. It was, by New Order's standards, a grueling outing, 34 dates (but an awful lot of travelling) spreading through till mid-July, and tapes of the shows catch the band sounding 'off' a lot more often than 'on.' The Poplar Creeks date is one of the few exceptions, and 'Fine Time' ripples across the stage with electrifying intent.

Already, however, the band knew that the end of the road was close. Hook later recalled, 'the saddest moment of my life that I can remember – close family apart – was when we sat in a hotel room in Los Angeles prior to playing Irvine Meadows [16 June]. We held a meeting about Factory because they were having such financial problems [and] it was there that Bernard announced he was going off to do his own thing. That gave me the shock of my life. I never expected that. I never expected not to have New Order.'

Back from the longest tour they had ever undertaken, New Order found themselves headlining the Reading Festival, bad-tempered with both the songs and each other. They proceeded to turn in one of the best shows of their lives – and the worst of their careers. Afterwards, Hook returned to the stage alone and tried to set fire to his guitar.

The bastard wouldn't burn and, as he stared at the scarcely-smoking instrument, suddenly he was seeing New Order there as well, calm, complacent and determinedly non-combustible. He returned to the dressing room and, before the day was through, announced that he, too, was leaving the band.

(SINGLE) Run 2
8907 Run 2
8907a Run 2 (extended mix)
8913 MTO
8913a MTO (Minus Mix)
ORIGINAL RELEASE: Factory FAC 273 – September 1989
UK CHART POSITION: 9 September 1989 – #49 (12 weeks)
COMMENTS: An odd choice for a single, that was treated with all the bemusement it deserved in the marketplace. The b-side 'MTO' is little more than a

New Order, Jan 1986. (Tom Sheehan)

Joy Division's Ian Curtis, Rainbow Theatre, London, November 1979. (Barry Plummer)

Electronic, Le Palace, Paris, 06 Dec 1991. (Fabrice Chassery)

Revenge, Paris, 26 Jan 1990. (Fabrice Chassery)

Bernard Sumner, La Mutualite, Paris, 08 Dec 1987. (Fabrice Chassery)

Peter Hook, La Mutualite, Paris, 08 Dec 1987. (Fabrice Chassery)

Stephen Morris, La Mutualite, Paris, 08 Dec 1987. (Fabrice Chassery)

Gillian Gilbert, La Mutualite, Paris, 08 Dec 1987. (Fabrice Chassery)

New Order, Finsbury Park, London, 09 June 2002. (David Sultan)

New Order, Finsbury Park, London, 09 June 2002. (David Sultan)

New Order, Le Zenith, Paris, 26 May 2002. (David Sultan)

Peter Hook and Pottsy (formerly Monaco). (David Sultan)

New Order, Paris, May, 1993. (David Sultan)

curio, either.

(SINGLE) PETER HOOK/REVENGE: 7 Reasons
r01 7 Reasons
r02 Jesus…I Love You
r03 …Love You Too
r04 Bleach Boy
ORIGINAL RELEASE: Factory FAC 247 – November 1989
COMMENTS: 'I don't know what it was, but when I was presented with New Order having some time off, I wasn't very happy about it, I didn't want the time off, I was quite happy touring. So I think Revenge was a rebellion thing, against that. I thought "right, I'll show you, I'm going to do something that doesn't sound a bit like New Order."

'So, I got two guys in, on guitar and keyboards, who really weren't that great, and the whole thing was a bit of a struggle. It felt very manufactured, it didn't feel natural, I didn't feel confident, and that came across in the music. Which was kind of foolish because... Bernard did Electronic, and people said it sounded just like New Order without the bass, which must have driven him crazy!' – Peter Hook, 1997

Bucking conventional rock lexicography, New Order insist their solo activities are *not* spin-off projects, although there's little doubt that they serve the same purpose – that is, to allow the individual band members to let off steam beyond the confines of the group and, as Morris put it, absorb ideas they might never otherwise have been exposed to.

'Our outside projects don't affect New Order, except in that they allow you personally to gain a wider perspective on what you're doing.' Hook continued. 'You get so used to being a part of New Order that it's very easy to start thinking there's nothing outside of it. It's nice to discover new people.'

In 1987, Hook purchased the old Cargo Studios wherein Joy Division spent so much time and, having renamed them Suite 16, he began toying with the notion of a solo album – despite his own admission that he really didn't want to do it. 'I don't really have any interest in the studio,' he told *Q*. 'I don't know whatever possessed me to buy one. I must be bleeding mad.'

Nevertheless, the next few months saw the project take shape as Hook teamed up with Chris 'CJ' Jones, the studio's resident engineer, and Nyam Nyam's Dave Hicks, and late in 1987 he admitted, 'I'm doing something with a friend of mine now (Hicks) but doing it solo doesn't interest me at all. I like the way we work together. I like the way, particularly, Bernard and me play together. For me that's what keeps New Order, the whole thing, alive.' Now, however, New Order seemed distinctly *not* alive, and it was time to bring the side project, already dubbed Revenge, out of the shadows.

The intention was for all three members to involve themselves in every aspect of the band, although Hook later acknowledged that, 'if I wasn't around, they stopped working. I had to be the leader all the time. It wore me out.' The group's ambition, too, was to prove fatal – discussing Revenge for the *One True Passion v2.0* 2CD anthology in 2004, Hook described this, the group's debut, as their most streamlined release. 'There were just miles too many layers [on everything else], which is unfortunate. Revenge's stuff was intricate and complicated. I didn't want to let anything go, because I wasn't 100% confident about anything. I put everything in, just in case somebody liked some bit. I couldn't bear to throw anything away.'

In fact, he never needed to. As *Uncut* announced some 15 years later, following the release of *One True Passion V2.0*, 'Truth is, Hook's DNA (shared with Bernard Sumner, Stephen Morris and Gillian Gilbert) prevents him from creating anything that's less than gorgeously dolorous, while those bowels-of-heaven bass lines here underpin two hours' worth of mournful melodies and Hook's lyrical declamations of despair and self-doubt.'

> **(SINGLE)** BERNARD SUMNER/ELECTRONIC: Getting Away With It
> e01 Getting Away With It
> e01a Getting Away With It (extended)
> e01b Getting Away With It (7-inch edit)
> e01c Getting Away With It (Vocal Remix)
> e01d Getting Away With It (Nude mix)
> e01e Getting Away With It (Instrumental)
> e02 Lucky Bag
> e02a Lucky Bag (edit)
> e02b Lucky Bag (Miami edit)
> **ORIGINAL RELEASE:** Factory FAC 257 – December 1989
> **UK CHART POSITION:** 16 December 1989 – #12 (9 weeks)
> **COMMENTS:** Five years after Bernard Sumner and the Smiths' Johnny Marr first recorded together, on Quando Quango's 'Atom Rock' single, the pair reunited during 1988 to concentrate on songwriting. Their activities were necessarily halted by other commitments – New Order's *Technique* album, and Marr's involvement with The The's *Mind Bomb*. The following year, however, they reconvened for what initially looked like a simple one-off project, combining with Pet Shop Boy Neil Tennant for this unimpeachably frothy 45.

A joy to encounter, 'Getting Away With It' truly was the sum of at least some of its parts – co-writer (with Marr and Sumner) Neil Tennant's backing vocals are inescapably Pet Shoppy, Bernard Sumner's lead is the newest order you could hope for, and there were plenty more such puns awaiting as 'Getting Away With It' travelled through the review pages. Its chart success, meanwhile, ensured that, whatever the principals' original intentions might have been, Electronic was destined to continue sparking.

1990

> **(ALBUM)** PETER HOOK/REVENGE: various artists *HOME*
> r05 Wende
> **ORIGINAL RELEASE:** Sheer 001 April 1990
> **COMMENTS:** A violent instrumental (demo of 'Slave', since gathered onto *One True Passion v2.0*.

(SINGLE) PETER HOOK/REVENGE: Pineapple Face
r06 Pineapple Face
r06a Pineapple Face's Revenge
r06b Pineapple Face's Last Lunge
r06c Pineapple Face's Big Day (same as r06e)
r06d Pineapple Face's Big Day (US remix)
r06e Pineapple Face Calls It A Day
r06f Pineapple Face's Edit
r06g Pineapple Face (Pickering & Park Remix) (same as r06e)
r07 14k
ORIGINAL RELEASE: Factory FAC 267 – May 1990
COMMENTS: Hey, forget what you've read elsewhere... this is good stuff.
True to Hook's word, it doesn't sound like New Order (not too much, anyway); and,
true again, there's an awful lot going on around the song itself. But there's a bass
line running through it that could sink ships, the ghost of 60s radio filtering through
the fade, and enough little hooks and snarls that Revenge's US label not only found
themselves with a major club hit, they even let the group make a video, a romp
through a seedy red light scenario that was promptly banned for being too sexy for
TV.

The b-side '14k,' meanwhile, has been described by Hook as 'my favourite
Revenge song of all. The lyrics express what I was trying to say better than anything
else I've ever done. I love it. I still listen to it.'

(SESSION) PETER HOOK/REVENGE: outtakes/demos etc
r08 Underworld
r09 Hot Nights/Cool City
r10 Surf Bass
r11 Soul
r12 Precious Moments
r13 Pumpkin
ORIGINAL RELEASE: *One True Passion V2.0*

(ALBUM) PETER HOOK/REVENGE: *ONE TRUE PASSION*
r06 Pineapple Face
r14 Big Bang *aka* The Trouble With Girls
r15 Kiss The Chrome
r16 Slave
r17 Bleachman
r18 Surf Nazi
r19 Fag Hag
r20 It's Quiet
ORIGINAL RELEASE: Factory FAC 230 – June 1990
COMMENTS: Hook himself is rarely kind to *One True Passion*, arguing that it
sounded far better live than it ever did on record, complaining about its fussiness...
pah, what does he know? From the reworked versions of 'Wende' ('Slave') and

'Bleach Boy' (the proto-industrial clatter of 'Bleachman') that gave pre-'Pineapple Face' fans something to cling to, and onto the shimmering, and so simplistic closer 'It's Quiet,' *One True Passion* overcomes so many of the bassist's personal objections that one could almost believe he's reacting to the album's commercial fate, as opposed to its musical invention, when he delivers his dour pronouncements.

(SINGLE) World In Motion
9001 World In Motion
9002 The B-Side
9001a World In Motion (No Alla Violenza Mix)
9001b World In Motion (Subbuteo Mix)
9001c World In Motion (Subbuteo dub – 4.13)
9001d World In Motion (Carabinieri mix – 5.40)
ORIGINAL RELEASE: Factory FAC 293 – May 1990

UK CHART POSITION: 2 June 1990 – #1 (12 weeks)
COMMENTS: Although the band was broken, there was to be one final act, one that would see New Order go to sleep on a full stomach, if nothing else.

The recording, the previous year, of the 'Best And Marsh' TV theme attracted attention far beyond the band's traditional catchment area; it drew in ears from the Football Association as well, as they pondered the once-every-four-years (if they're lucky) dilemma of selecting the song with which the country will sing England into the World Cup.

It was a traditionally fraught area; although such releases were guaranteed hits (1970's 'Back Home' even topped the chart), they were also regarded as crass, unlistenable and wholly embarrassing. Indeed, the idea of inviting a 'real' rock group to humiliate themselves in such shark-filled waters was as absurd as the average football record itself, but an invitation went out to New Order and, though few would ever have predicted it, a positive response came back almost immediately.

Later, Sumner explained, 'we recorded "World In Motion" because it was such an unexpected thing for us to be doing. But we wanted to bring some respectability to a disgraced musical genre.' They may or may not have succeeded in that aim, but 'World In Motion' did indeed become the most successful football record since 'Back Home,' topping the chart for a month that summer, and faltering only when England's time in the tournament ended with defeat to the Germans in the semi-final.

Co-written with comedian Keith Allen, the Stephen Hague-produced single paired New Order with a clutch of the 1990 England World Cup squad – Peter Beardsley, Paul Gascoigne, Steve McMahon, Chris Waddle, Des Walker, Craig Johnston and a rapping John Barnes among them. But not every participant was as enthusiastic as the Liverpool star, as Manchester United's Brian McClair explained, as he recalled a conversation he had with England captain Bryan Robson.

Robson: 'We've just made a record for the England World Cup Squad with some blokes called New Order.'

McClair: 'You'll have a #1 there, no problem.'

Robson: 'Never, no way! There's no way that rubbish is going to get to #1.'

T-shirts promoting the single, inscribed *EnglandNewOrder: Express Yourself*, were assigned the catalogue number FAC 283.

(LIVE) BERNARD SUMNER/ELECTRONIC: Dodger Stadium, LA 4/5 August 1990 (both dates)
UNR Gangster
UNR Try All You Want
UNR Reality
UNR Get The Message
UNR The Patience Of A Saint
UNR Getting Away With It
UNR Idiot Country
UNR Tighten Up
UNR Soviet
COMMENTS: Electronic would make a virtual virtue of their refusal to gig, turning in no more than seven shows throughout their decade-long career – with even Bernard Sumner, Mr Tour-Hater himself, eventually expressing some frustration at their situation. In August 1990, however, they appeared as special guests of Depeche Mode, and tapes of the event suggest that, given time, Electronic might have emerged a formidable live act. The line-up was completed by percussionists Kesta Martinez and A Certain Ratio's Donald Johnson, and keyboard player Andy Robinson.

The band's other live dates comprised Hacienda January 1991, Manchester's Cities In The Park festival in August 1991, and shows in Paris, Glasgow and London in December 1991.

(SINGLE) PETER HOOK/REVENGE: I'm Not Your Slave
r16 I'm Not Your Slave
r16a Slave (7-inch edit)
r16b Slave (extended remix)
r16c Slave (remix edit)
r16d Slave (Bonus Beat)
r16e Slave (instrumental)
r16f Slave (dub mix)
r16g Slave (alternate mix)
r16g Slave (club mix)
r15a Kiss The Chrome (edit)

r21 Amsterdam
ORIGINAL RELEASE: Factory FAC 279 – September 1990

(ALBUM) PETER HOOK/REVENGE: various artists *FUNKY ALTERNATIVE SIX*
r16h Slave (Smooth Mix)
ORIGINAL RELEASE: Concrete CPROD 016
COMMENTS: The basis for 'Slave' was a reworking of the giveaway 'Wende' instrumental, a great choice for single that was rendered even greater by the b-side cover of John Cale's 'Amsterdam,' and more intriguing by the host of remixes that circulated around the world.

The single was released as an expanded, five piece version of Revenge toured the US to generally high spirits – drummer Ash and bassist, and later guitarist, David Potts joined the team, with Hook recalling how, just months earlier, the latter had been working in a Manchester record store, where his greatest thrill was designing window displays which showed off the albums he liked the most.

He applied for a Tape Op job at Suite 16, during the recording of *One True Passion*; 'He came in to label the tape boxes and make tea, basically. Then, while we were recording, he'd be showing the guitarist how to play certain riffs, he'd be showing the keyboard player... and I thought "hang on a minute, he's better than both these guys!".' Potts was recruited into the live band – 'and the music got a hundred times better.'

Guitarist Dave Hicks was not convinced of that. As thoughts turned towards Revenge's next album, Hicks was adamant they record it as the original trio; when his bandmates refused, Hicks quit and Potts was in. With bassist Brian Whittaker moving in to enable Potts to switch to guitar, and new drummer Mike Hedges, the band spent much of 1991 in the studio, writing and demoing, but venturing out for the occasional live show as well, both to preview new material, and revive some older classics – New Order's 'Dreams Never End' was now the group's set-closer.

(SINGLE) Confusion 90
8720a Confusion (alternative mix)
8720b Confusion (essential mix)
8720c Confusion (trip 1-ambient confusion)
8720d Confusion (a capella)
8720e Confusion (con-om-fus-ars-ion)
8720f Confusion (ooh-wee dub)
ORIGINAL RELEASE: 12": US 1990 (Minimal Records QAL-249) – 1990

(ALBUM) various artists *VOLUME ONE*
8720g Confusion (remix by Dmitri for Dance Club Music)
ORIGINAL RELEASE: Limited edition for Dance Club Music members only.
Reissued on *Volume One* – Oct 1991
COMMENTS: A series of remixes added little to any previous version.

1991

(ALBUM) various artists *SELECT FACTORY TAPE*
e02b Lucky Bag (Miami edit)
r22 The Trouble With Girls (David Bianco remix)
ORIGINAL RELEASE: FACT 305c (CASSETTE FREE WITH *Select* magazine)
COMMENTS: A reasonable, and rare, Electronic remix, and a stunning new Revenge cut.

(SINGLE) BERNARD SUMNER/ELECTRONIC: Get The Message
e03 Get The Message (FAC 287/7a2 matrix)
e03a Get The Message (FAC 287/7a matrix – withdrawn mix)
e04 Free Will (7" edit)
e03a Get The Message (DNA Groove Mix)
e03c Get The Message (DNA Sin Mix)
e03b Get The Message (DNA Groove Mix edit) (promo only)
e03d Get The Message (DNA Sin Mix edit) (promo only)
e03e Get The Message (Extended Mix) (album version)
e04a Free Will (Extended Mix) (12" full length version)
ORIGINAL RELEASE: Factory FAC 287 – April 1991
UK CHART POSITION: 27 April 1991 – #8 (7 weeks)
COMMENTS: It's Marr's acoustic guitar bed that powers this single, as Electronic shrug off the year-plus that had elapsed since their last/first single, and simply pick up where they left off, commercially and musically. Opening doors that neither New Order nor the Smiths had ever truly bothered in their own pursuit of their private pop visions, 'Get The Message' is unspeakably garrulous, even as its actual melody chases somewhat more introspective directions, and the percussion races off towards Primal Scream territory – that band's Denise Johnson, incidentally, throws in some characteristically captivating backing vocals.

(ALBUM) BERNARD SUMNER/ELECTRONIC: *ELECTRONIC*
e05 Idiot Country
e06 Reality
e07 Tighten Up
e08 The Patience Of A Saint
e09 Gangster
e10 Soviet
e03 Get The Message
e11 Try All You Want
e12 Some Distant Memory
e13 Feel Every Beat
INTERNATIONAL (& UK REMASTERED) CD BONUS TRACK
e01 Getting Away With It
ORIGINAL RELEASE: Factory FAC 290 – May 1991

UK CHART POSITION: 8 June 1991 – #2 (16 weeks)

COMMENTS: Electronic's debut album was a sharp, frenetic offering, undeniably influenced by recent events of the electro/club scenes but, the opening 'Idiot Country' an honourable exception, rarely allowing itself to be swallowed whole by the hybrid. Nor could either of Electronic's composite parts be said to have over-stepped the boundaries of their collaboration; of course Sumner's vocal (and songwriting) is unmistakable; of course there are flourishes of guitar that could only have been Marr.

But only 'The Patience Of A Saint' truly has you throwing your hands into the air and declaiming the validity of these supergroups, as Neil Tennant returns with bandmate Chris Lowe in tow, and winds up with a reminder of the great little singles that the Pet Shops used to sling out when they started.

Highlights, however, there are aplenty – the urgent clanging of 'Gangster,' the careful subtlety of 'Soviet,' the familiar textures of the duo's last single and, closing the show, the next one, 'Feel Every Beat.' ('Getting Away With It' would subsequently be added to the album's remastered version; there is also a US promo single featuring a unique edit of 'Tighten Up.')

(SINGLE) BERNARD SUMNER/ELECTRONIC: Feel Every Beat
e13a Feel Every Beat (7-inch remix)
e13b Feel Every Beat (12-inch remix)
e13c Feel Every Beat (Dub Mix)
e13d Feel Every Beat (Tactile Mix)
e13e Feel Every Beat (Downstairs Mix)
e13f Feel Every Beat (Downstairs Dub)
e13g Feel Every Beat (Dave Shaw 12-inch Remix #1)
e13h Feel Every Beat (Dave Shaw 12-inch Remix #2)
e13i Feel Every Beat (DNA Mix)
e14 Lean To The Inside
e15 Second To None
ORIGINAL RELEASE: Factory FAC 328 – September 1991
UK CHART POSITION: 21 September 1991 – #39 (4 weeks)
COMMENTS: A braver choice of single than one might have expected, 'Feel Every Beat' marries barrelhouse piano with pulsating rhythm, and spread across the DNA 12-inch mix like floodwaters over farmland. The instrumental 'Lean To The Inside' sounds like the basis for just as great a song.

(SINGLE) MORRIS + GILBERT/THE OTHER TWO: Tasty Fish
o01a Tasty Fish (A Mix)
o01b Tasty Fish (Pascal Mix)
o01c Tasty Fish (Pascal 12-inch Mix)
o01d Tasty Fish (OT Mix)
o01e Tasty Fish (The Almond Slice Mix)
ORIGINAL RELEASE: Factory FAC 329, October 1991
UK CHART POSITION: 9 November 1991 – #41 (3 weeks)
COMMENTS: Quite frankly, one of the greatest records in the entire New Order
catalogue and one which, had it been released under the band's own name, would
have proved one of the biggest as well. Gillian Gilbert's vocals are quite sublime,
the electronics behind her are almost ruthlessly intriguing and, though too many
people have already used the words 'fish' and 'hook' in the same pun packed
sentence, still 'Tasty Fish' ranks among the best-baited 45s of the year.

The remixes, so integral to the record's US club success, detract somewhat (okay,
quite a lot) from the absolute purity of the original version, but they did the job they
were given, and that's probably all that counts.

(SINGLE) PETER HOOK/REVENGE: *Gun World Porn EP*
r23 Deadbeat
r23a Deadbeat (Gary Clail remix)
r23b Deadbeat (Gary Clail remix 2)
r24 Cloud Nine
r25 State Of Shock
r25a State Of Shock (Liverpool edit)
r25b State Of Shock (Paralyzed Mix)
r26 Little Pig
r26a Little Pig (Extended Mix)
r27 [untitled telephone answering machine message]
ORIGINAL RELEASE: Factory FAC 327 – January 1992 (US Capitol 98479
– December 1991)
COMMENTS: For all the new material and high hopes heaping up around the
band, *Gun World Porn* became Revenge's swansong, as a conventional four song
EP and revised across a clutch of (largely promotional) remixes.

(ALBUM) PETER HOOK/REVENGE: various artists: *HEAVEN AND HELL: A
TRIBUTE TO THE VELVET UNDERGROUND VOL 2*
r28 White Light White Heat
ORIGINAL RELEASE: Imaginary ILLCD 017
COMMENTS: One of *the* all-time definitive Velvet Underground retreads, hard
and sharp enough to eclipse either Joy Division or New Order's takes on 'Sister
Ray'; up there, in fact, with such gems as Bowie's 'Waiting For The Man,' Bryan
Ferry's 'What Goes On' or…actually, it's shocking to realise just how pitifully few
great Velvets covers there are out there. Certainly nothing else on this tribute fits the
bill, but 'White Light' was worth the price of admission anyway.

1992

(SINGLE) BERNARD SUMNER/ELECTRONIC: Disappointed
e16 Disappointed (Original Mix)
e16a Disappointed (7-inch Mix)
e16b Disappointed (12-inch Mix)
e05a Idiot Country Two (*aka* Ultimatum mix)
e09a Gangster (FBI Mix)
ORIGINAL RELEASE: Parlophone R 6311 – June 1992
UK CHART POSITION: 4 July 1992 – #6 (5 weeks)
COMMENTS: Pulled from the *Cool World* movie soundtrack, it was third time's the charm for Electronic's passing partnership with Neil Tennant. Yes, of course it still sounds like the Pet Shop Boys, but this is the Pet Shops at their best, with a keening chorus, a battalion of electronics, and so many hooks that no depth of remix could ever have dented its majesty.

Indeed, if there's any disappointment to be taken from the remixes, it's that not one of them bothered adding more than a minute or two to the song's original dimensions, when they could have been taking lessons from the Art Of Mix/Ultra Hot Razor team (John M Pillin and Steve Smith); their FBI Mix of 'Gangster' is utterly compulsive.

(ALBUM) *REPUBLIC – ADVANCE CASSETTE*
UNR Pre-mix instrumental versions of songs intended for the new album.
ORIGINAL RELEASE: Factory FAC 300 – October (?) 1992. Collectors estimate that no more than five copies were manufactured.
COMMENTS: 'World In Motion' was New Order's last new recording for close to three years. Indeed, for a time, it seemed as though they might never reconvene. 'Quite simply,' designer Peter Saville reflected, 'they were sick of the sight of each other. They needed [a] break to recover.'

Of course, not one of the quartet was idle during the lay-off, as Sumner's Electronic, Hook's Revenge and the other two's The Other Two proved. By mid-1992, however, the band had reconvened in the studio, to begin working towards a new album.

Much had changed since New Order's last appearance, most notably the elevation of Mad/Manchester as the music capital of the immediate universe – even before the temporarily world-conquering emergence of Oasis, the spirit of the Happy Mondays and Stone Roses still roamed the streets. By their own confession, the group absorbed all this, then attempted to put their own spin on it.

It was not, however, destined to be an easy process. The album sessions were themselves so intense that, when New Order were invited to rerecord Joy Division's 'Love Will Tear Us Apart' and 'Dead Souls' for the movie soundtrack *The Crow*, they turned it down, partly became Sumner considered it a backward step, but also because they simply didn't have the time.

For the album was not the only thing occupying their minds. The Haçienda was lurching from crisis to crisis, while the group was also labouring beneath the glowering shadow of Factory's demise, as a decade long party finally began to wind down. The label declared bankruptcy on November 24, 1992, just months before the scheduled release date for *Republic* – advance cassettes of the unmixed music had already been manufactured, a catalogue number was set aside for the proposed first single. And then....

Tempers within the band's own camp were strained, too. Hook explained, 'we were so pissed off with each other because we'd been together so long, and there'd been problem after problem. On top of that, we were having crisis meetings about the Haçienda twice a week, while we were trying to record an album. That's not exactly a great environment to write in — and because we weren't getting on anyway, we weren't writing very quickly.

'We were out drowning our sorrows in all types of ways, which meant a lot of the time, we weren't able to work because we were completely twatted — not that we were particularly willing to work anyway. What happened was, if there was nobody in the studio you'd go in for a bit and, as soon as someone else turned up, you'd run off. It was awful. And Factory were trying to rush us to do the LP because they needed money.'

'In the past,' continued Morris, 'everyone on Factory had the same kind of arrangement as us, no contracts and an understanding that they could leave when they wanted to. So OMD and the Railway Children buggered off, and it was only us daft sods who stuck it out. Then Factory started doing contracts with the Happy Mondays and trying to be a real record company. But they never got record company-ish enough, and now they're in the hands of the liquidators.'

But the label's demise, Sumner continued, was also 'the story of our times,' exacerbated by the company's own, self-confessed obsession with ambitious recording projects – Cath Carroll was estimated to have spent close to $400,000 on her Factory album, and she wasn't alone. The label also gave away too much in terms of recording agreements, which paid too much attention to the comfort of the artist, but very little to that of the label. Everything was falling... indeed, had already fallen... apart.

And then, as the *Observer* put it, 'in the midst of the carnage, someone found a piece of paper signed by the Factory directors that read: "The musicians own the music and we own nothing" – which meant that the bands could sign huge publishing deals for all the tunes they'd already written, as well as recording contracts for future music.'

The liquidators, Sumner grinned, 'just couldn't believe this piece of paper existed. But it did. No contract, just this bit of paper. They tried to make out that we'd written it a couple of days earlier, but honest to God we didn't.'

The finger-pointing that erupted when this was made public, the suggestion that New Order could, maybe even should, have thrown in their lot with the label, cut little ice with New Order themselves. Sumner admitted outright that the band would have happily remained a bargaining chip, 'if Factory hadn't already owed us so much money.' Instead, the band shifted their affections to London Records in the UK... and it was business as usual.

Sumner continued, 'we signed to London Records because, when Factory went down, they went down owing us a *lot* of money. A lot of money. Basically, as far as I'm concerned, they went down without paying us for *Technique*. That amount of money. So we signed to London Records because they offered to pay back the Factory debt plus, to complete the recording of *Republic*. Factory Records went down half way through *Republic*, so London offered to pay us the money that Factory owed us, plus finish the recording of *Republic*. So we didn't get paid an advance, we just got paid back the money that we were owed.'

(SESSION) MORRIS + GILBERT/THE OTHER TWO: TV *America's Most Wanted*
o02 *Theme*
COMMENTS: One of the most-heard US television themes of the 1990s – certainly up there with the Rembrandts' 'I'll Be There For You' (*Friends*) and Inner Circle's 'Bad Boys' (*COPS*) anyway – the Other Two's dramatic overture isn't simply their own best-known track, it's probably the most frequently whistled number in this entire book. And most people don't even know it's in here.

They Might Be Giants have been known to cover it live, incidentally.

1993

(SINGLE) Regret
9301 Regret (album version)
9301a Regret (New Order mix)
9301b Regret (Fire Island mix)
9301c Regret (Junior Dub mix)
9301d Regret (Sabres' Slow'n'Low)
9301e Regret (Sabres' Fast'n'Throb)
ORIGINAL RELEASE: Centredate NUO 1 – April 1993
UK CHART POSITION: 17 April 1993 – #4 (7 weeks)
COMMENTS: In the past, Morris revealed, 'the New Order method of titling [songs was] just writing down words that are completely abstract and don't relate to anything; then, when you've written the songs, it's just like pin the tail on the donkey.' This time around, they decided to do something different. 'Let's name the songs!,' Gilbert laughed. 'For instance, "Regret" was always "Regret".'

Originally scheduled for release on Factory, with the catalogue number FAC 323, 'Regret' ranks among the most direct songs New Order have ever recorded, with its signature guitar riff cutting through daytime radio like a knife, to captivate the listener without any to do. This wasn't one of those records that grows on you, it wasn't one that you hear a dozen times before you finally discern its unimpeachable graces. It just shot out both hands and grabbed you round the throat, and didn't stop shaking till you laid out your cash.

The remixes, spread across the now obligatory slew of 7-inch, 12-inch, CD and promotional singles, allowed the song to spread its wings further. Not all were especially exciting (or even necessary), but among the best, the 'Fire Island Mix' mixed the guitar overture down to ambient inaudibility, slowed the song to balladic proportions, and allowed Sumner's vocal to carry the punch, while New Order's own eponymous mix reduced the intro to a succession of crunchy keyboard flourishes, and the percussion to a sound not unlike the beating of a damp carpet (!). But Andy Weatherall and his Sabres Of Paradise's 'Slow'n'Low' mix was the most revolutionary, as it dispensed with much of the lyric, most of the melody and wound up all but unrecognisable.

Discussing remixes in general, Sumner mused, 'I think some remixers write a whole new track and, in the last half hour in the studio, they get the vocal and plonk it on. [But] listening to remixes means I know what's going on in the clubs, because I don't go clubbing any more. It's a good way of learning off other people.'

(ALBUM) *REPUBLIC*
9301 Regret
9302 World
9303 Ruined in a Day
9304 Spooky
9305 Everyone Everywhere
9306 Young Offender
9307 Liar
9308 Chemical
9309 Times Change
9310 Special
9311 Avalanche
ORIGINAL RELEASE: Centredate 828413, May 1993

UK CHART POSITION: 15 May 1993 – #1 (19 weeks)

COMMENTS: Embracing every rhythm pattern currently blaring out of club speakers (with jungle and drum & bass predominating), *Republic* emerged the ultimate, glorious, dance floor disc. Yet its gestation was so slow that there were times, Peter Hook confessed, when it felt as though the album would never be complete. '*Closer* took two weeks from start to finish and, ever since then, it's taken longer and longer and longer, until you get to *Republic*, when you're talking about 7 months!'

'When a band records its first album,' Sumner continued, 'it does it quick and makes it good. There's a lifetime of experience being poured into it, and a lifetime of songs. Once things take off, though, that life experience narrows, because you're either in the studio or you're being interviewed, or you're on the road staggering around drunk and shagging lots of girls. So, what do you write songs about? Either you're going to start writing shit songs about nothing, or you start to use your fucking head, stop doing it for a while, and live a little.'

He insisted that 'the most important thing is to deliver a piece of music which means something to you, and isn't just the focus of the next sales campaign.' It was vital, too, to shake things up a little and *Republic* itself made two very determined attempts to shrug off any past formulae New Order might have worked towards – writing the songs before entering the studio, and employing a proper producer, 'World In Motion' overseer Stephen Hague.

Gillian Gilbert explained, 'we chose him because when we first met him, he said he never wanted to produce an album because it took too long. He didn't want to spend a lot of time on it, which is a good attitude to have.' But *Republic* still took 'too fucking long,' complained Hook, 'and the idea of writing songs before we went into the studio didn't work either.'

Rather than blame themselves, however, Morris reckoned technology was at fault. 'In Ye Olde Days, you just plugged in a guitar, added drums and that was it. Now you've got computers and such like, and you can spin the whole thing out for bleeding years if you want to.'

And New Order, it appeared, wanted to.

'No, it just happened like that,' Morris continued. 'Times change, music changes, things which bands can do now, they could never have got away with in the past and *vice versa*.'

As usual, the album cover was designed by Peter Saville, who was astonished to discover that, after the years of *laissez-faire* distance that had been his past experience with the band, 'this time, they all wanted to have approval of it.'

The result, a collage of imagery that erupts around what started life as a holiday brochure photo of a young couple playing with a rubber ring on a sun-soaked golden beach, emerged one that Saville continues to regard fondly. Not only, he says, was it the first time that he and his partner, Canadian Brett Wickens, ever employed a computer to blend pictures together, it was also the first time they ever found all four band members to be in total agreement over something.

'New Order is a complete democracy. With other groups, there is always someone who's "in charge" and, if you're a designer or a video director or whatever, you have to identify who has the power and that's the person you have to deal with. [But] with New Order, that doesn't happen and, whenever an individual personality tries to be that, the others gang up against them. So you have the four band members to consider, and traditionally they would never agree on anything, which is one of the reasons why I would wander off and do the cover by myself.

'In fact, not only would they never agree, they would also deliberately disagree. So, if somebody said "I think the cover should be red," another would say it ought to be blue. And that's when I'd thank them for their input, then go away and make it green. But they loved the rubber ring, all four of them' – and not necessarily for the sheer whimsicality of the image. With Factory's slow implosion now in full swing, and the label's suitors and detractors alike descending upon the still twitching body, to make off with the jewelry, the sight of that bright rubber ring being wrestled over by two laughing, carefree people – 'almost torn apart by them,' was how Saville described it – seemed somehow analogous to the band's own situation.

The rubber ring remained, to be joined by a succession of other images... a burning house, a *Twin Peaks* lake scene, a forest by night, scene upon scene piling up [around the happy vacationers to leave the viewer feeling physically assaulted by the sheer wealth of information. By the time the sleeve was completed, one of Saville's colleagues was moved to describe it as 'CNN directed by David Lynch.' Saville himself, however, preferred to call it 'a fast forward collage; if it reminds me of anything, it's sitting in an LA hotel room with 52 channels and nothing to watch.'

Good job there was a new New Order album to listen to, then. Or was it? A decade later, Sumner admitted, 'I think [*Republic*] is a mixed bag. I think there are some really good tracks on it and some mediocre tracks on it. Yeah, that's what I really think.' In the notes to *Retro*, he reveals that 'Everyone Everywhere' was his favorite track after 'Regret,' even if the chord shapes were so awkward that playing it hurt his hand. 'But the thing that overjoyed me about *Republic* was that we actually finished it. The thing I'm proud of – apart from [the fact that] there *are* some great tracks on it – the thing I'm really proud of is that we actually soldiered through and finished it. Because if we'd really had any sense, we had so much trouble and strife recording it, we should've gotten the fuck out of there until all the business affairs were sorted out to our satisfaction. But we didn't, we soldiered on. And I'm very proud of [that].'

(SINGLE) Ruined In A Day
9303a Ruined in a Day (radio edit)
9303b Ruined in a Day (12 inch Bogle mix)
9303c Ruined in a Day (Bogle mix)
9303d Ruined in a Day (Dancehall Groove)
9303e Ruined in a Day (instrumental)
9303f Ruined in a Day (K-Klass edit)
9303g Ruined in a Day (live mix)
9303h Ruined in a Day (Reunited in a Day remix)
9303i Ruined in a Day (Rhythm Twins dub)
9303j Ruined in a Day (Sly & Robbie radio edit)
9303k Ruined in a Day (the ambient mix)
9312 Vicious Circle (New Order mix)
9312a Vicious Circle (Mike Haas mix)
ORIGINAL RELEASE: CentreDate NUO 2 – June 1993
UK CHART POSITION: 3 July 1993 – #22 (4 weeks)
COMMENTS: Maybe it's churlish; and, almost certainly, it evinces a complete lack of understanding of the nature of the modern dancefloor (a mix for every mood – how super). But is any song so good that it requires upwards of a dozen different mixes, before it can be let out on its own? Especially one like 'Ruined In A Day' which, on album, stood as a moody oasis that already sparkled as much as it needed to.

Part of New Order's intention, Sumner admitted, was simply to grasp the opportunity to lock horns with artists they admired. K-Klass, for example, were 'a band from Liverpool... we all liked the stuff they did.' Other remixes were suggested by the label – one of the London staffers was a dance DJ 'who told us who was hot and who's not hot.' And others were unleashed because... again, Sumner put it best. Pairing up with Jamaican rhythm section Sly Dunbar and Robbie Shakespear could... indeed, should... have been a phenomenal move. But 'we didn't think that the Sly and Robbie remixes were the most *fantastic* thing we'd ever done. But we thought it was one of the funniest things we'd ever heard! So that's why we put it out. I mean, we don't have to take everything we do absolutely seriously. But, we thought it was so ridiculous, we'd put it out.'

(LIVE) Starplex Amphitheatre, Dallas, Texas, 21 July 1993
UNR Ruined In A Day
UNR Regret
UNR Dream Attack
UNR Round And Round
9313 World (The Price Of Love)
UNR As It Is When It Was
UNR Everyone Everywhere
UNR True Faith
UNR Bizarre Love Triangle
UNR Temptation
UNR The Perfect Kiss
UNR Fine Time
ORIGINAL RELEASE: Box set *Retro*
COMMENTS: New Order kicked off their latest world tour in Dublin on 5 June, ploughing on through three well-spaced European festivals during July, and then into a short (nine date) American tour in July. This recording dates from the opening night in Dallas, a 116 degree sweatbox that left the audience exhausted before the two opening acts (Stereo MCs and 808 State) had even completed their own performances; and saw tempers so frayed that, the moment it became apparent that New Order intended playing just one encore ('Fine Time'), a mini-riot ensued.

Riding its subtitle so hard that its eventual titling certainly marked a major compromise on the band's behalf, 'World' itself was one of the highlights of the 1993 set list – as, indeed, it was of *Republic* as a whole.

(SINGLE) World (The Price Of Love)
9302a World (radio edit)
9302b World (Perfecto edit)
9302c World (Perfecto mix)
9302d World (Pharmacy dub)
9303e World (the Price of Dub)
9303f World (Sexy Disco dub)
9303g World (Spike's mix)
9303h World (Stephen Hague mix – same as radio edit)

9303i World (the Brothers Dubstrumental)
9303j World (the Brothers in Rhythm mix)
9303k World (World in Action mix)
ORIGINAL RELEASE: CentreDate NUO 3 – August 1993

UK CHART POSITION: 4 September 1993 – #13 (5 weeks)
COMMENTS: Beyond the above, an unreleased US promo also promised so-called 'Price Of Love' remixes by Danny Tenaglia, although the dozen revisions that did make it out were probably more than enough for most tastes.

(LIVE) Reading Festival, August 1993
UNR Ruined In A Day
9314 Regret
9315 As It Is When It Was
UNR Round & Round
UNR Everyone Everywhere
UNR Temptation
UNR The Perfect Kiss
UNR World
UNR Fine Time
UNR Blue Monday
ORIGINAL RELEASE: Box set *Retro*
COMMENTS: In early August, at a meeting in New York, Sumner told Hook, 'if I never see your face again, it'll be too soon.' Less than a month later, he got his wish. 'We'd just finished the tour... we were all falling out with each other.' When the gig finally ended, 'we all walked off, went to bed, and didn't speak to each other for five years.'

The tragedy of that was, Reading 93 ranks as one of the greatest gigs New Order ever played. 'I remember someone playing a bootleg of the gig at a clothes shop and it sounded fantastic,' Sumner continued, while Hook admitted that, when he heard the tapes of the show back, 'I was nearly in tears... thinking, "oh shit, what a waste".'

The two Reading tracks that have seen official release so far bear out the band's post-mortem enthusiasm. 'Regret' has a tightness that allies it alongside its studio counterpart; and, if 'As It Was...' seems a little looser, then that is the nature of the song itself. It is harsh, however, that New Order have not (yet) seen fit to release the entire show. Fans and collectors might prefer to see and hear an early performance. But they would certainly enjoy this one more.

(SINGLE) MORRIS + GILBERT/THE OTHER TWO: Selfish
o03 Selfish (The Single Mix)
o03a Selfish (That Pop Mix)
o03b Selfish (East Village Vocal Mix)
o03c Selfish (Junior Style Dub)
o03d Selfish (East Village Dub)
o03e Selfish (Fire Island Mix)
o04a Moving On (Waterfront Mix)
ORIGINAL RELEASE: London TWO 1 – October 1993
UK CHART POSITION: 6 November 1993 – #46 (2 weeks)
COMMENTS: Already heralded as one of the highlights on the approaching
The Other Two album, the near-symphonic 'Selfish' followed 'Tasty Fish' into the
lower echelons of the chart… and then, absurdly, dropped like a stone.

Once again, the remixes took more than they gave to the song itself, but pounding
onto the nightclub floor, pop genius really doesn't need to show itself too often.

(ALBUM) MORRIS + GILBERT/THE OTHER TWO: *THE OTHER TWO AND
YOU*
o01 Tasty Fish
o05 The Greatest Thing
o03 Selfish
o04 Movin' On
o06 Ninth Configuration
o07 Feel This Love
o08 Spirit Level
o09 Night Voice
o10 Innocence
CD BONUS TRACK
o11 Loved It (The Other Track)
ORIGINAL RELEASE: London (520028) – November 1993

COMMENTS: Originally scheduled for a late 1992 release on Factory (FACT
330), the album was ultimately delayed until after *Republic* had run its course.
Regarded as the most obscure of the New Order spin-offs, the Other Two quickly
revealed themselves, contrarily, to be the most commercial, as the album spirals out
from the vibrant electronica of the immortal 'Tasty Fish,' to embrace an entire
barrage of textures and techniques that – yes, might sound more like New Order

than either Electronic or Revenge – but also reveal Gilbert to have the best voice in the entire band. In fact, the whole thing makes you despair, sometimes, of whatever it is that goes on in record company boardrooms… they spend all that time and money manufacturing the next pop sensation, then overlook the best 'new band' of them all, though they've been on the books all along.

From the almost-sultry 'Feel This Love' to the brightly bleeping 'Loved It'; from the compulsive 'Movin' on' to the spectral glow of the instrumental 'Ninth Configuration,' *The Other Two And You* draws on all the innovation that New Order were famed for, all the pop genius that they were occasionally capable of, and winds up with ten songs that… let's not beat around the bush here; they leave the bulk of *Republic* in the dust.

(SINGLE) Spooky
9304 Spooky (album version)
9304a Spooky (radio album edit)
9304b Spooky (Fluke edit *aka* Minimix)
9304c Spooky (Magimix)
9304d Spooky (Moulimix)
9304e Spooky (Neworder in Heaven)
9304f Spooky (Night Tripper mix)
9304g Spooky (Out of Order mix)
9304h Spooky (Boo! Dub mix)
9304i Spooky (Stadium instrumental)
9304j Spooky (Stadium mix)
ORIGINAL RELEASE: Centredate NUO 4 – December 1993
UK CHART POSITION: 18 December 1993 – #22 (4 weeks)
COMMENTS: Opening on a robotic pulse that is the closest New Order have ever come to a musical acknowledgement of the influence of Kraftwerk, 'Spooky' then drifts into a suitably haunted ballad and, even with no band to promote it, 'Spooky' – the fourth and final single from *Republic* – was strong enough to at least shove the band into the Top 30.

1994

(SINGLE) True Faith 94
8722c True Faith-94
8722d True Faith-94 (radio edit *aka* radio mix)
8722e True Faith-94 (Eschreamer dubbier)
8722f True Faith-94 (Perfecto radio edit)
8722g True Faith-94 (Eschreamer dub)
8722h True Faith-94 (Perfecto mix)
8722i True Faith-94 (Sexy Disco dub)
8722j True Faith-94 (TWA Grim Up North mix)
ORIGINAL RELEASE: Centredate NUO 5 – November 1994
UK CHART POSITION: 19 November 1994 – #9 (8 weeks)
COMMENTS: The original single was so sublime that a remix really seems

unnecessary – or, maybe, that was why London Records deemed it essential, as perfection was tweaked a little bit tighter and a record that everybody should already have owned suddenly became an essential purchase all over again. Originally treated for the forthcoming *? (The Best Of New Order)* compilation, 'True Faith 94' took on such a life of its own that it came close to eclipsing the success of the 1987 version.

8723e 1963 95 (Lionrock Full Throttle mix)
8723f 1963 95 (Lionrock M6 Sunday Morning mix)
8723g 1963 95 (Lionrock Sparse 'n' Fast mix)
8723h Let's Go (new vocal version) *aka* Let's Go (Nothing For Me)

1995

(SINGLE) Nineteen63
8723a 1963 94 (album mix)
8723b 1963 95 (Arthur Baker radio remix)
8723c 1963 95 (Joe T Vanelli Dubby mix)
8723d 1963 95 (Joe T Vanelli Light mix)
8723e 1963 95 (Lionrock Full Throttle mix)
8723f 1963 95 (Lionrock M6 Sunday Morning mix)
8723g 1963 95 (Lionrock Sparse'n'Fast mix)
8724 Let's Go (new vocal version) *aka* Let's Go (Nothing For Me)
ORIGINAL RELEASE: CentreDate NUO 6 – January 1995
UK CHART POSITION: 21 January 1995 – #21 (4 weeks)
COMMENTS: How divided opinions remain over the virtues of all these remixes and remodels, with the urge to keep up with technology seemingly outstripping any need to keep pace with the band's own history.

Whereas 'True Faith 94' merited all the attention it deserved, the renewed attention granted its 1987 b-side ('a waste of a song,' remember?) was less obvious. Originally reworked, once again, for inclusion on *? (The Best Of New Order)* – the '94 Album Mix,' it was reapproached the following year, with Baker and the rising Lionrock's remixes alone truly justifying the operation.

(SINGLE) Blue Monday 95
8805c Blue Monday (Andrea mix)
8805d Blue Monday (Brain mix, *aka* Corleone mix)
8805e Blue Monday (Hardfloor mix)
8805f Blue Monday (Hardfloor radio edit)
8805g Blue Monday (Jam & Spoon Manuela mix)
8805h Blue Monday (Starwash mix)
8805i Blue Monday (Plutone dub)
8805j Blue Monday (Plutone mix)
ORIGINAL RELEASE: CentreDate NUO 7 – July 1995
UK CHART POSITION: 5 August 1995 – #17 (4 weeks)

(ALBUM) various artists *FROM MANCHESTER WITH LOVE*
8805m Blue Monday (Richie Hawtin mix)

ORIGINAL RELEASE: Love.net L NET4CD – 1995

COMMENTS: 'If a job's worth doing,' Todd Rundgren once remarked, 'it's worth over-doing.' Having escaped the remixer's attentions as *? (the Best Of New Order)* came together, 'Blue Monday' (the 1988 remake) was pulled out for a make-over the following year regardless. There was never any attempt made to improve on the form of either past version, however; rather, 'Blue Monday 95' was intended simply to let a clutch of the day's hottest remix names show how they would handle a song that undoubtedly influenced almost all of them.

Retro's inclusion of the Jam & Spoon Manuela Mix is representative of the final results, while the Razormaid mix, though certainly in keeping with the often dramatic scenarios best associated with that particular brand name, is nevertheless one of their less essential efforts. An evening spent with the multitudinous remixes, then, is regrettably recommended for technicians and masochists only.

(SINGLE) Everything's Gone Green – The Advent remixes
8113b Show me Green Mix
8113c Green For Help Mix
8113d Green Gone Hard Mix
8113e Electric Green
ORIGINAL RELEASE: Internal LIARX 32 – 1996
COMMENTS: While the cat's away...New Order were dead, but the back catalogue was hopping. Sadly, this scarce 12-inch really doesn't go anywhere that the original didn't suggest.

(SINGLE) MORRIS + GILBERT/THE OTHER TWO: Innocence
o10a Innocence (Love To Infinity's Deep Love 12-inch)
o10b Innocence (Love To Infinity's Deep Dub)
o01f Tasty Fish (K Klass Klub Mix)
o01g Tasty Fish (K Klass Pharmacy Dub)
o12 Satisfied
ORIGINAL RELEASE: US single Qwest 41737 – February 1995
COMMENTS: With Warner Brothers thoroughly enthused by the club success of the Other Two's other two singles-so-far, a third track is pulled from the album, remixed and then unleashed. Surprisingly, 'Innocence' did not hit as hard as it might have, but the classy K-Klass takes on 'Tasty Fish' were both unavoidable for a time.

1996

(SINGLE) BERNARD SUMNER/ELECTRONIC: Forbidden City
e17 Forbidden City
e18 Imitation Of Life
e19 A New Religion
ORIGINAL RELEASE: Parlophone R6436 – June 1996
UK CHART POSITION: 6 July 1996 – #14 (4 weeks)
COMMENTS: 'New Order meets the Smiths, Manchester supergroup, how soon is blue Monday... you know the drill, you imagine the thrill and, first time out

(back in 1991, grandchildren), both the timing and the writing were spot on.

But what a difference five years makes. Post Grunge, post Britpop, and way past the post for the Cackhanded Electrodance Shuffle, messrs Sumner and Marr reconvened, and simply carried on as if history hadn't happened, not even realising that half the people who bought the first album have probably bought the farm since then. Dance-pop for the dead... what a novel concept.' (*Alternative Press*)

Point taken. But it really wasn't that bad.

(ALBUM) BERNARD SUMNER/ELECTRONIC: *RAISE THE PRESSURE*
e17 Forbidden City
e20 For You
e21 Dark Angel
e22 One Day
e23 Until The End Of Time
e24 Second Nature
e25 If You've Got Love
e26 Out Of My League
e27 Interlude
e28 Freefall
e29 Visit me
e30 How Long
e31 Time Can Tell
JAPANESE CD BONUS TRACK
e32 All That I Need
ORIGINAL RELEASE: Parlophone PCS 7382 – July 1996

UK CHART POSITION: 20 July 1996 – #8 (5 weeks)
COMMENTS: Or maybe it was.

Electronic, mused *Alternative Press*, really was 'the kind of band which exists best on paper.' Ferret through rock's archives and a thousand such superstar collaborations leap out and scream, and the only difference is, Electronic not only got off the paper, they got off the starting blocks too. So, though no-one would call their second album a Second Coming, in terms of commonplace occurrences, it's certainly up there with hen's teeth and fish-headed babies, a carnival freakshow of passing-by superchums, and a vivacious pop bounce which will roost in your skull forever.

Neil Tennant was occupied elsewhere, but Denise Johnson makes a welcome return, and Kraftwerk's Karl Bartos pops up to power the spotty 'Second Nature.'

But the music... oh, the music. *Raise The Pressure* lowers all expectations, an almost carbon-copy return to the pastures of its predecessor, with a couple of added bonus guitar solos ('Forbidden City' has the best of them), and Sumner's talky-mope vocals visibly wavering between the heartbreak soul he wants to sing, and the bucket and mop combo he so often becomes. He does have a nice voice, but has he not heard of conviction? 'Oh yeah, Hooky's got a few of them.'

So what you expect is what you get, no shocks, no surprises, no 'Panic' or 'Blue Monday,' and scarcely even a 'Getting Away With It.' But a lot of songs that sound like they'd like to be one of them and, really, one has to ask – what's the point of leaving a band, if you're just going to carry on making their records?

(SINGLE) BERNARD SUMNER/ELECTRONIC: For You
e20 For You
e20a For You (radio edit)
e32 All That I Need
e33 I Feel Alright
e34 Free Will (12-inch mix)
e16 Disappointed
e35 Get The Message (DNA Mix)
ORIGINAL RELEASE: Parlophone R6445 – September 1996
UK CHART POSITION: 28 September 1996 – #28 (2 weeks)
COMMENTS: Electronic's debut was remarkable because it rarely sounded anything like its composite parts. Their second disappointed because that's all it did, and 'For You' is the first of the Smiths-y songs. Which isn't a bad thing – the Smiths are great if you like the Stranglers' 'Golden Brown,' and 'For You' frolics with the best of the old band's intentions. But is that enough?

(SINGLE) Confusion
8720h Confusion (Pump Panel Reconstruction Mix)
8720i Confusion (Pump Panel Flotation Mix)
ORIGINAL RELEASE: FFRR/London FX 260 – 1996
COMMENTS: Lifted from the recently released remix collection, *? (The Rest Of New Order)*, further manipulations of 'Confusion' were undertaken by and, on the record label, credited to Pump Panel, a four man (Alexi Delano, Cari Lekebusch, Dan Zamani, Tim Taylor) techno band that had recently signed to London.

1997
(SINGLE) BERNARD SUMNER/ELECTRONIC: Second Nature
e24 Second Nature
e24a Second Nature (7-inch edit)
e24b Second Nature (Journey Mix Radio Edit)
e24c Second Nature (Extended Journey Mix)
e24d Second Nature (Modern Mix Radio Edit)
e24e Second Nature (Extended Modern Mix)
e24f Second Nature (Plastic Vox)

e24g Second Nature (Plastik Mix)
e24h Second Nature (Sweet Remix)
e24i Second Nature (Trance Atlantic Dub)
e24j Second Nature (Edge Factor Dub)
e24k Second Nature (Alternative Mix)
e36 Turning Point
e13b Feel Every Beat (12-inch mix)
ORIGINAL RELEASE: Parlophone R6455 – February 1997
UK CHART POSITION: 15 February 1997 – #35 (2 weeks)
COMMENTS: One of the album's New Orderly moments. And not even one of the better ones.

(SINGLE) PETER HOOK/MONACO: What Do You Want From Me
m01a What Do You Want From Me? (single version)
m01 What Do You Want From Me?
m01b What Do You Want From Me? (instrumental)
m02 Bicycle Thief
m03 Ultra
ORIGINAL RELEASE: Polydor 573 190 – March 1997
UK CHART POSITION: 15 March 1997 – #11 (6 weeks)
COMMENTS: Quite simply, one of the greatest songs any member of New Order has ever put his name to, individually or collectively. A soaring chorus, an unshakeable riff, a breathless blast of passion, power and rocking danceability, 'What Do You Want From Me' was one in the eye for everybody who wrote off Peter Hook after Revenge, who wrote off New Order after 'Regret,' who reckoned that all the good stuff was now in the past. Clearly, there was a lot more still to come.

Having abandoned Revenge after the *Gun Word Porn* EP, Hook and Potts spent eight months of writing songs and playing tapes to friends; and another ten months searching for the right kind of management. (In the midst of this, he also played bass on Durutti Column's 1995 *Sex & Death* album.)

Hook explained, 'we were doing it for ourselves, basically, but we'd play things to friends and they'd say "why don't you put it out, you daft bastard?" But, it was just something we did for fun... it really was music for pleasure, which is why we called the album that.' And even after they did start taking things seriously, the project remained on a back burner somewhere. 'We got this manager, a girl from Manchester, and she did nothing but hold us up for six months. Then we tried managing ourselves, and that didn't work, and finally we bumped into the Charlatans' manager, he took us on board, got us a deal, and that got us going. But eighteen months had passed by then.'

Although the line-up would double in size for live work, Monaco was essentially Hook and Potts alone, and he enthused about the division of labour. 'It's strictly 50-50, which means I have twice as much say in this band than I ever had in New Order.'

The single was released on the eve of Monaco's live debut at Dundee Grand Hall on April 28, the opening night of a full UK tour with the Charlatans.

(SINGLE) PETER HOOK/MONACO: Sweet Lips
m04 Sweet Lips
m05 Shattered
m04a Sweet Lips (Tony De Vit Trade Mix)
m04b Sweet Lips (Farley and Heller's Ambient Mix)
m04c Sweet Lips (Joey Negro East Coast Groove)
m04d Sweet Lips (Joey Negro Main Slice Mix)
m04e Sweet Lips (Fire Island Vocal Mix)
m04f Sweet Lips (instrumental)
ORIGINAL RELEASE: Polydor 571 054 – May 1997
UK CHART POSITION: 31 May 1997 – #18 (4 weeks)

(ALBUM) PETER HOOK/MONACO: *MUSIC FOR PLEASURE*
m01 What Do You Want From Me?
m06 Shine
m04 Sweet Lips
m05 Buzz Gum
m06 Blue
m07 Junk
m08 Billy Bones
m09 Happy Jack
m10 Tender
m11 Under The Stars (bonus track on US & Japan CDs only)
m12 Sedona
ORIGINAL RELEASE: Polydor 537 242 – June 1997

UK CHART POSITION: 21 June 1997 – #11 (3 weeks)

(SINGLE) PETER HOOK/MONACO: Shine
m06 Shine (new single mix)
m06a Shine (instrumental)
m13 Coming Round Again (GLR radio session)
m10b Tender (original mix)
ORIGINAL RELEASE: Polydor 571 418 – September 1997
UK CHART POSITION: 20 September 1997 – #55 (1 week)
COMMENTS: Monaco begins where Peter Hook's day job ended, but while
some of the songs would slot nicely into New Order's lexicon, most are forays into

unexpectedly new territory, all underpinned by some superbly melodic bass and the duo's unerring ear for hooks. The single "What Do You Want From Me" is up there with the best of New Order, and it isn't alone. Exceptional.

At the time of release, with New Order's career still very much in the air, Peter Hook himself wouldn't say whether or not the band had actually broken up. But ask him why his last side-project, Revenge, was so icky, while his latest one, Monaco, was so damned good, he admitted it was because he was back doing what he's best at. And if what he's best at is sounding like New Order, then obviously he had no fear of comparison. Or competition. The best bass-led electronic dance band of the Eighties may be dead. Long live the best bass-led electronic dance band of the Nineties.

'I went through this phase with Revenge, where I was really paranoid about sounding like New Order, and I think I shot myself in the foot a bit. The music came from my head, not my heart.' With Monaco, on the other hand, he was back to doing what only he can do, a return which he credited the remainder of the band with – David Potts, a mercurial vocalist/guitarist, who could switch from maudlin dancefloor mopester to shining star of BritPop: The Next Generation in the blink of an eye.

'What Do You Want From Me,' Monaco's first single, would have graced any New Order album since *Low Life*; 'Buzz Gum' sounded like Stone Roses playing Oasis, then wiping up the mess with the Lightning Seeds. In short, though Hook admitted, 'if someone heard one of our songs on the radio, they'd probably think it's New Order,' *Music For Pleasure*, remained a startlingly fresh, and remarkably dynamic collection.

Plus, Hook himself sounded happier than he had in aeons. 'I've gone from one extreme to the other. I've decided I enjoy playing the way I played with New Order, so I should let other people enjoy it again as well. It isn't a hang up anymore. It really was a hang up during the Revenge era, striving to be different.

'With David, with Monaco, it's like going back to the start, going back to something I'm happy with and feel proud of, and you can tell the difference. The whole record sounds bright, sounds more confident, it comes from the heart. It's more... how can I describe it? It's "in yer face," whereas Revenge was like "hiding behind yer shoulder." It's the difference between hiding round the corner going "I hope somebody likes it," and leaping out in front of people going, "I KNOW you're going to like it".'

But first, Hook needed to be reminded of what he was truly capable of. 'We sat down one day and David just went "why? Why don't you play bass like you used to?" It was like a revelation – why don't I play the bass like that? I'd forgotten!'

The early delays and hiccups notwithstanding, Monaco were swift to mark out their territory: two hit singles – 'Sweet Lips' followed 'What Do You Want From Me' into the Top 20; a British tour with the Charlatans, and a handful of their own headlining shows, led up to a summer full of British festivals.

'Touring this year, though, it's been amazing, really exciting. It's just gone from strength to strength, and in a way... in lots of ways actually, it feels like the first time all over again. And, at 41 years of age, that really can't be bad.'

(SINGLE) BERNARD SUMNER/ELECTRONIC: Until The End Of Time
e23a Until The End Of Time (K-Klass Mix)
e23b Until The End Of Time (Fluffy Dice Mix)
e23c Until The End Of Time (Sweet Dub)
e23d Until The End Of Time (Soulboy Collective 7-inch Version)
ORIGINAL RELEASE: Parlophone 12RDJ 6483 – October 1997
COMMENTS: Released as a promo only, on 12-inch and CD.

1998

Ever since Reading '93 banged the final nail into New Order's coffin, offers for the band to reform to play a few summer festivals had been falling onto Rob Gretton's desk. Most of the time he tried to ignore them but, finally, the sheer weight of offers (and the amount of money being waved before him) became too great to overlook any longer.

Convening a meeting between the four band members in January 1998, 'Rob sort of demanded that we get together,' Hook explained. 'He lived and breathed New Order and never wanted anything apart from it — he always said to us, "If you put as much bloody effort into New Order as you do your solo projects, you'd be fucking bigger than U2." And I suppose in some ways he was right. He was very frustrated by it all, so he got us together in a meeting.

'So he got us all together again and, lo and behold, it was like going home at Christmas. You're terrified before you go, but when you get there it's fine. Because all the business stuff… had been sorted out, we found that a lot of the anger we had inside ourselves about each other seemed a bit misguided. By being away for so long, you realise that it wasn't the people that were to blame for our unhappiness. It was more to do with [the business]. The music side of it – the New Order side – was the simplest part. We used to make music when we wanted to, we'd gig when we wanted to and we used to enjoy and feel like we were getting something from it.'

In January, 1998, the four members met together to discuss a possible reunion, not only built around the band's own credibility, but also the recent release of the Joy Division boxed set *Heart And Soul*, a package whose sales were already running far in excess of expectations. And, from the outset, the quartet's enthusiasm was boundless.

Hook continued, 'the New Order thing is nice because, after saying goodbye to Joy Division and all those songs, I'd hate to do it twice. I have no idea what it will be like, though. In the past, I think New Order was so close, and so together for so long, that it's obviously going to breed resentment and a bit of contempt because we were in each others' pockets for 18 years and we desperately, desperately, needed to get out of it. All of us felt the same way, Bernie and I, Stephen and Gillian, we were all so close that we honestly didn't know our ass from our elbow.

'The nicest thing in the world has been to step back and be able to appreciate what we've done, and see that was a good part, that was a bad part, and honestly I don't think the personality problems we had in the past will come up because we're much older and much wiser. And we know how well we work together; it's like I said to Bernie, "God, it's a gift. We had a gift together." And, as a musician, you can't really ask for anything more.'

(LIVE) Reading Festival August 30 1998
9801 Regret
9802 Touched By The Hand Of God
9803 Isolation
9804 Atmosphere
9805 Heart and Soul
9806 Paradise
9807 Bizarre Love Triangle
9808 True Faith
9809 Temptation
9810 Blue Monday
9811 World In Motion
ORIGINAL RELEASE: DVD *3 16* London Records 90 Ltd 8573-84802-2 –
2001
COMMENTS: Having rehearsed a fabulous, hits-heavy, live set (with a couple
of Joy Division surprises thrown in for good measure), the revitalised New Order
announced their return with a (relatively low-key) Manchester Apollo show on 16
July. The official comeback was set for the Phoenix Festival, and when that event
was cancelled due to low ticket sales, both New Order and co-headliners Prodigy
were readily absorbed into the following month's Reading Festival.

Overlooking the song's absence from the Reading set list, Hook confessed later,
'I have a hard time getting my head around the idea of playing "The Perfect Kiss"
in my 50s. I can't quite get there. But you can only do what feels right. I still think
we're the greatest band. How can you turn your back on that?'

The Reading performance bore out all his optimism. Opening with 'Regret,' a
number whose chiming guitar intro was tailor-made for kicking off a concert, the
band piled through more-or-less every hit you'd hope to hear, and wound up less
than exhilarating, surprisingly, only on one of the songs that might have been
expected to emerge the best of all – one doesn't want to complain that the
rearrangement of 'Isolation' failed to treat the old dog with the 'respect' that it
deserved, but the bpm battering that replaces the original moodiness is no
replacement for the song's original styling.

One might groan, too, at the presence of 'World In Motion' as an encore. But its
status as New Order's first ever #1 demanded its inclusion, and the massed
singalong that accompanies it could raise the hair on the nape of the saddest cynic.

(ALBUM) PETER HOOK/MONACO: various artists *GOTTA GET A
MESSAGE TO YOU*
m14 You Should Be Dancin'
ORIGINAL RELEASE: Polydor October 1998
COMMENTS: A Bee Gees' tribute album, featuring further tracks by the Orb,
Lightning Seeds, 911, Ultra Nate, Space, Louise, Cleopatra and more. Monaco
made three stabs at completing their contribution, with Polydor's artist development

manager, Peter Lorraine, reflecting, 'the first version was a bit frightening to tell the truth. Hooky was singing on it. In the end they enlisted the help of a session singer. Hooky really liked the song. It's great, it starts off with a disco type thing and all the time you're just waiting for that New Order bass sound to come in.'

(ALBUM) PETER HOOK/MONACO: various artists *STREETWISE*
m05a Buzz Gum (FC Kahuna Exclusive Remix)
ORIGINAL RELEASE: NCH 0006 – October 1998
COMMENTS: A middling remix of the album cut.

(SESSION) *John Peel Show* recorded 24 November 1998, broadcast 30 December 1998
9801 Regret
9805 Heart and Soul
9807 Bizarre Love Triangle
9810 Blue Monday
9812 Isolation
9813 Touched By The Hand Of God
9814 True Faith
9815 Paradise
9816 Atmosphere
ORIGINAL RELEASE: 9812-16 on *In Session*, Strange Fruit SFRSCD 128
COMMENTS: Four songs from the Reading Festival, and a short but entertaining interview, paved the way for a truly dynamic studio session. Once again, 'Isolation' is a little disconcerting in its new electrodrag, but 'Atmosphere' is beautiful, stately and momentous, while the new look 'Touched By The Hand Of God' packs an almost acerbic edge.

(ALBUM) various artists *COLLECTED*
9817 Temptation 98
ORIGINAL RELEASE: London Records 90 Ltd. COLCD 1, 1999
COMMENTS: A new recording, cut as part of the celebrations surrounding the handover of the Commonwealth Games from Kuala Lumpur to Manchester.

1999

New Order wrapped up the first stage of their comeback with a 28 December return to Manchester, followed by a massive Alexandra Palace bash on New Year's Eve, triumphant events that saw them reclaiming, as the *New Musical Express* put it, 'their title as British rock's most erratic elder statesmen, speeding from banality to brilliance in the space of a heartbeat.'

Working around the members' extra-curricular commitments, plans were now afoot for New Order to record a new album during the summer of 1999, as Hook told Radio One. 'We're doing a new album in the new year. We're getting on very well. It's the first time in years that we've actually enjoyed each other's company, and I'm very pleased about it indeed. I'm looking forward to it and it's not been very often I've been able to say that!' Sumner, however, was quick to sound a note of caution. 'We're kind of taking it one day at a time. If you think too far into the future, you get stressed out. The project at the moment is these gigs. We'll see how they go and then think about writing together in the future.'

Imminent, too, was the long-rumoured New Order box set, tentatively titled Recycle and scheduled for release early in 1999. A 22 CD round-up of all the band's singles-so-far, advance reports suggested the inclusion of several unreleased tracks dating back to the Western Sound demos in 1980, plus one further disc devoted entirely to the 1998 Reading Festival show. Artwork, of course, would be by Peter Saville. The original release date came and went, however, before it was finally announced that the entire project had been canned as it was not 'financially viable.'

All the group's plans, meanwhile, were thrown into absolute disarray by the unexpected death of manager Rob Gretton, from a heart attack on 15 May. A statement issued jointly by the band and Gretton's management company two days later described their 'shock' at his death, continuing, 'We are sure that all who have dealt with him as a colleague share with us our feelings that we have a unique and genuine friend. His loyalty, generosity and the strength of his principles combined with his love of life will remain an inspiration to us all. Our thoughts are with his partner Lesley and children Benedict and Laura at this time.'

It would ultimately be October before the band completed any recording, a single track, 'Brutal,' for the forthcoming Leonardo Di Caprio vehicle *The Beach*.

(SINGLE) MORRIS + GILBERT/THE OTHER TWO: You Can Fly
o13a You Can Fly (Cevin Fisher's Mile High Club Mix)
o13b You Can Fly (Cevin Fisher's Frequent Flyer Dub)
o13c You Can Fly (Quake Vocal Mix)
o13 You Can Fly (Quake Dub)
o13 You Can Fly (Radio Edit)
o14 Voytek *aka* Jonno
ORIGINAL RELEASE: Centredate TWCD 2 – unreleased (scheduled March 1999)
COMMENTS: A series of mixes prepared for the planned first single from the forthcoming *Super Highways* album.

(ALBUM) MORRIS + GILBERT/THE OTHER TWO: *SUPER HIGHWAYS*
o13 You Can Fly
o15 Super Highways
o16 The River
o17 One Last Kiss
o14 Voytek
o18 Unwanted
o19 New Horizons *aka* Common As Muck
o20 Cold Feet
o21 The Grave
o22 Hello
o23 Ripple

o24 Weird Woman
JAPANESE CD BONUS TRACKS
o13a You Can Fly (Cevin Fisher Mile High Club Mix)
o15a Super Highways (Andy Votel mix)
ORIGINAL RELEASE: London 566018 – March 1999

COMMENTS: *SuperHighways* suffered the same fate as the planned singles –
and, indeed, as Peter Hook's Monaco project, as the Other Two were informed
they'd been dropped from the label on the eve of the album's release. (But at least
it was released.) Very much the follow-up to its predecessor, the addition of Sub
Sub's Melanie Williams to very effectively add her vocals to Gilbert's, prompted
the duo to admit 'we almost considered doing our first live dates.' *Almost.*

Critical response to the album was as muted as its release, but the handful of
reviews it did receive tended towards the spellbound: 'this album is stunning,'
announced the on-line *All Music Guide*; 'absolutely brilliant, with incredible hook-
filled melodies, mesmerizing vocals...and tight production. In a just world, this
album would top the charts and be available wherever CDs are sold; It hasn't, and
it isn't, but it is well-worth the search. You will not be disappointed.'

(SINGLE) BERNARD SUMNER/ELECTRONIC: Vivid
e37 Vivid
e37a Vivid (Radio Edit)
e38a Prodigal Son (Harvey's mix aka Harvey's Greatly Deluded mix)
e38b Prodigal Son (Two Lone Swordsmen Mix)
e38c Prodigal Son (Inch Mix)
e38d Prodigal Son (Harvey's A Star In Your Mind mix)
e39 Radiation
e40a Haze (alternative mix)
ORIGINAL RELEASE: Parlophone R6514 – April 1999
UK CHART POSITION: 24 April 1999 – #17 (3 weeks)
COMMENTS: Chastened by the charnel house that was *Raise The Pressure*'s
fate among the critics, Sumner and Marr reconvened three years later to lay down a
far rockier selection whose greatest drawback turned out to be the proximity of the
New Order reunion. How, after all, could anyone get excited about the support act,
when the orchestra was already tuning up?

Divorced from the momentous news rolling down the road, however, 'Vivid'
lays out the album's stall from the outset, a vast improvement... a major step

forward… a rebirth for an idea that still has a lot to say. Catch the 'Prodigal Son' remixes as well. Originally issued in their own right as a clear-vinyl promo 12-inch, electro-grunge has never sounded better. And, as for that chart position… it deserved a lot more.

(ALBUM) BERNARD SUMNER/ELECTRONIC: *TWISTED TENDERNESS*
e41 Make It Happen
e40 Haze
e37 Vivid
e42 Breakdown
e43 Can't Find My Way Home
e44 Twisted Tenderness
e45 Like No Other
e46 Late At Night
e38 Prodigal Son
e47 When She's Gone
e48 Flicker
US CD BONUS TRACKS
e41a Make It Happen (Darren Price mix)
e49 King For A Day
e50 Warning Sign
US DELUXE CD BONUS DISC
e41a Make It Happen (Darren Price mix)
e49 King For A Day
e50 Warning Sign
Haze (Alternative Mix)
e39 Radiation
e40a Come Down Now (Cevin Fisher Mix)
e38b Prodigal Son (Two Lone Swordsmen Mix)
e38c Prodigal Son (Inch Mix)
e38d Prodigal Son (Harvey's A Star In Your Mind mix)
e38a Prodigal Son (Harvey's Greatly Deluded Mix)
ORIGINAL RELEASE: Parlophone 498345 – April 1999
UK CHART POSITION: 8 May 1999 – #9 (3 weeks)
COMMENTS: The more you hear it, the better it gets. Electronic's masterpiece might have been doomed to be overlooked… was, in fact, bumped several times from the schedules as the New Order reunion gathered pace. But once it did hit the streets, in '99 in Britain and a full year later in the United States, it proved to be well worth the wait. Recorded with a full band line-up for the first time (Black Grape's Jed Lynch and Doves' Jimmy Goodwin), *Twisted Tenderness* was recorded as quickly as was humanly possible, as Sumner explained. 'We've worked really hard over a short period of time. Having a band has meant that we could work ideas far quicker than normal. It also means the end result is a lot more live sounding than before. We're both really happy with it.'

'It's got an energy about it,' agreed Marr, 'which is something you can't really design. You can strategize as much as you like, but unless what you do has got the x factor – the moments that make you go "yes!" even as they first come to you – there's no way you can expect it to have that effect on anyone else.'

In fact, that energy was the first thing you noticed, whether peeling out of the return to 'Idiot Country' that was the opening 'Make It Happen,' or the frenetic guitar jam of 'Breakdown'… or even the oddly placed, but so-strangely affecting cover of Blind Faith's 'Can't Find My Way Home.' A great album… but hey, where'd it go?

(SINGLE) MORRIS + GILBERT/THE OTHER TWO: Super Highways
o15 Super Highways
o13a You Can Fly (Cevin Fisher Mile High Club Mix)
o15a Super Highways (Andy Votel mix)
ORIGINAL RELEASE: London TWO 2 – June 1999
COMMENTS: Replacing first, 'Weird Drum Woman,' and then 'You Can Fly' on the schedules, the release of 'Super Highways' was itself shattered after London announced they were dropping the Other Two from the roster; the single was released, without fanfare (let alone remixes) 'to fulfil contractual obligations' only.

(SINGLE) BERNARD SUMNER/ELECTRONIC: Late At Night
e46 Late At Night
e46a Late At Night (radio edit)
e41 Make It Happen
e41a Make It Happen (Darren Price mix)
e49 King For A Day
e51 Come Down Now (Cevin Fisher mix)
e50 Warning Sign
ORIGINAL RELEASE: Parlophone R6519 – July 1999
COMMENTS: One of the hardest hitting songs on the album but also, sadly, one of the most ordinary, 'Late At Night' was actually withdrawn from release in the UK and, compared to what they could have released, deservedly so.

It would mark the group's final release, although they had not necessarily said goodbye. 'I think Electronic will make [another] record at some point because we work so well together and we have such a great time,' Marr mused. 'There are things that Electronic do that I can only do with Bernard Sumner and Bernard can only do with me. There are reasons for Bernard and I to work together, that he and I know about and there is a shared influence that we have that we only have with each other.

'We have an agenda that we share. I don't think people quite realise that about Bernard and myself. I think people think I was on Venus and Bernard was on Pluto but it wasn't really like that. I think the Smiths and New Order actually were more similar than people think. No matter what kind of framework the music was in, it was emotive.'

(ALBUM) original soundtrack *THE BEACH*
9901 Brutal
ORIGINAL RELEASE: Sire 31079 – February 2000
COMMENTS: Filmed by the Danny Boyle led team who were also responsible

for *Trainspotting*, *The Beach* was based on the cult novel by Alex Garland, as a group of twenty-something backpackers (led by Leonardo Di Caprio) search for an alternative paradise in Thailand. According to Hook, 'we were asked to write something new for that film… really late on, so by the time we'd done it, it just about made the film. It was a warm-up for us to try and start working again. It was the first thing we wrote. Also, seeing as we got on with each other, we wanted to try different producers out. There was Rollo from Faithless who really, really enjoyed working with us, but it wasn't the sound we were after. We were after a really hard sound.'

In fact, 'Brutal' doesn't sound too far removed from that ideal, a firm indication of the new resolve that helped dictate New Order's decision to return – so many other reformations, after all, are content merely to retain the blueprint that had served them so well in the past. 'Brutal' was recognisably New Order. But it was recognisably *new* as well – plus, it packed a guitar solo that must have made Sumner's fingers bleed.

Leftfield, Moby, Underworld, Unkle and Faithless were among the other bands involved in the soundtrack album, while Sumner reappeared alongside the Chemical Brothers, via their 'Out Of Control' collaboration.

According to Sumner, 'The Chemicals thing came after one of them called me and asked if I'd be interested. Of course I was, I love what they do.' The Chemical Brothers themselves continued, 'we had that track in quite a different form, including a quite spectacular synth riff, which doesn't exist anymore, followed by a big sitar drop. All the way through, though, the song had that hi-energy break and that crackly snare drum which always made us think of New Order.

'Rather than mucking around, we wanted to try and get [Sumner]. He's a total hero to us, New Order are a band we both love, so… we sent him a tape and he liked it. We spoke to him, got on okay, he came down and put in a lot of work on it. He's always been writing lyrics and melodies against just rhythms and that's a particular skill that he has.

'We probably wouldn't have phoned up Bernard Summer for our first record, that's probably one of those things that comes out of having confidence and success – the fact that we believed we wouldn't be overpowered by someone who's so strong. He's an inspiring person because he loves making music – he was there until 8am.'

(ALBUM) original soundtrack *MANCHESTER UNITED BEYOND THE PROMISED LAND*
   8724f Touched by the Hand of God (Touched by the Hand of Bias)
   ORIGINAL RELEASE: Circa Records Ltd. VTCD 350 – 1999
   COMMENTS: Back in 1976, Manchester United's resurgence on the football field was symbolic of Manchester's own rebirth as a musical force. Since that time, the music had maintained its supremacy – from Joy Division to the Smiths, from the Happy Mondays to Oasis. The football team, however, had faltered – three Cup Finals in four years were followed by just three more in a decade and, as the 1990s got underway, United seemed doomed forever to fall short at the final hurdle. But 1992 brought their first championship in a quarter of a century and, in the decade-plus since then, 'failure' for Old Trafford means the team didn't win every trophy they tried for. And that didn't happen too often.

Sumner's own avowed support for Manchester United may or may not have been instrumental in drawing New Order into the soundtrack for this documentary tribute to the Red Devils, conceived as they journeyed where no English side ever had, and won the treble of the League Championship, FA Cup and European Cup.

(ALBUM) original soundtrack *SPLENDOR*
8609e Bizarre Love Triangle
ORIGINAL RELEASE: Astralwerks 6282 – September 1999
COMMENTS: The soundtrack to the latest Greg Araki movie was a remarkably well-conceived electro feast that merged seamlessly (or otherwise... Lionrock vs Suede is pretty scary) into latter day Britpop, as the giants of one field remixed the monsters of the other. Hague's attempt on 'Bizarre Love Triangle' closes the set in fine style.

(SESSION) October 1999?
UNR Atmosphere?
UNR Blue Velvet?
UNR Escape While You Can?
UNR Falling?
UNR It's Your Fate?
UNR Off The Record?
UNR Out of Order?
UNR Synthesized?
UNR Tell Me?
UNR The Deepest Sea?
COMMENTS: The first reports out of the studio allegedly found New Order essentially jamming around their instincts. Few of the songs were even halfway complete... 'Off The Record' and 'Synthesized' were still instrumentals, while 'Tell me' was little more than synthesizer patterns. Elsewhere, sources described music that ranged in sound between *Closer* era Joy Division ('It's Your Fate'), and a Hook-filled Electronic ('Escape While You Can'), topped off by nine minutes of near ambience, 'The Deepest Sea.'

However those in the know believed this session never took place and the reports were simply made up.

The spirit of Joy Division resurfaced, meantime, in a rumoured rerecording of 'Atmosphere,' intended for inclusion on the then-gestating *Cohesion* benefit album. Ultimately, however, the group would hand over a live version of the same song.

Elsewhere, Hook alone was involved during this time in sessions for a concept album being prepared by Arthur Baker; he featured on two tracks, a reworking of the old Jewish hymn 'Avinu Malkenu,' recorded with Mogwai, and 'Love Hymn' featuring Stuart Braithwaite and Pharoah Sanders.

Sumner, too, had outside commitments, linking with Primal Scream to contribute to their forthcoming *Xtrmntr* album. 'I've got loads of respect for Bobby Gillespie,' he mused at the outset of the session. 'It's hard to say what [the track is] going to sound like when it's finished but at the moment it's pretty raw.'

With the collaboration eventually emerging as the album's 'Shoot Speed/ Kill Light,' Gillespie himself explained, 'We wrote this song that was really Germanic – real Joy Division, real noisy, psychedelic driving music. Then we thought, we need some guitar on this and the best guy to do it was fucking Barney. So we asked him to play and it was perfect.'

'It was me entering the spirit world and getting in touch with Ian Curtis,' bandmate Mani continued; 'getting him right involved.'

Taking a break from this wealth of activity, New Order attended the tenth annual *Q Music Awards*, to receive the Inspiration gong from Keith Allen. The BBC interviewed Hook immediately after, and found him in expansive, if self-confessedly less-than-sober mood.

'The weird thing is, when we actually started the group, right, twenty years ago, there was no awards. And we went through fifteen years of being a group when we achieved loads and loads of things and there was no awards. Now the awards thing seems like cheap television to me. We have wiped the floor with them bands out there, I tell ya. We have wiped the floor with ALL them bands out there… haven't we?'

2000

(SINGLE) PETER HOOK/MONACO: I've Got A Feeling
m15 I've Got A Feeling
m15a I've Got A Feeling (edit)
m16 Heaven
m17 Barfly
m15 I've Got A Feeling (CD-Rom video)
ORIGINAL RELEASE: Papillon Roadrunner RR 2078-3 0004 – August 2000
COMMENTS: Monaco had already completed work on their second album, provisionally titled *Be Careful What You Wish For*, when London Records announced that the band was being dropped, following the company's merger with Universal.

A spokesman for the band's management said: 'It came as bolt out of the blue because, track by track, [London] accepted the album and loved it.' Hook, however, continued, 'Getting a record deal isn't a problem, people are listening to it and saying, "We'll have it." There's no animosity, it's probably a blessing in disguise. The reason they're dropping bands is, they're trying to focus on the pop market. They don't want to concentrate on guitar music.'

He confessed, of course, that the dropping was 'a bit of a setback… but, seeing as they signed Adam Rickitt (the former *Coronation Street* actor) after us, I think we got our own back really. So bollocks to them. It was quite interesting. Well it wasn't at the time, because it was heart-rending. We delivered the record and we just didn't hear anything back for ages. We were trying to get it out for summer and it was just really weird; it was like your girlfriend doesn't phone you so you think something's wrong. And then you find out she's going out with Adam Rickitt!'

Close to a year elapsed before the band announced its new home, at Papillon Records, but the album wasn't out of the woods yet, as the first single from the set, 'I've Got A Feeling,' was withdrawn after sample clearance could not be obtained in time for a loop used on one of its b-sides, 'Heaven Seven' – the single had already been manufactured and was ready to ship when the news came through.

2001

(ALBUM) various artists: *COHESION: MANCHESTER AID TO KOSOVO & MINES ADVISORY GROUP BENEFIT*
9804 Atmosphere
m18 Ballroom
o12a Superhighways (Andy Votel mix)
ORIGINAL RELEASE: i-CollectiV.com IC 00001 – February 2001
COMMENTS: Plans for this ambitious 36 track benefit album were first laid in mid-1999, at which time New Order were confidently rumoured to be preparing a new studio version of 'Atmosphere' for inclusion. Ultimately they delivered the Reading Festival version, while the Other Two handed over a remix and Monaco turned in 'Ballroom,' as companions to material (new, remixed and otherwise) from fellow Mancunians Happy Mondays, Ian Brown, the Clint Boon Experience, Badly Drawn Boy, Doves, Lamb and Elbow (among many more.)

(SINGLE) PETER HOOK/MONACO: See Saw
m19a See Saw (Lab Rats Let Loose On The See Saw Vocal Mix)
m19b See Saw (Lab Rats Dub Mix)
m19c See Saw (Solaris Club Mix)
m19d See Saw (Solaris Dub Mix)
ORIGINAL RELEASE: Papillon DJFLY 151/152 – March 2001

(ALBUM) PETER HOOK/MONACO: *MONACO*
m15 I've Got A Feeling
m20 A Life Apart
m21 Kashmere
m22 Bert's Theme
m18 Ballroom
m19 See-saw
m23 Black Rain
m24 It's A Boy
m25 End Of The World
m26 Marine
ORIGINAL RELEASE: Papillon BTFLYCD 0005 – August 2000

COMMENTS: Originally to be titled *Be Careful What You Wish For*, Monaco's second album was already underway as the New Order reunion took shape, with Hook enthusing at that time, 'it's going quite well. It's so much nicer doing it this time, now we have a name for the group and we know what we want to do. The last time was very much searching in the dark, very much fledglings, so now it feels a lot stronger, and a lot more positive, because we know what we want to achieve.'

No sooner was the album complete, however, than Monaco were dropped by Polydor, with Hook later confessing, 'It was a bit like being jilted at the altar because we'd finished the LP and we were waiting for them to bring it out when we parted. It was a bit of a blow and it took quite a few months for us to get over that, Pottsy and I, but I've got confidence in the record and I'm very happy with it and very proud of it.'

Rightly so. While no individual track leaped out with the radio-friendly immediacy of 'What Do You Want From Me,' still *Monaco* was at least as strong as its predecessor, with its ensuing obscurity more down to Hook's New Order commitments, than any problem with the record. Still, Hook resignedly observed, 'England has a very strange attitude towards my solo projects, whether they're all crap or not I don't know. They look at you strangely, and they did it with Bernard for doing Electronic, they don't particularly seem to like it.....'

Hook subsequently utilised the abandoned album title for the second half of Revenge's *One True Passion V2.0* reissue.

(SINGLE) True Faith 2001
8722l True Faith (video edit)
8722m True Faith (Morel's Pink Noise Club Mix)
8722n True Faith (Morel's Pink Noise I've Taken Too Much Dub)
8722o True Faith (Morel's Calling Shifty Dub)
8722p True Faith (Morel's Extra Dub)
8722r True Faith (Morel's Pink Noise "My Fear of Dub mix")
8722q True Faith (Morel's Pink Noise mix edit)
8722s True Faith (Philip Steir Club Mix)
8722t True Faith (Philip Steir Dub)
8722u True Faith (Philip Steir edit)
8722v True Faith (Philip Steir Re-order mix)
8722w True Faith (Philip Steir Reprise)
8722x True Faith (vocal up)
ORIGINAL RELEASE: US promo 12-inch and CD singles: unavailable to general public
COMMENTS: Another year, another compilation (*International*), another barrel-load of remixes. Is there a point to all this?

(SINGLE) Crystal
0101 Crystal (original version)
0101a Crystal (radio edit)
0101b Crystal (full length version)

0101c Crystal (7 minute edit)
0101d Crystal (Bedrock dub)
0101e Crystal (Bedrock radio edit #1)
0101f Crystal (Circumstance mix) [video]
0101g Crystal (Digweed & Muir Bedrock Main Remix Edit)
0101h Crystal (Digweed & Muir Bedrock radio edit)
0101i Crystal (Digweed & Muir Bedrock remix)
0101j Crystal (dub)
0101k Crystal (John Creamer & Stephane K Intro mix, *aka* Intro mix)
0101l Crystal (John Creamer & Stephane K Main mix)
0101m Crystal (John Creamer & Stephane K remix edit)
0101n Crystal (Lee Coombs dub)
0101o Crystal (Lee Coombs remix)
0101p Crystal (remix by Spike)
0101q Crystal (video)
0102 Behind Closed Doors
ORIGINAL RELEASE: CentreDate NUOCD 8 – August 2001

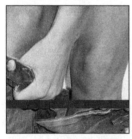

UK CHART POSITION: 25 August 2001 – #8 (4 weeks)
COMMENTS: The choice of 'Crystal' as the first single was, insisted Hook, inevitable. The song 'just came... seemed dead obvious, really up front, really different sounding but dead powerful.'

Indeed. Of course, a myriad of remixes quickly put a stop to that, as 'Crystal' found itself subjected to some quite impenetrable revisions – and a handful of solidly excellent ones. Granted a wider audience via its inclusion on *Retro*, Lee Coombs' effort mashed the original performance with an intricate web of explosive percussion, while John Digweed's assault, too, met with Hook's approval. 'It's a really deep house version. It's great actually and nothing like the record. He's used quite a lot of the vocal and even some of the bass, which is amazing for a remix.'

(TV) *Later... With Jools Holland*
0103 Crystal
ORIGINAL RELEASE: DVD *Later... Louder* (Warner 0927 49254-2 – May 2003)

Although 'Crystal' was granted a wonderful video, the band made a handful of live TV appearances to support its release, including this well-received showing. (The band also performed 'Regret', '60 Miles an Hour' and 'Love Will Tear Us

Apart'.)

(ALBUM) *GET READY*
0101 Crystal
0104 60 Miles an Hour
0105 Turn My Way
0106 Vicious Streak
0107 Primitive Notion
0108 Slow Jam
0109 Rock the Shack
0110 Someone Like You
0111 Close Range
0112 Run Wild
ORIGINAL RELEASE: London 8573 89621 – August 2001

UK CHART POSITION: 8 September 2001 – #6 (4 weeks)

COMMENTS: Looking back on the *Get Ready* sessions, Hook smiled, 'that was probably the happiest I've ever been with these fuckers. Sumner was right all along. We needed time to find ourselves. Now, if something's on our minds, we just say so. Miles better.

'I think the album as a whole was recorded much more confidently. By going off, working on your own and breaking the New Order mould, it's made us – or at least me – a little bit more confident. You know you're going to get somewhere now, whereas on *Republic…*'

The album was recorded at Morris and Gilbert's own studio, at their farm, in Derbyshire. 'They came in and tore my studio to bits,' Morris reported after it was all over. 'Going, "ooh, I don't like that kind of milk, and I don't like these sandwiches, they're a bit runny".'

Anxious not to rush the record for the sake of it, however, the group eased into the recording process by simply hanging out together and jamming. 'That was the thing about being apart for so long,' Hook continued. 'It made us appreciate that the strength of New Order was in the playing together. Once we started playing together again, we found that the chemistry was still there and it felt like we were moving on.'

'Brutal,' of course, was the first manifestation of that forward momentum; 'and immediately after that,' Sumner said, 'came "60 miles per hour". We wrote the two songs as a pair. In fact, they shared the same drum beat at one stage… I think they still do share the same drum beat.' Several other songs were completed before the sessions began as the band made what Morris described as a conscious effort 'not to make the same mistake we made for the last three or four fucking times. We actually gave Bernard (Sumner) more songs than he needed, which was also a first.'

The presence of producer Steve Osbourne was similarly inspirational, as Hook explained. 'He... made us work and repeat things over and over again, he'd still be looking for his mystical thing. He was a little like Martin Hannett sometimes, he'd go off on [a tangent] and push and push, then all of a sudden, it would work.'

It really did. Like 'Brutal' and 'Crystal,' *Get Ready* is unmistakeably New Order. But it has a freshness... even a rock-iness... that its predecessors had only mustered in part, as the quartet not only relaxed into playing together, they also relaxed out of their old habits of playing *against* one another – an electrifying subtlety in the early days, of course, but a virtual liability by the time they arrived at *Republic*. Songs like 'Primitive Notion,' 'Close Range' and (best of all) 'Slow Jam' might not have seemed out of place on past albums, but they would never have been enacted quite so brilliantly.

Neither were the band alone in the studio, as they recruited a handful of guests to add their own distinctive timbre to the proceedings. Having already made an indelible impression across 'Crystal,' singer Dawn Zee worked further magic on 'Close Range' and 'Run Wild,' while Primal Scream's Bobby Gillespie gives the band some irascible front across the corrosive 'Rock The Shack,' as he repays Sumner for guesting on the Scream's own most recent album, *Xtrmntr*.

More surprising was the appearance of Smashing Pumpkins frontman Billy Corgan, at that time still finding his feet following the demise of that band, but a long time friend of New Order's – Hook remembers meeting him for the first time when Corgan was just 15, turning up at one of their shows as a friend of the promoter, and talking about the band that he hoped one day to form. Since that time, his devotion has remained alive, as his Starchildren alter-ego contributed a version of 'Isolation' to the mid-1990s Joy Division tribute album *A Means To An End*, and took to incorporating 'Transmission' into the Pumpkins' own live set.

Sumner returned his enthusiasm. 'I just like Smashing Pumpkins and I like Billy's voice,' he explained. 'Nothing to do with him being a fan of ours, or playing "Transmission." I just like the records and my son is into him. He gave me some CDs, and made me a compilation tape and I just really dug it. I like Billy's voice. He's got a kind of metallic timbre to it. He sounds high and low at the same time. You can't tell if he has a high or a low voice. He's got a metallic tone to it. We just wrote a track on the album and I could hear him singing on it. I just said "I can hear Billy sing on that".

'Hooky knows him a bit better than I do and said "well, I've got his number here, why don't we just call him". So we called him up and he said "That's really weird man. I just went out and bought the *Peel Sessions* Joy Division album, and I was listening to Joy Division when you called". He said he was coming over to Europe the next week and would do it then.'

(LIVE) Olympia, Liverpool, 18 July 2001

UNR Atmosphere
UNR Slow Jam
UNR Crystal
UNR Regret
UNR Love Vigilantes
UNR Isolation
UNR Your Silent Face
0113 Turn My Way
UNR Close Range
UNR Touched By The Hand Of God
UNR Bizarre Love Triangle
UNR True Faith
UNR Temptation
UNR Love Will Tear Us Apart
UNR Ruined In A Day
UNR 60 Miles An Hour
UNR Blue Monday
ORIGINAL RELEASE: Box set R*etro*
COMMENTS: New Order's return to action was also their first ever show without Gillian Gilbert. Grace, the Morris' daughter, was seriously ill and needed one of her parents to remain at home with her. 'It was a difficult decision to make,' Morris admitted, 'but that's what we decided. I mean it was either... it had to be one of us, really, and it ended up being Gillian.'

She was replaced for live work by Phil Cunningham, but the reality of the situation did not hit home until this, the first show. She felt, she complained later, 'Like the ghost in *Randall & Hopkirk*. I should turn up in a white suit, going, I'm not dead!'

Cunningham was not the only new face on stage, as Billy Corgan expanded his studio role to bring some extra guitar to the proceedings – and, without deviating too far from his performance on *Get Ready*, Corgan transformed live renditions of 'Turn My Way' into a personal triumph. According to Sumner, 'we mentioned that we were going out on tour and needed a guitarist and he said "hey, I'm out of a job with Pumpkins so I'll come on tour with you. I'll play guitar". It was great. He enjoyed it so much that he wanted to come to England and Europe with us, but we had already asked Bobby Gillespie (Primal Scream) to do some dates with us. We didn't want too many "names" on the stage. [But] Billy was great and he really added something with his guitar.'

The concert itself, Hook confessed, 'was a bit nerve-wracking. It's always worse playing near home. We thought for some magical reason that, by playing Liverpool, none of our drunken mates would turn up. But needless to say, our drunken friends are very resilient and turned up. But, no, it was a bit like a homecoming and I really enjoyed it.'

(LIVE) AreaOne Festival, Devore CA – 5 August 2001
0114 New Dawn Fades [with Moby]

ORIGINAL RELEASE: *24 Hour Party People* soundtrack

COMMENTS: From Liverpool, New Order travelled to Japan for a phenomenal appearance at the Mount Fuji Festival; and thence to the US, for four more massive open air events.

ArenaOne was the last in this sequence, and saw New Order perform both their own set and make a guest appearance alongside Moby – accompanied, for the first time, by Gillian Gilbert. Ahead of the trip, Sumner admitted, 'We obviously miss her, but you can't take your kids everywhere touring… it's just impossible really. I don't think it's fair. You go through all these time changes. It gets a bit too much for kids. Besides, there are all these drunken roadies around.' She did, however, fly out for the band's last week in the US, and lined up with her bandmates on a magnificently, turbulently emotional version of a number Moby first appropriated in the mid-1990s, for the *A Means To An End* Joy Division tribute album.

(SESSION) radio *Steve Lamacq Evening Session* broadcast 17 October 2001
0115 Slow Jam
0116 Your Silent Face
0117 Close Range
0118 Rock The Shack

ORIGINAL RELEASE: *In Session*, Strange Fruit SFRSCD 128

COMMENTS: If New Order's last BBC session was obsessed with the past, this set concentrated almost wholly on the present, with only a near-perfect 'Your Silent Face' hurtling the listener (very expertly) back to an earlier age. With Phil Cunningham maintaining his live role in the band, and both Dawn Zee and Bobby Gillespie reprising their *Get Ready* roles, the session adds little to the familiar versions of the songs, but is a lot of fun for all that.

The session was recorded midway through a fresh spate of gigging, with the Manchester Apollo show on October 4 subsequently included among *Q* magazine's 'greatest gigs ever' feature, at #75. 'It was the night they... revisited greatness. Always patchy live, this might have been a nervous return to their native city (they hadn't played there for three years). Instead, the Apollo's fans were treated to a virtual greatest hits set, including some seldom-aired Joy Division material.'

(SINGLE) 60 Miles An Hour
0104a 60 Miles an Hour (radio edit)
0104b 60 Miles an Hour (Supermen Lovers remix)
0104c 60 Miles an Hour [video]
0104d 60 mph (chorus vocal down)
0104e 60 mph (Dave Kahne mix)
0104f 60 mph (David Kahne mix 2)
0104g 60 mph (David Kahne mix recall 2)
0104h 60 mph (Recall Master mix)
0104i 60 mph (vocals down .5db)
0119 Sabotage
9808 True Faith

9809 Temptation
ORIGINAL RELEASE: CentreDate NUO 9 – November 2001
UK CHART POSITION: 1 December 2001 – #29 (2 weeks)
COMMENTS: A smart choice of single in its album/radio edit form and, in many ways, a better candidate for the remixes as well, as David Kahne, in particular, brings an even more punishing edge to the proceedings than the already brittle original envisioned. Scattered across the b-sides of the various formats, 'Sabotage' was a smart *Get Ready* out-take, but the real treat came in the shape of two live cuts from Reading 1998.

(SINGLE) Someone Like You
0110a Someone Like You (Funk d'Void remix)
0110b Someone Like You (Futureshock Stripdown mix)
0110c Someone Like You (Futureshock vocal remix)
0110d Someone Like You (Gabriel & Dresden 911 vocal mix)
0110e Someone Like You (Gabriel & Dresden voco-tech dub)
0110f Someone Like You (James Holden heavy dub)
ORIGINAL RELEASE: CentreDate NUO 10 – December 2001
COMMENTS: As one of the danciest numbers on *Get Ready*, 'Someone Like You' was always a strong candidate for both single status and a bucketload of remixes – although, arguably, its original format was already adventurous enough to deter a lot of people from having a go. In the event, none of the remixes truly match the first time you heard the album cut, although James Holden's heavy dub is, at least, well titled.

2002

(LIVE) Gold Coast Parklands, Gold Coast, Australia, 20 January 2002
0201 Crystal
UNR Transmission
UNR Regret
UNR Love Vigilantes
UNR 60 Miles An Hour
UNR Atmosphere
UNR Close Range
UNR Bizarre Love Triangle
UNR True Faith
0202 Temptation
UNR Love Will Tear Us Apart
UNR Blue Monday
ORIGINAL RELEASE: Box set *Retro*
COMMENTS: Having wrapped up 2001 with a three month UK and European tour, New Order began the new year in New Zealand and Australia, hitting some of the southern hemisphere's greatest festivals and venues. The Big Day Out was the second show, but all the tightness and power that had been built up over the past few months was still firmly in place – indeed, of all the shows revisited on the live

portion of *Retro*, this is the only one to contribute two tracks to the proceedings, a relatively straightforward 'Crystal,' but a brilliantly behemothic 'Temptation.'

(SINGLE) Here To Stay
0203 Here to Stay (full length vocal)
0203a Here to Stay (extended instrumental)
0203b Here to Stay (radio edit)
0203c Here to Stay (Felix da Housecat – Extended Glitz mix)
0203d Here to Stay (the Scumfrog Dub mix)
0204 Player in the League
ORIGINAL RELEASE: CentreDate NUO 11 – April 2002
UK CHART POSITION: 27 April 2002 – #15 (3 weeks)
COMMENTS: A sharply scintillating new single spirals off the soundtrack to *24 Hour Party People*, to prove that the colossal rebirth that was *Get Ready* was neither a fluke nor a one-off. How pleasing, too, that they didn't go overboard on the remixes, as Felix da Housecat and Scumfrog (following up his brilliant reinterpretation of David Bowie's 'Loving The Alien') alone got their paws on it – to prove that less is sometimes better.

Though neither has much to do with the original song, the 'frog's pounding bass-heavy loop might sound like it wants to turn into Gala's 'Freed From Desire' (*might* is the operative word), but it has a visceral impact all of its own, while Felix kicks off from the mid-rift of 'Blue Monday,' before plunging into a world all his own.

(LIVE) Finsbury Park, June 9 2002
0205 Crystal
0206 Transmission
0207 Regret
0208 Ceremony
0209 60 mph
0210 Atmosphere
0211 Brutal
0212 Close Range
0213 She's Lost Control
0214 Bizarre Love Triangle
0215 True Faith
0216 Temptation
0217 Love Will Tear Us Apart
0218 Digital
0219 Blue Monday
0220 Your Silent Face
UNR World In Motion
ORIGINAL RELEASE: DVD *5 11* Warner Video 0927 49366-2 – Dec 2002
COMMENTS: And if *you* had to select a New Order set list, wouldn't you end up with much the same set as this? There may be more New Order live footage out there than anyone could ever choose from, but if hot hits guide your cheque-writing

hand, it'll be *511* every time.

Four years earlier, Peter Hook lamented 'losing' the Joy Division catalogue when Curtis died and the band became New Order. Time and distance have healed much of the reasoning behind that loss; in reclaiming those songs, the group have reclaimed a slice of heritage whose enforced absence might even have hamstringed them in the past. No less than five Joy Division songs featured in the Finsbury Park set, including what Sumner insists is 'only the second time we've played ["She's Lost Control"] in 25 years' (in fact, it's at least the fifth, following a couple of shows during 1985, and two the gigs preceding this one), and the first encore, 'Digital,' which was indeed being given its first ever airing on a British stage since 1980. If you got to thank *24 Hour Party People* for one thing, it's this.

One can live without the DVD bonus features – a documentary interview and a snatch of the soundcheck. But the rainsoaked concert itself is essential, from the opening whirl of 'Crystal' and the angry insect pulse of 'Transmission,' through the hauntingly sparse 'She's Lost Control' and onto a truly triumphant closing salvo that lasts so long that every successive number feels like the last… and the last one emerges as such a surprise that even the anti-climax is a thrill. What would you have *preferred* them to play?

(SINGLE) World In Motion
9001 World In Motion
0221 Such A Good Thing
9001a World In Motion (No Alla Violenza Mix)
ORIGINAL RELEASE: CentreDate NUO 12 – June 2002
UK CHART POSITION: 15 June 2002 – #43 (2 weeks)
COMMENTS: 'Putting on my new shoes, stepping on the grass…' With the 2002 World Cup on the horizon, and English hopes as foolishly high as they ever are, reports that New Order were planning to rerecord 'World In Motion' were circulating as early as Christmas, swiftly followed by the rumour that David Beckham was being tapped up for the rap section.

The rerecording never happened; a timely reissue of the original single was nevertheless given a fan-shaped boost via the inclusion of the group's latest contribution to footballing rock lore, 'Such A Good Thing' – a document of the trials and terrors of being a World Cup fan in one time zone, having to rearrange their schedule for games in another, specially written as BBC Radio Five Live's own official World Cup Theme. And, for everyone who complains that, not only is it not the greatest New Order record ever made, nor even the greatest (second greatest) football song… what do you expect from a b-side?

(SINGLE) Confusion Remixes 2002
0222 Confusion (Arthur Baker 2002 version) [new vocal]
0222a Confusion (Electroclash version) [new vocal]
0222b Confusion (Koma + Bones mix)
0222c Confusion (Koma + Bones vocal)
0222d Confusion (Koma + Bones dub)

0222e Confusion (Larry Tees Electroclash mix) [new & old vocal]
0222f Confusion (Outputs Nu-Rocktro version) [new vocal]
0222g Confusion (Arthur Baker 2002 instrumental)
8720j Confusion (a capella and parts) [old vocal]
8720k Confusion (Arthur Baker 2002 version) [old vocal]
8720l Confusion (Asto Dazed mix) [old vocal]
8720m Confusion (Outputs Nu-Rocktro version) [old vocal]
ORIGINAL RELEASE: Whacked Records WACKT002 – November 2002
UK CHART POSITION: 30 November 2002 – #64 (1 week)
COMMENTS: No matter that 'Confusion' had not featured in New Order's live set since the very first comeback gig back in July 1998 and the same year's Reading Festival. It remained a club favourite, not to mention a remixer's dream – and there was another compilation coming (the *Retro* box set). Oh what the hell, let's knock out a new vocal (the best one yet, as it happens), then throw it to the wolves.

(LIVE) *40 Years At Radio One* – John Peel's party
0223 Transmission
ORIGINAL RELEASE: *In Session*, Strange Fruit SFRSCD 128
COMMENTS: 'If you hadn't played our record 20 years ago, we wouldn't have been here.' With those words (from Sumner), a clearly affectionate New Order kick into a frenetic take on the Joy Division oldie, shot in their rehearsal space for broadcast within DJ Peel's celebration *not* (despite the title) of 40 years at Radio 1, but of 40 in the DJ-ing business as a whole.

2003-04
(ALBUM) various artists *HOPE*
0301 Vietnam
ORIGINAL RELEASE: London Records 90 Ltd 50466 5846 2 – 2003
COMMENTS: The War Child charity's latest offering was a benefit for the children of Iraq, conceived as the American war drew inevitably closer. Some extraordinary performances resulted, including George Michael's exemplary reading of Don McLean's 'The Grave,' a lament for the dead of Vietnam. Sticking with that same simile, despite the war having yet to bog down into the precise historical echo that it was destined for, New Order turned to a remarkably faithful rendering of Jimmy Cliff's 'Vietnam' – a third person rendering, incidentally, of the scenario they themselves had broached in 'Love Vigilantes,' back on *Low Life*. Further resonance is added, incidentally, by the insertion of a few choruses of another Cliff hit, 'The Harder They Come,' into the song's fade.

(STUDIO) PETER HOOK/REVENGE: *ONE TRUE PASSION V2.0*
r29 Televive
r30 The Wilding
ORIGINAL RELEASE: *One True Passion V2.0*
COMMENTS: Putting the finishing touches to the almost-all-inclusive *One True Passion V2.0* compilation, Hook, New Order live guitarist Phil Cunningham

and programmer Roger Lyons recorded two of the songs that highlighted the original Revenge's live shows, but which had not been captured on tape before. Reworked lyrics marked Hook's own new-found love of singing and writing, but the greatest departure from the original Revenge sound was the employment of a characteristic Hook bass line. 'I haven't any inhibitions now about playing bass. When I had Revenge, I was really wound up about sounding like New Order. It was just daft.'

(SINGLE) The Peter Saville Show Soundtrack
0401 Soundtrack
ORIGINAL RELEASE: London Records 90 Ltd, SAVILLE1 – January 2004
COMMENTS: Originally titled 'Ambient,' a 30 minute instrumental piece produced for sale at the Peter Saville Show exhibition at the London Design Museum, as a limited edition of 3,000 copies. Showcasing Saville's album art and design work, the exhibition ran from January 23-April 18, 2004 and was dominated, naturally, by Saville's work for both Joy Division and New Order, a relationship so deeply embedded in both parties' career that the artist was frequently referred to as the band's fifth member.

(SINGLE) JOY DIVISION: Atmosphere
7952 Atmosphere
8037 She's Lost Control (12-inch version)
ORIGINAL RELEASE: FACUS 2 – Sept 1980
COMMENTS: Released as the follow-up to 'Love Will Tear Us Apart,' and notable not only for restoring an already hard-to-find a-side to the racks, but also for the so-called '12-inch' version of 'She's Lost Control.' In fact, beyond clearly being a different take to the familiar album version, there is little to choose between the two, including their length.

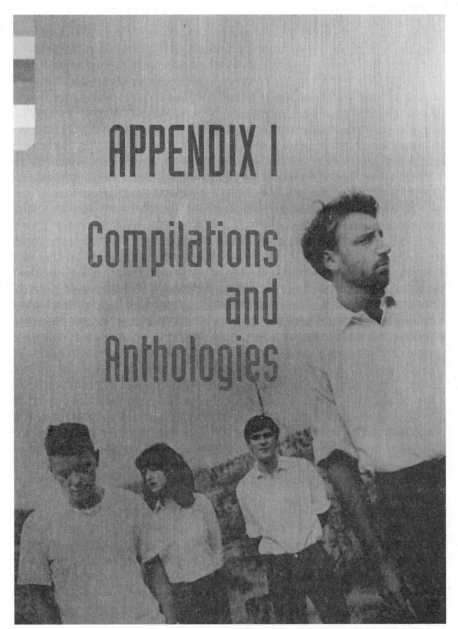

APPENDIX I

Compilations
and
Anthologies

1981

(ALBUM) JOY DIVISION: *STILL*
7924 Exercise One
7926 Ice Age
8033 Sound Of Music
7906 Glass
7927 The Only Mistake
7928 Walked In Line
7925 The Kill
7946 Something Must Break
7943 Dead Souls
8050 Sister Ray
8051 Ceremony
8052 Shadowplay
8053 A Means To An End
8054 Passover
8055 New Dawn Fades
8056 Twenty-Four Hours
8057 Transmission
8058 Disorder
8059 Isolation
8060 Decades
8061 Digital
ORIGINAL RELEASE: Factory FACT 40

UK CHART POSITION: 18 October 1981 – #5 (17 weeks)

COMMENTS: The first and, to many fans' minds, the greatest Joy Division compilation prior to *Heart And Soul*, *Still* was issued as a double album, partly as a tribute to Curtis (and an epitaph for Joy Division), and partly to try and still the flood of bootlegs that was now pouring out. ('I'm amazed! I've never seen so much *shit*,' Hook shuddered. 'Some of it is good and some of it's bad but on the whole the recordings are horrible. I'm fascinated though. It's so repetitive, so monotonous. The same songs, over and over again.')

While the first two sides of vinyl functioned as a basic round-up of Joy Division's non-album catalogue, plus the odd out-take, sides three and four remarkably preserved the group's last ever concert, a move that drew down commentary from both sides of the fence – heartwarming tribute, or ghoulish exploitation? The concert itself, of course, didn't care – it had no idea what the future held, and it plays through well.

1982

(VIDEO) JOY DIVISION: *HERE ARE THE YOUNG MEN*
7955 Dead Souls
7956 Love Will Tear us Apart
7957 Shadowplay
7958 Day Of The Lords
8004 Digital
8005 Colony
8006 New Dawn Fades
8007 Autosuggestion
7960 Transmission
7961 Sound Of Music
7962 She's Lost Control
7963 Walked In Line
7964 I Remember Nothing
8036a Love Will Tear Us Apart (promo video)
ORIGINAL RELEASE: VHS Factory FACT 37 – September 1982
COMMENTS: First the good news. *Here Are The Young Men* corrals virtually every piece of extant Joy Division stage footage into one place and, even more than the live recordings, illustrates precisely why the in concert experience was regarded with such awe by so many people. And now the bad. None of this footage was shot with public consumption in mind, little of it makes even pretence towards professional quality and the sound is a muddy mess at the best of times. The band is visible primarily as a blur, while the camera spends almost as much time searching for focus as it does actually focusing on the players.

But still *Here Are The Young Men* is an essential document, an opportunity to witness how the Curtis persona so entranced a generation, as he half dances, half vibrates through his own mental images of how the band sounded.

(ALBUM) NEW ORDER: *81-82*
8201 Temptation
8202 Hurt
8113 Everything's Gone Green
8131 Procession
8132 Mesh
ORIGINAL RELEASE: US Factory/Rough Trade FACTUS 8 – Nov 1982
COMMENTS: A handy round-up of recent singles, aimed at giving the Americans an easy entrée to the soon-to-be-touring band's recent activities.

1986

(SINGLE) JOY DIVISION: *THE PEEL SESSION (31.1.79)*

7901 Exercise One
7902 Insight
7903 Transmission
7904 She's Lost Control
ORIGINAL RELEASE: Strange Fruit SFPS 013 – November 1986

(ALBUM) NEW ORDER: *1981-85*
8510 The Perfect Kiss
8513 Love Vigilante
8201 Temptation
8304 Blue Monday
8310 Your Silent Face
8401 Thieves Like Us
8314 Confusion
8114 Dreams Never End
ORIGINAL RELEASE: Japan, Factory/Columbia TD-3072 – April 1985
COMMENTS: A well-rounded promotional compilation issued to coincide with
the group's Japanese tour

1987

(ALBUM) NEW ORDER: *SUBSTANCE 1987*
8719 Ceremony
8113 Everything's Gone Green
8721 Temptation
8304 Blue Monday
8720 Confusion
8401 Thieves Like Us
8510 Perfect Kiss
8516 Sub-culture
8601 Shellshock
8603 State of the Nation
8609 Bizarre Love Triangle
8722 True Faith
8106 In A Lonely Place
8112 Procession
8131 Mesh
8202 Hurt
8305 The Beach
8314b Confusion Instrumental
8402 Lonesome Tonight
8403 Murder
8401a Thieves Like Us (instrumental)
8510c Kiss of Death
8603a Shame Of The Nation
8723 1963

ORIGINAL RELEASE: Factory 200 – August 1987

UK CHART POSITION: 29 August 1987 – #3 (37 weeks); reissue 17 July 1993 – #32 (2 weeks)

COMMENTS: A handy round-up of the singles (A and B sides)-so-far, marred (at least for completists) only by the latter-day reassessments of 'Ceremony,' 'Temptation' and 'Confusion.' There is no denying, however, that the rerecordings do lend the overall sound a stronger sonic continuity, an advantage that the collection justified when it became the first album to be released in the new DAT audio tape format which the industry was then convinced was the medium of the future.

Unfortunately, the industry was wrong. The vast majority of the album's 400,000 UK sales were spread between traditional vinyl and the slowly emergent CD, however, and DAT returned to the recording studio where it belonged.

Promotional rulers, inscribed *12 Inches Of New Order* were assigned the catalogue number FAC 203.

(SINGLE) JOY DIVISION: *THE PEEL SESSION (26.11.79)*
7968 Sound Of Music
7969 Twenty-Four Hours
7970 Love Will Tear Us Apart
7971 Colony
ORIGINAL RELEASE: Strange Fruit SFPS 033 – November 1987

COMMENTS: Prior to its release, the first *Peel Session* EP was among the most avidly anticipated in the entire archive. Bootlegs had long familiarized collectors with its contents, but the sound was generally poor and off-air, all hand-held mikes and insistent 'hush' sounds from the tapers. Pulled straight from the BBC's own reference recordings, the January 1979 session was revealed in all its original stark glory – and lived up to all the hopes that preceded it. Then the second session repeated the process, to prove that some things really were as great as you remembered them.

1988

(SINGLE) JOY DIVISION: Atmosphere
7952 Atmosphere
8035 Love Will Tear Us Apart
7943 Transmission (live)
7931 The Only Mistake
8033 Sound Of Music
ORIGINAL RELEASE: Factory FACD 213 – June 1988
UK CHART POSITION: 18 June 1988 – #34 (5 weeks)

COMMENTS: Issued alongside the *Substance* compilation, the greatest hits EP. 'Sound of Music' appears on the cassette and 12-inch versions only.

(ALBUM) JOY DIVISION: *SUBSTANCE*
7702 Warsaw

7704 Leaders Of Men
7805 Digital
7922 Autosuggestion
7947 Transmission
8037 She's Lost Control (12-inch version)
8048 Incubation
7953 Dead Souls
7952 Atmosphere
8036 Love Will Tear Us Apart
CD BONUS TRACKS ('APPENDIX')
7703 No Love Lost
7705 Failures
7806 Glass
7923 From Safety To Where...?
7948 Novelty
8047 Komakino
8034 These Days
ORIGINAL RELEASE: Factory FACD 250 – July 1988
UK CHART POSITION: 23 July 1988 – #7 (8 weeks)
COMMENTS: Confusingly sharing its title with a near-simultaneous New
Order compilation, Peter Hook relates an amusing anecdote. When New Order
toured the US around the time of *Lowlife* (August 1985), 'we played things from
Movement and *Power, Corruption And Lies*, neither of which had been released in
America, and people thought it was new material.' A couple of years later,
following the release of the Joy Division *Substance* compilation, 'kids were writing
to us from America, asking when we were going to tour. The band had been gone
for seven years, but if people don't have access to the material, they don't have
access to the history either.'

In fact, it was possible to envy those naïve *ingénues*, reveling in their first ever
taste of Joy Division. After eight, nine, almost ten years, fans of the band had grown
accustomed to the ruthless discipline and icicle glare; could never be surprised by
any of the sonic shards that shot out from the speakers. But imagine coming to that
sound for the first time, comfortable in your world of REM and Robyn Hitchcock,
Sonic Youth and the Pixies – aware, perhaps, of the link to New Order, but unaware
of just how brutally that link had been severed. Then forget all your personal
complaints about this album's contents ('wot? No rare stuff?') and start to live
again.

(VHS) JOY DIVISION: *SUBSTANCE*
7804 Shadowplay
7909 She's Lost Control
7910 Shadowplay
7911 Leaders Of Men
7950 She's Lost Control
7955 Dead Souls

8036a Love Will Tear us Apart
7947 Atmosphere
Interviews (previously released as 17 minute promo *Wired*)
ORIGINAL RELEASE: US Factory/Qwest 277 – promo copies only.1988
COMMENTS: A companion piece to *Here Are The Young Men*, as the group's *Granada Reports* and *Something Else* TV appearances are added to the stew, together with Malcolm Whitehead's footage from the Bowdon Youth Club, and a specially commissioned 'Atmosphere' video, newly directed by Anton Corbijn. As a partner to the *Substance* CD, it's a shock – those same ears that were opened to the studio material would surely have recoiled from the distant clatter of the live footage. But the moments of magic far outweigh the waste and, until the definitive Joy Division DVD finally arrives (as it someday certainly will), this bruised and battered old video tape will remain an essential document.

1989

(VHS) NEW ORDER: *SUBSTANCE 1989*
8314 Confusion
8511 The Perfect Kiss
8601 Shellshock
8609 Bizarre Love Triangle
8722 True Faith
8724 Touched by the Hand of God
8805 Blue Monday 1988
8901 The Happy One
ORIGINAL RELEASE: Factory/Virgin FACT 225 – September 1989
COMMENTS: A little prematurely, perhaps, bearing in mind how few (surprisingly so) videos New Order had made to date, *Substance 89* offers a straightforward rendering of the group's videos-to-date, only a handful of which ('True Faith' and 'Blue Monday 88') truly step out of the realms of the obvious to match the music with genuinely captivating videos. The unannounced inclusion of 'The Happy One' is a bonus-of-sorts, albeit one that can only be enjoyed if you like your music in seconds-long snippets.

1990

(ALBUM) NEW ORDER: *THE PEEL SESSIONS*
8101 Truth
8102 Senses
8103 ICB
8104 Dreams Never End
8203 Turn The Heater On
8204 We All Stand
8205 Too Late
8206 5-8-6
ORIGINAL RELEASE: Strange Fruit SFRCD 110 – September 1990
COMMENTS: An unadorned assemblage of the two 12-inch EPs already

released in the *Peel Sessions* series, but still remarkable for that exemplary 'Turn The Heater On.'

(ALBUM) JOY DIVISION: *THE PEEL SESSIONS*
7901 Exercise One
7902 Insight
7903 Transmission
7904 She's Lost Control
7968 Sound Of Music
7969 Twenty-Four Hours
7970 Love Will Tear Us Apart
7971 Colony
ORIGINAL RELEASE: Strange Fruit SFRCD 111 – 1990
COMMENTS: Single CD reissue of the two earlier EPs.

1993

(ALBUM) NEW ORDER: *IN ORDER*
8304 Blue Monday
8306 Age of Consent
8510a The Perfect Kiss (extended version)
8609a Bizarre Love Triangle (extended dance mix)
8722a True Faith (morning sun extended remix)
8905a Round & Round (12" version)
ORIGINAL RELEASE: Qwest PRO-A-5970 (vinyl) – 1993
COMMENTS: Released in the protracted lead-up to the following year's *? (The Best Of New Order)* compilation, an American vinyl promo, primarily serviced to DJs, and highlighting a well-conceived selection of New Order dancefloor fillers.

(ALBUM) NEW ORDER: *IN ORDER*
8114 Dreams Never End
8304 Blue Monday
8306 Age of Consent
8510 The Perfect Kiss
8609 Bizarre Love Triangle
8722 True Faith
8905 Round & Round
ORIGINAL RELEASE: Qwest PRO-CD-5970 (CD) – 1993
COMMENTS: Well aware that not everybody likes to dance... the stay-at-home journalist's version of the above, cosily contained upon a single CD and demanding nothing more strenuous than the occasional tapping toe. Both versions of *In Order*, by the way, are considered eminently collectible, despite the lack of any 'new' music.

(VHS) JOY DIVISION/NEW ORDER: *THE NEW ORDER STORY*
7903 Transmission

8036a Love Will Tear Us Apart
8128 Ceremony
8130 Temptation
8805 Blue Monday 88
8724 Touched by the Hand of God
8609 Bizarre Love Triangle
8314 Confusion
8601 Shellshock
8603 State Of The Nation
8511 Perfect Kiss
8722 True Faith
8905 Round & Round
9001 World in Motion
8806 Fine Time
9301 Regret
9303 Ruined in a Day
9302 World
7952 Atmosphere

ORIGINAL RELEASE: London/PolyGram Video 087 134-3 – September 1993

COMMENTS: It could probably have been better, but it could scarcely have been more complete, as the full complement of New Order videos to date is supplemented with live material, chat, and even a look back at the Joy Division days, via the too-seldom-seen 'Love Will Tear Us Apart' film, plus a pair of shorts from Anton Corbijn.

1994

(ALBUM) NEW ORDER: *? (THE BEST OF NEW ORDER)*
8722c True Faith-94
8609c Bizarre Love Triangle-94
8723a 1963-94
9301 Regret
8806 Fine Time
8510 The Perfect Kiss
8601 Shellshock
8401 Thieves Like Us
8809 Vanishing Point
8907 RUN
8905e Round & Round-94
9302 World (The Price Of Love)
9303 Ruined in a Day
8724 Touched by the Hand of God
8805 Blue Monday 1988
9001 World in Motion

ORIGINAL RELEASE: London Records 90 Ltd 828580.1 – Nov 1994

UK CHART POSITION: 3 December 1994 – #4 (17 weeks)

(ALBUM) NEW ORDER: *? (THE BEST OF NEW ORDER)*
8802 Let's Go (Nothing for Me)
8114 Dreams Never End
8306 Age of Consent
8513 Love Vigilantes
8722c True Faith-94
8609c Bizarre Love Triangle 94
8723b 1963-95
8806 Fine Time
8809 Vanishing Point
8907 Run
8905e Round & Round-94
9301 Regret
9302 World (The Price Of Love)
9303 Ruined in a Day
8724 Touched by the Hand of God
8805 Blue Monday-88
9001 World in Motion
ORIGINAL RELEASE: US Qwest/Warner Bros. 9 45794-4 – Nov 1994

COMMENTS: Not until you hear the hits crashing one upon another does it become apparent just what a fine repertoire New Order developed. From the still-stunning 'Age Of Consent,' through the corny (but okay, it's captivating) 'Love Vigilantes,' 'True Faith,' 'World'.... even 1988's remix of the already perfect 'Blue Monday' fits a pattern.

Surprisingly reprised from the customarily overlooked *Salvation!* soundtrack, a new version of 'Let's Go' hops out to remind us that 'Touched By The Hand Of God' was not the only boon bestowed upon that luckless collection, while a total disdain for chronology only adds to the album's constantly shifting moods.

Cunningly designed to neither negate 1987's mammoth *Substance* catcher-upper, nor replace the simultaneously released, but very different variation issued for the US market *?* is a stunning career resume. The absence of a few of *Substance's* choicer early singles does prevent this album from truly living up to its title, but *some of* the best? Definitely.

(VHS) NEW ORDER: *? THE BEST OF NEW ORDER*
8722c True Faith-94
9301 Regret
8907 Run 2
8609c Bizarre Love Triangle-94
8806 Fine Time
8511 The Perfect Kiss
8601 Shellshock
8314 Confusion
8805 Blue Monday 1988
8905e Round & Round-94

9302 World (The Price Of Love)
9303 Ruined in a Day
8603 State of the Nation
8724 Touched by the Hand of God
9001 World in Motion
9304 Spooky
8722 True Faith
ORIGINAL RELEASE: London Records 90 Ltd. 633 730-3 – December 1994
COMMENTS: And, if you need to do something with your eyes while you're listening, here's much the same selection again, in video form.

1995

(ALBUM) NEW ORDER: *? (THE REST OF NEW ORDER)*
8805f Blue Monday (Hardfloor mix)
8306a Age of Consent (Howie B remix)
8609d Bizarre Love Triangle (Armand Van Helden mix)
8113a Everything's Gone Green (Dave Clarke mix)
8724d Touched by the Hand of God (Biff & Memphis remix)
8721a Temptation (CJ Bolland mix)
CASSETTE BONUS TRACKS
9302b World (Perfecto mix)
8722a True Faith (Shep Pettibone mix)
8720h Confusion (Pump Panel Reconstruction mix)
9303f Ruined in a Day (K-Klass remix)
9301c Regret (Fire Island mix)
CD BONUS TRACK
9304c Spooky (Magimix)
BONUS CD
8304 Blue Monday
8805f Blue Monday (Hardfloor vocal mix) **
8805c Blue Monday (Andrea mix)
8805 Beach Buggy
8805m Blue Monday (Richie Hawtin mix)
8805h Blue Monday (Jam & Spoon Manuela mix)
8805i Blue Monday (Starwash mix)
8805k Blue Monday (Plutone mix)
ORIGINAL RELEASE: London Records 90 Ltd 828657 – Aug 1995
COMMENTS: Despite the efforts of some definitely trendy names, 'Round And Round' and 'Bizarre Love Triangle,' are functional, but neither more nor less preferable to the originals.

(SINGLE) JOY DIVISION: Love Will Tear Us Apart
8036b Love Will Tear Us Apart (remix by Don Gehman)
8036 Love Will Tear Us Apart
8036c Love Will Tear Us Apart (remix by Arthur Baker)

8034 These Days
7952 Atmosphere
7943 Transmission (live)
ORIGINAL RELEASE: London YOJ 1 – May 1995
UK CHART POSITION: 17 June 1995 – #19 (3 weeks)
COMMENTS: Back in 1984, when singer Paul Young announced he intended covering 'Love Will Tear us Apart,' a great roar of protest arose from the pages of the music press. Ian Curtis was dead just four years at the time, and the song – *his* song – still had a resonance that bordered on the sacrosanct.

What a difference a decade makes. Did anybody even raise an eyebrow as this pair of remixes plopped into view; did a single spine tingle with horror at the thought of Arthur Baker's beats running roughshod over Saint Ian's epitaph? And has anyone played either of them more than once or twice since they first picked up the single? Answers on a postcard, please….

(ALBUM) JOY DIVISION: *PERMANENT*
8035 Love Will Tear Us Apart
7947 Transmission
7917 She's Lost Control
7918 Shadowplay
7913 Day Of The Lords
8039 Isolation
8040 Passover
8043 Heart And Soul
8044 Twenty-Four Hours
8034 These Days
7948 Novelty
7953 Dead Souls
7927 The Only Mistake
7946 Something Must Break
7952 Atmosphere
8036b Love Will Tear Us Apart (remix by Don Gehman)
ORIGINAL RELEASE: London Records 8286242 – August 1995
UK CHART POSITION: 1 July 1995 – #16 (3 weeks)
COMMENTS: A terribly straightforward Joy Division 'best of,' with nothing to recommend it to anyone armed with a more-than-passing awareness of who the group was. Of course, that still rendered it a crucial acquisition to an entire generation of new kids, tempted and teased by a new wave of 90s acts whose own love of Joy Division was flown brightly from their mastheads… from Nine Inch Nails down through the entire industrial scene; from the Smashing Pumpkins on to Low… entire Joy Division tribute albums were falling from the sky now; of *course* it was time the kids heard the real thing.

1996

(BOX SET) JOY DIVISION: *HEART AND SOUL*

7805 Digital
7806 Glass
7912 Disorder
7913 Day Of The Lords
7914 Candidate
7915 Insight
7916 New Dawn Fades
7917 She's Lost Control
7918 Shadowplay
7919 Wilderness
7920 InterZone
7921 I Remember Nothing
7926 Ice Age
7924 Exercise One
7947 Transmission
7948 Novelty
7925 The Kill
7927 The Only Mistake
7945 Something Must Break
7922 Autosuggestion
7923 From Safety To Where...?
8037 She's Lost Control (1980 version)
8033 Sound Of Music
7952 Atmosphere
7953 Dead Souls
8047 Komakino
8048 Incubation
8038 Atrocity Exhibition
8039 Isolation
8040 Passover
8041 Colony
8042 A Means To An End
8043 Heart And Soul
8044 Twenty-Four Hours
8045 The Eternal
8046 Decades
8036 Love Will Tear Us Apart
8034 These Days
7702 Warsaw
7703 No Love Lost
7704 Leaders Of Men
7705 Failures
7801 The Drawback
7802 Interzone
7803 Shadowplay

7901 Exercise One
7905 Insight
7906 Glass
7907 Transmission
7944 Dead Souls
7946 Something Must Break
7908 Ice Age
7928 Walked In Line
7929 These Days
7930 Candidate
7931 The Only Mistake
7932 Chance (Atmosphere)
7970 Love Will Tear Us Apart
7971 Colony
8049 As You Said
8062 Ceremony
8063 In A Lonely Place
7933 Dead Souls
7934 The Only Mistake
7935 Insight
7936 Candidate
7937 Wilderness
7938 She's Lost Control
7939 Disorder
7940 Interzone
7941 Atrocity Exhibition
7942 Novelty
7949 Autosuggestion
7965 I Remember Nothing
7966 Colony
7967 These Days
8022 Incubation
8025 The Eternal
8026 Heart And Soul
8028 Isolation
8030 She's Lost Control

ORIGINAL RELEASE: London 828 968-2 – December 1997

UK CHART POSITION: 7 February 1998 – #70 (1 week)

COMMENTS: If Ian Curtis hadn't stepped out for a metaphorical pizza, that night in May, 1980, where would Joy Division be today? Probably not too far away from where they are anyway, universally feted for two classic albums; cited as an influence on everything from Nine Inch Nails to the price of tea; and finally getting the boxed set treatment. Well, if Style Council deserve one....

Joy Division had it all. In the years immediately following the punk explosion, they emerged from hometown Manchester with a staccato, icy drone, spreading doom, gloom and the unbearable weight of hopelessness wherever they went. Not since the heyday of Leonard Cohen, bemused critics wrote, had any band sounded so suicidal and, though the clichés swiftly came back to haunt those who wrote such wearisome words, so did Joy Division. Arguably, Joy Division remain the most insularly influential band of the post-Pistols 70s. And *Heart And Soul* is the ultimate exposition of their legacy.

Four discs compile together pretty much everything Joy Division released during their two year existence: two complete albums, a bunch of rare and hard to find single tracks, a few radio sessions (more are available elsewhere), a bunch of demos dating back to almost-their-first; and a disc of unreleased live material which *Goldmine* grumbled 'makes a fine Frisbee,' but is, in fact, worth a little more than that. After all, one can never have too many Joy Division live recordings, can one?

The first thing one notices is, Joy Division were never the doomy despair mongers of popular legend. So Curtis sang like a man with a more than sore head, but the band had a polar power and polarized passion which defied, and ultimately denied, the hopelessness which Curtis allegedly imparts: Joy Division rocked, dude, and a cat with no ears could tell you that. No matter that they ultimately turned into New Order; nor that 'Love Will Tear Us Apart' has since been subject to so many earnest dissertations that it has lost all its original meaning. Through the first two discs at least, Joy Division are what Iggy should have done next, if he'd really meant *The Idiot*; and what Bowie could have done, if he'd retired right after *Heroes*; it's what the 80s wanted to be, and the 90s (Nine Inch again) tried so hard to be. And it's that which would have destroyed the group, regardless of whether Curtis lived or not. No band can carry that much promise; no band should be expected to. *Heart And Soul* is more than a great boxed set; it's also a warning.

Though the liner notes flatter to deceive, this is not quite the Complete Works Of.... The live portions of *Still*, for example, are very under-represented; also absent are the majority of tracks recorded for the BBC's John Peel Show, and previously released across the *Peel Sessions* mini-album. A handful of other, and not necessarily lesser, odds and ends are also missing.

What we do get, however, is completely overwhelming nevertheless. Opening, with Martin Hannett's first productions for the band, *Heart And Soul* traces the Joy Division story through to its final pages... the demos of 'Ceremony' and 'In A Lonely Place' which would, with a minimum of rearrangement, eventually surface as New Order's first single.

Unreleased material abounds: aside from the live disc, most of disc three's 24 tracks emanate either from demos or long unheard radio sessions, but little of it is the kind of workaday filler which normally meets that description. Neither is the accompanying booklet a standard issue. Suitably blurry photographs accompany a clutch of lengthy essays (a little over-elegiac, but that is only to be expected), but it's the lyrics and collector information which predominates, confirming Joy Division's long held status as one of the most collectible bands of their era. As for their other reputation, as the most meaningful band of their age – well, the music answers that question.

1999

(ALBUM) BERNARD SUMNER/ELECTRONIC: *THE BEST OF*
e01a Getting Away With It (Full Length Version)
e07 Tighten Up
e08 Patience Of A Saint
e03 Get The Message
e12 Some Distant Memory
e13 Feel Every Beat
e17 Forbidden City
e20 For You
e24 Second Nature
e28 Freefall
e31 Time Can Tell
e01 Getting Away With It
e18 Imitation Of Life
e33 I Feel Alright
e16 Disappointed
ORIGINAL RELEASE: EMI Japan WPCR10570 – unreleased (scheduled Dec 1999)
COMMENTS: It's all very well labels releasing a spoiler compilation when one of their old acts has a new album out… but not when nobody cares about either of them. An excellent collection drawing both album tracks and b-sides from Electronic's two album EMI career, *The Best Of* was ultimately shelved, around the same time as it became apparent that Electronic themselves were not long for this world.

2000

(ALBUM) JOY DIVISION: *COMPLETE BBC RECORDINGS*
7901 Exercise One
7902 Insight
7903 Transmission
7904 She's Lost Control
7968 Sound Of Music
7969 Twenty-Four Hours
7970 Love Will Tear Us Apart
7971 Colony
7950 Transmission
7951 She's Lost Control
ORIGINAL RELEASE: Fuel 302 061 084 – July 2000
COMMENTS: A straightforward reissue of the *Peel Sessions* album, with the added bonus of the September 1979 *Something Else* performance, plus the interview (but not, sadly, the music) from the Richard Skinner/*Rock On* broadcast. This disc was subsequently repackaged alongside New Order's *BBC Radio 1 In Concert*

album as *New Order & Joy Division: Before & After – The BBC Sessions* (Fuel 302 061 213).

2002

(ALBUM) NEW ORDER: *INTERNATIONAL*
8719 Ceremony
8304 Blue Monday
8314 Confusion
8401 Thieves Like Us
8510 The Perfect Kiss
8601 Shellshock
8609a Bizarre Love Triangle (extended dance mix)
8722 True Faith
8724a Touched By The Hand Of God (original 12 inch)
8905 Round And Round
9301 Regret
0101 Crystal
0104 60 Miles An Hour
0203 Here To Stay (radio edit)
BONUS DVD
9810 Blue Monday (live)
8511 The Perfect Kiss
8722 True Faith
ORIGINAL RELEASE: US Warner/Rhino R2 73835 – Oct 2002
COMMENTS: No matter that New Order had released just one new album since the last hits collection, this US compilation rounded all the oldies up once again, with the added attraction of the three most recent hits. The bonus DVD was more interesting, drawing in the Reading 98 rendition of 'Blue Monday,' plus two of the group's most popular past promos – 15 years on, 'True Faith' still shows up on Stateside VH-1 with uncanny regularity.

(ALBUM) JOY DIVISION/NEW ORDER: original soundtrack *24 HOUR PARTY PEOPLE*
7947 Transmission
7952 Atmosphere
8037 She's Lost Control
8036 Love Will Tear Us Apart
0114 New Dawn Fades [with Moby]
8721 Temptation
8304 Blue Monday
0203 Here to Stay
ORIGINAL RELEASE: WEA/London Records 0927 44930 2 – Apr 2002
COMMENTS: With Tony Wilson's memoir, *24 Hour Party People*, having proven one of the most entertaining, if not altogether trustworthy, accounts of post-punk Manchester yet published, the movie was awaited with anticipation and

nervousness in more or less equal quantities – both among its featured cast and casual onlookers.

The end result would live up to all expectations, emerging one of the finest rock-related movies of recent years, and one of the most nostalgia-stirring ever – no matter that the truth was not necessarily adhered to. The legend was far more emotive, and it was the legend that dominated the proceedings.

New Order, for all the chaos that surrounded their 'official' break with Wilson and his Factory empire, were involved throughout the movie production, 'helping them out and... advis[ing] them on the script,' as Hook put it as the film came together. 'And we've lent them a load of props from the Haçienda... and my best friend's firm has done the catering for it – he keeps bringing them round to my house. The most interesting thing to me will be to see what they get wrong. I was there, so I don't want to see a documentary on it, I'd rather see someone else's take on it.'

One of the most fascinating aspects, from the band's own point of view, was the rebuilding of the Haçienda, just weeks after Hook ceremoniously started up the first of the bulldozers that were to tear down the original. A near exact replica, the building was so lifelike, laughed Hook, that 'Steve [Morris] didn't go, because he thought they wouldn't let him in again like they used to at the original. "I'm the drummer out of New Order"; "Yeah, you and thousands of others. Piss off!"'

'The little bits they got wrong made it seem like you were in a dream,' he continued. 'It was mind-boggling. And all the people in Manchester who used to go to the Haçienda... made sure they got in, so when you were walking round it was like New Year's Eve because you knew everyone there. It was the most bizarre moment of my life. The strangest thing of all was when I went up to Barney after a few sherbets and said, "The only thing that's missing is Rob Gretton." And he tapped me on the arm... and there was Rob with his glasses on, or at least the actor playing him. Then Ian Curtis walked past — he looked at me and ran off... three times. He had the same mac on, the same badge and the same shirt and he really fucking looked like him.'

New Order and Joy Division dominated the soundtrack, their eight songs not only representing close to half of the 18 track album, but also serving up the only new recordings, a live 'New Dawn Fades,' recorded on their most recent US tour with Moby, and 'Here To Stay,' their next single. Elsewhere, the Sex Pistols, the Buzzcocks and the Clash represented the bands that 'started' it all; the Happy Mondays stood for those that ended it; and Durutti Column, A Guy Called Gerald, 808 State and Marshall Jefferson stood in for all the music that passed by in-between times.

In these days when picking your way through a movie soundtrack is akin to spending half your life watching *Top Of The Pops*, and wondering just what the hell a ghastly remake of Bowie's 'Changes' has to do with a film about fat green ogres, *24 Hour Party People* catapulted us back to an age when the music wasn't simply reflective of the film (sallow, crass and eminently forgettable? Shut up, at the back there), it was an integral part of it.

(ALBUM) JOY DIVISION: various artists: *FABRICLIVE.07 JOHN PEEL*

8036c. Love Will Tear Us Apart (remix)
ORIGINAL RELEASE: Fabric FABRIC14, December 2002
COMMENTS: Actually less a remix, more a case of overlaying the song amidships with a snatch of commentary from the 1978 European Cup Final, as Liverpool defeated FC Bruges to take the trophy. Unlike other volumes in the Fabric series, #7 allows its contents to stand all but unaltered, an excellent collection for anybody stranded far from Peel's nearest radio broadcasts that swoops through a wealth of genres and time spans, from bluegrass to noise and back again. *Fabriclive.07* reminds us just how he has survived for so long at the top of his game.

(BOX SET) NEW ORDER: *RETRO*
8806 Fine Time
8201 Temptation
8722 True Faith
8510 The Perfect Kiss
8105 Ceremony
9301 Regret
0101 Crystal
8609 Bizarre Love Triangle
8720 Confusion
8095 Round and Round
8304 Blue Monday
9901 Brutal
0108 Slow Jam
9305 Everyone Everywhere
8405a Elegia
8106 In a Lonely Place
8112 Procession
8310 Your Silent Face
8512 Sunrise
8802 Let's Go
8607 Broken Promise
8114 Dreams Never End
8132 Cries and Whispers
8610 All Day Long
8515 Sooner Than You Think
8313 Leave Me Alone
8402 Lonesome Tonight
8612 Every Little Counts
0112 Run Wild
0222b Confusion (koma & bones mix)
8604a Paradise (robert racic mix)
9301e Regret (sabres slow 'n' low mix)
8609a Bizarre Love Triangle (shep pettibone mix)
8601b Shell Shock (john robie mix)

8806b Fine Time (steve 'silk' hurley mix)
8723b 1963 95
8724a Touched by the Hand of God
8113 Everything's Gone Green
8805h Blue Monday (jam & spoon manuela mix)
9001b World in Motion (subbuteo mix)
0203a Here to Stay (extended instrumental)
0101p Crystal (lee coombs remix)
8404 Ceremony
8518 Procession
8303 Everything's Gone Green
8107 In a Lonely Place
8602 Age of Consent
8718 Elegia
8715 The Perfect Kiss
8912 Fine Time
9313 World
9314 Regret
9315 As It Is When It Was
0201 Crystal
0113 Turn My Way
0202 Temptation

ORIGINAL RELEASE: London Records 0927 49499 2 – Dec 2002

COMMENTS: A beast of a box, guaranteed to satisfy… who, exactly? Four discs, each selected by a different band associate, pick up on four different aspects of the band – their pop side (journalist Miranda Sawyer), their cult edge (journalist/DJ John McCready), their remixes (Haçienda DJ Mike Pickering) and their concerts (Bobby Gillespie) – each of which surely demands a box set all to itself, none of which is truly explored in the depth it deserves.

There again, had the decision been left to Hook, there wouldn't have been any music whatsoever. People don't buy box sets to listen to, he insists. They leave them unopened on the shelf, in the hope that one day they'll be worth lots of money. You could put four blank discs in there, or even none at all, and nobody would be any the wiser. And, if you don't believe him, ask Stephen Morris. 'I buy a box-set every Christmas. I never play them. They just sit there looking nice. That's all I want from them.'

Should you break through the plastic, however, *Retro* revealed what Hook determined to be 'a nice bookend to a career.' The original impetus came from the late Rob Gretton, who had been agitating for New Order to repackage their entire singles catalogue on CD, with each individual release restored with its original artwork and b-sides. A similar approach had proven very successful with Depeche Mode in the early 1990s (and would again in 2004), but London Records baulked at the idea. A more conventional box set, however, did meet with their approval, and a straightforward historical package, tentatively titled *Recycle*, was on the schedules for January 1999.

In the event, it did not appear, as New Order themselves changed their approach, announcing their intention to distance themselves almost completely from the project. They would choose the people who chose the tracks. And that was it.

In the event, they did collaborate with Bobby Gillespie on the live portion, but still they were rewarded for their trust when Mike Pickering emerged with a clutch of remixes that even Hook claimed he'd never heard before.

Elsewhere, both Sawyer and McCready came up with the most intelligent gatherings yet assembled under the banner of a New Order compilation, dwelling on the necessary hits, but unafraid to pull in some less familiar album tracks (and b-sides) as well. There is still room, of course, for a New Order box that treats their history as well as it examines their various aspects – but, for the time being, *Retro* will please no-one – but it won't piss them off either.

RETRO BONUS CD – available with a limited quantity of the above London Records boxset

9817 Temptation 98

0224 Transmission (Live) Recorded by Triple J at the Big Day Out, Gold Coast. Live sound by Dian Barton.Recording date 20th January 2002

0221 Such a Good Thing

8911 Theme from Best & Marsh

8802 Lets G (Extract from Instrumental used on Salvation motion picture sound track)

8722m True Faith (Pink Noise Morel Edit) Additional Remix and Production by Richard Morel

0112 Run Wild (Steve Osborne Original Mix)

8511 The Perfect Kiss (Live take recorded at video shoot) Recorded Live on Manor Mobile at Cheetham Hill Manchester 27th March 1985

8405 Elegia (Full Version)

COMMENTS: A magnificent (if somewhat brief) round-up of rarities, most dignified by the inclusion of the full-length 'Elegia,' and one previously unreleased cut, the Big Day Out airing for 'Transmission.'

2004

(ALBUM) NEW ORDER: THE RADIO ONE SESSIONS

9812 Isolation

9813 Touched By The Hand Of God

9814 True Faith

9815 Paradise

9816 Atmosphere

0115 Slow Jam

0116 Your Silent Face

0117 Close Range

0118 Rock The Shack

0223 Transmission (2002 Live Video)

ORIGINAL RELEASE: Strange Fruit SFRSCD 128, April 2004

COMMENTS: Combines the 1998 John Peel and 2001 Steve Lamacq sessions, plus video of the performance filmed for John Peel's 40th anniversary party in 2002.

This release means just one New Order BBC studio performance remains under-wrapped, the more-or-less disgraced 1984 set broadcast during the *Rock Around The Clock* marathon.

(ALBUM) PETER HOOK/REVENGE: *ONE TRUE PASSION V2.0*

r29 Televive
r30 The Wilding
r23 Deadbeat
r25 State Of Shock
r26 Little Pig
r24 Cloud Nine
r02 Jesus... I Love You
r06 Pineapple Face
r14 Big Bang
r16 I'm Not Your Slave
r07 14k
r17 Bleachman
r18 Surf Nazi
r01 7 Reasons
r21 Amsterdam
r20 It's Quiet
r08 Underworld
r24a Deadbeat (Gary Clail Dub)
r26 State Of Shock (US edit)
r06c Pineapple Face's Big Day Out
r22 The Trouble With Girls
r05 Wende
r16d Slave (Bonus Beats)
r16h I'm Not Your Slave (US remix)
r09 Hot Nights/Cool City
r10 Surf Bass
r04 Bleach Boy
r11 Soul
r15 Kiss The Chrome
r19 Fag Hag
r12 Precious Moments
r13 Pumpkin
r06g Pineapple Face (Pickering & Park Remix)

ORIGINAL RELEASE: LTMCD 2375 – January 2004

COMMENTS: Nobody was as surprised as Peter Hook, it seems, when James Nice's LTM label approached him about remastering and reissuing the Revenge back catalogue for a 2CD anthology – his spoken word outro to disc one chimes with gratitude and astonishment, before kicking into one of the two tracks he hauled out of absolute obscurity, to rerecord for inclusion.

Not exactly the *complete* works of Revenge, this seriously upgraded version of the *One True Passion* album nevertheless rounds up the vast majority of the group's work, including several non-album b-sides, the entire *Gun World Porn* EP and a clutch of tracks previously available only as scarce promo remixes, if at all. A handful more, had lain unreleased since Revenge's heyday, and reviews of the ensuing package expressed their own amazement at the decade-plus that the band had spent in the doldrums: as *Q* magazine's review so eloquently put it, 'while Hooky's certainly no Ian Curtis, he's still heartfelt and distinctive on his own, and much of what follows lays claim to the fact that Revenge were a truly underrated band. A well-rounded portrait of his first 'other band' and one whose memory ought to be recalled with rather more reverence.'

Incidentally, disc one of the 2CD package alone bears the *One True Passion* title. The second disc adopts the title Hook originally intended for the second Monaco album, *Be Careful What You Wish For*.

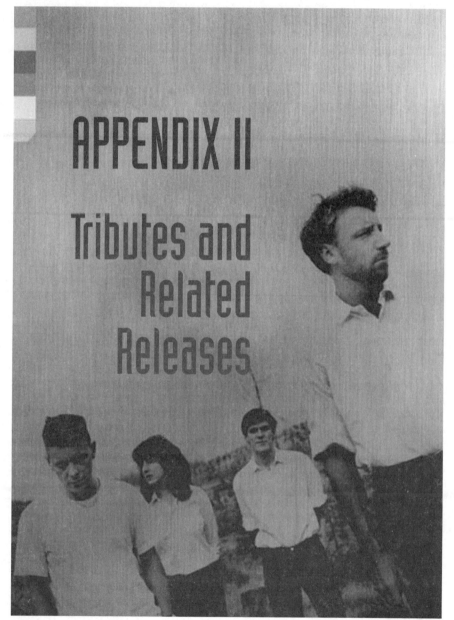

APPENDIX II

Tributes and Related Releases

(ALBUM) *ART OF MIX ULTRA HOT ART DISC TWO*
   Bored Of Pepsi (Steele version) – Joan Crawford (000 BPM)
   Ruined In A Day (LB Mayer edit) – New Order (112 BPM)
   Slave (Lucky mix) – Revenge (124 BPM)
   Touched (Dear Tina Dub) – New Order (114 BPM)
   Getting Away (Mrs. Craig Mix) – Electronic (126 BPM)
   Round & Round (Blanche's Mix) – New Order (130 BPM)
   Tasty Fish (Cape Cod Mix) – The Other Two (130 BPM)
   World (Queen Bee Mix) – New Order (131 BPM)
   How Does It Feel (Beach Blue Mix) – Electroset (136 BPM)
   1963 (Air Force One Mix) – New Order (138 BPM)
   Love Will Tear Us Apart (Literal Mix) – Joy Division (152 BPM)
   Bizarre Love Triangle (Mildred's Mix) – New Order (124 BPM)
ORIGINAL RELEASE: CD 2841 Corporation, Inc. UHACD02, 1998 (bootleg)

COMMENTS: Through the mid-late 1980s, and on into the 1990s, a thriving market for dance remixes was met by a number of specialist remix teams. The boom was, ultimately, quashed by the record labels' own growing appreciation of remixes, released both generally and promotionally, alongside individual bands' new singles and albums; prior to that, extremely limited edition 12-inch, white-label style remixes had the market to themselves, as well as a very well-defined corner of the collectors' market.

A number of DJ remixes exist that were released only for club consumption, in extremely limited quantities, and generally elude public consumption. This CD collection rounds up a mere fraction of the New Order-and-related mixes, and was itself produced in a limited edition of 1,000 copies. Its dedication, however, is fairly universal: 'This CD is dedicated to Gillian, Peter, Stephen & Bernard with the hopes that they will continue to bring us crossover dance excellence in the new millennium and beyond.' Because like many DJ remixes, these mixes were just edits and cut-ups of the records, not using the multi-track masters, it should be treated like a bootleg.

   (TRIBUTE) various artists: *SOMETHING ABOUT JOY DIVISION*
   Colony – The Difference
   Love Will Tear Us Apart – The Carnival Of Fools
   Ceremony – Allison Run
   Heart And Soul – Orange Party
   She's Lost Control – Silver Surfers
   Interzone – Speed Blue
   Decades – Comic Spoilers
   Shadowplay – Afterhours
   Atrocity Exhibition – Subterranean Dining Room
   Dead Souls – Sundowners
   Atmosphere – Hitchcock's Scream
   Warsaw – Definitive Gaze

CD BONUS TRACKS
A Means To An End – Jackie Stewart Said
The Drawback – The Pow!
I Remember Nothing – Magick Y & Uncle Tybia
Transmission – T & The Starburst
ORIGINAL RELEASE: Vox Pop (Italy) VP 3 – 1989
COMMENTS: All-Italian tribute contains a few interesting arrangements, but more slavish imitation.

(TRIBUTE) various artists: *CEREMONIAL: A TRIBUTE TO JOY DIVISION*
Shadowplay – Ikon
Isolation – Trance to the Sun
Atmosphere – Wreckage
Dead Souls – Decaf
Heart And Soul – Sub Version
Ceremony – Child
Love Will Tear us Apart – Trance to the Sun
In A Lonely Place – Lycia
The Eternal – Shadow Light
Shadowplay – Phobia
Warsaw – You Shriek
Atmosphere – Corpus Delecti
Love Will Tear Us Apart – Opium Den
New Dawn Fades – The Last Dance
ORIGINAL RELEASE: Mere Mortal Prod. MMP-1 – 1995
COMMENTS: There was a time, and not too long ago either, when the idea of a tribute to Joy Division would have warranted approaching with nothing more than caution, and a certain gleeful curiosity.

Not any longer. Even if you don't regard Joy Division as the Holiest of Holies, sacred ground upon which none should walk, the atrocities committed in their name through the early-mid 1990s were a hanging offence at the least, making one positively yearn for the days when Paul Young's vapid recreation of 'Love Will Tear Us Apart' was the only sin in sight.

So, where does that leave *Ceremonial*?

Untouched, actually. From the moment Ikon's 'Shadowplay' flows into earshot, unerringly faithful but unfamiliarly joyful, *Ceremonial* shoves everything else from your mind, to the point where it seems disrespectful even to call this a tribute album. Highlighted by Decaf's rocking 'Dead Souls' (which suffers only by comparison with NIN's darker, denser, effort); Shadow Light's Spector-esque 'The Eternal' (that's Spector-esque when compared to the hyper-minimal original); Lycia's funereal 'In A Lonely Place' and Corpus Delicti's dryly New Orderly 'Atmosphere,' it's a return to basics for a dozen bands, most of whom flow around Goth Central, and all of whom are smart enough to know that Joy Division themselves were never Goths. Miserable buggers, yes; but Goths? Not on your nelly.

They laid the relevant groundrules, though; and, in acknowledging that, *Ceremonial* wrenches Joy Division's memory away from the sentimental sordidness of current contemplation, and restates what it was that made them matter in the first place. They didn't give a damn about the past, and they didn't care much for the future, either. It wasn't love which tore us apart, after all.

(TRIBUTE) various artists: *A MEANS TO AN END: A TRIBUTE TO JOY DIVISION*
She's Lost Control – Girls Against Boys
Day Of The Lords – Honeymoon Stitch
New Dawn Fades – Moby
Transmission – Low
Atmosphere – Codeine
Insight – Further
Love Will Tear us Apart – Stanton-Miranda
Isolation – Starchildren
Heart And Soul – Kendra Smith
24 Hours – Versus
Warsaw – Desert Storm
They Walked In Line – GodheadSilo
Interzone – Face To Face
As You Said – TORTOISE
ORIGINAL RELEASE: Hut D29 – 1995
COMMENTS: The main problem with *A Means To An End* is, you want to like it a lot more than it's actually possible *to* like it. By the standards of mid-90s Alternative Americana, after all, it certainly hauls in enough major names to at least be worth a listen... Girls Against Boys, electro-jester Moby, the minimalist Low, Codeine and Billy Corgan's Starchildren conceit paramount among them. But the contributions themselves fail, with just a handful of exceptions, so deeply into so-so territory that you do wonder, how many of the bands involved actually knew who Joy Division were (let alone what they sounded like) before the record company cheque fell onto the doormat?

The exceptions are the obvious ones – Moby's 'New Dawn Fades' isn't simply excellent, it was also co-opted onto the *Heat* movie soundtrack, where it bristles with even more delirious intent. (It turns up again on his *I Like To Score* collection.) Starchildren, too, are respectful without being overly stand-offish, and Low were themselves cruising in such high gear at this time that it was unlikely they could ever put a foot wrong. Elsewhere, however, *A Means To An End* simply mills around the most obvious moves, and pays tribute to Joy Division only in as much as it sends you screaming back to the original versions, simply to wash the taste of these terrors from your ears.

(TRIBUTE) various artists: *BALANCE: A TRIBUTE TO JOY DIVISION*
Transmission – Subgud
Twenty Four Hours – Empty Lives

Love Will Tear Us Apart – Peltz
Atmosphere – Beyond Dawn
Disorder – The Tubs
Heart and Soul – Crave
Passover – Bever
Decades – Theatre Of Tragedy
Ceremony – Planet Bee
The Eternal – Skog
New Dawn Fades – Anno Domini
ORIGINAL RELEASE: Ego Development 001 – 1997
COMMENTS: A fair bash at a tricky theme by a gathering of Norwegian Goths.
Skog would later be better known as Kings of Convenience.

(TRIBUTE) various artists: *WARSAW: UN HOMENAJE*
Atmophere – Automatics
Love Will Tear Us Apart – Pribata Idaho
Passover – Senor Chinarro
The Only Mistake – Explosivos Acme
Transmission – Submarine
The Eternal – Sweetwater
Dead Souls – Honey Langstrumpf
Twenty Four Hours – Yellowfin
Disorder – Los Planetas
The Drawback – Supernova
She's Lost Control – El Nino Gusano
Something Must Break – Lord Sickness
Wilderness – Long Spiral Dreamin'
Ceremony – Mercromina
No Love Lost – The Flow
Failures – Alias Galor
New Dawn Fades – Strange Fruit
ORIGINAL RELEASE: El Colectivo Karma 011, 1997
COMMENTS: Spain's dark souls pay their own respects to Joy Division. Best
left alone.

(TRIBUTE) various artists: *BLUE ORDER: A TRANCE TRIBUTE TO NEW
ORDER*
Confusion – Martin N
Blue Monday – Flipside
Touched by the Hand of Dub – Coercion
Spooky – Endorphin
Young Offender – Martin O
1963 – THC
Finetime – Bug-eyed Funk
Everything's Gone Green – Sandowski

The Beach – Flipside
Bizarre Love Triangle – Judson Leach
Regret – Casey Stratton
ORIGINAL RELEASE: Hypnotic CLP 99852, 1997
COMMENTS: Part of an on-going series of trance and electro tributes to the giants of the recent rock past, *Blue Order* is typical of its bedfellows in that few of the bands involved are household names – unless, of course, you happen to share a house with Martin N, Liva Akselbo or Tek Hed, of course. Neither are their takes on New Order's greatest hits and bits precisely what one would regard as traditional: 'Confusion,' 'Blue Monday,' 'Bizarre Love Triangle,' 'Regret'... one recognises the titles before the sounds make sense, but wasn't that always the way with New Order? Rather, the best of these tracks actually stand alongside the group's own sanctioned remixes in terms of teaching old dogs new tricks, while the remainder at least *try* to do something new.

(TRIBUTE) NAU ENSEMBLE: *THE ETERNAL – VARIATIONS ON JOY DIVISION*
The Eternal
Atmosphere
Decades
Interlude (original composition)
Luz Aeterna
Atmosphere
The Eternal
ORIGINAL RELEASE: Atrium 22108, April 1999
COMMENTS: 'The music of Joy Division as you've never heard it before, adapted by the Nau Ensemble for strings, medieval choir, and ambient sonics.' A spellbinding creation, the five songs merged together around a recurrent theme of 'The Eternal,' and suffering only when you accuse it of riding the same wave of hybrid curiosity that has produced so many symphonic rock and string quartet tributes over the years. It doesn't – rather, *The Eternal* is that so incredibly rare thing, a borrowed notion that is absolutely original.

(ALBUM) various artist tribute – *THIEVES LIKE US*
Age Of Consent – Thursday 29
Ruined In A Day – Echo Stylus
Touched By The Hand Of God – Strange Angels
True Faith – Satellite Circle
Hurt – Sensoria
Dream Attack – MinGys
In A Lonely Place – Fadestation
Mesh – Florentine Cruise
Confusion – Suzuki Kid
Round & Round – Vegasphere
Regret – Radiate

World In Motion – International Jewel Thieves
Angel Dust – Neutered Faith
Times Change – Larry Petrov
ORIGINAL RELEASE: Something Invited Records – January 2000
COMMENTS: A harsh electro-driven stab at reappraisal that succeeds only in reminding us that, for every great idea New Order prompted their musically inclined listeners to try out, there were a lot of lousy ones as well. And this collection, sadly, seems to overflow with the things.

(ALBUM) various artists: *BACK TO MINE*
Big Eyed Beans From Venus – Captain Beefheart
Higher Than The Sun – Primal Scream
The Rain – Missy Elliot
Venus In Furs – Velvet Underground
M62 Song – The Doves
In Every Dream Home A Heartache – Roxy Music
Was Dog A Doughnut – Cat Stevens
Bassline – Massonix
Cherry Red – Groundhogs
Energy Flash – Joey Beltram
I Feel Love – Donna Summer
Mushroom – Can
The Dance – Rhythim Is Rhythim
E=MC2 = Giorgio vs Talla @XLC
ORIGINAL RELEASE: DMC BACKCD 11 – 2002
COMMENTS: One more in the so-admirable *Back To Mine* series, New Order's selection of 14 songs that influenced or otherwise affected them was, according to the liners, 'researched, created and completed with the full and frank co-operation of the band themselves, who were all on stage/on planes/in boats at the time.'

It's an eccentric mix – more so than such other series highlights as Faithless, Everything But The Girl, Orbital and Tricky – but there is scarcely a cut in sight that one cannot, in some way, tie back to either Joy Division or New Order's own musical journey, whether it's the primal impact of the Velvets, Can and Roxy Music (what, no Iggy?); the direct cultural input of Donna Summer and Giorgio Moroder, or the more modern vitality of Primal Scream and Missy Elliott... even the Groundhogs cut is excused with the observation, 'Peter Hook will probably tell you that Tony McPhee says more about his life than JG Ballard.'

(ALBUM) Soulwax – *2 MANY DJS*
The Beach
ORIGINAL RELEASE: Pias – April 2002
COMMENTS: Mixed with the a capella portion of Detroit Grand Pubah's 'Sandwiches'

(ALBUM) *IN HINDSIGHT VOLUMES 1 + 2*

Subculture (Sarm West Mix/Razormaid remix #1)
Touched by the Hand of God
Bizarre Love Triangle
Everything's Gone Green
5-8-6
Subculture (Berlin Mix/Razormaid remix #3)
True Faith
Fine Time
Blue Monday
Subculture (Deborah Lyall Mix/Razormaid remix #2)
Confusion
Everything's Gone Green
Your Silent Face
Round & Round
State of the Nation
Thieves Like Us
Vanishing Point
Spooky
Mr. Disco
Perfect Kiss
Ultraviolence
ORIGINAL RELEASE: Razormaid – no cat/CDR
COMMENTS: By no means a full accounting of all the New Order remixes issued during this period, the two volume *In Hindsight* concentrates on those produced by Razormaid, the undoubted market leaders. Some can become a little irritating as they go on, but their impact on the American club scene of the time is undeniable.

(TRIBUTE) *THE STRING QUARTET TRIBUTE TO JOY DIVISION AND NEW ORDER*
Love Will Tear Us Apart
She's Lost Control
Isolation
New Dawn Fades
Bizarre Love Triangle
Blue Monday
Love Vigilantes
True Faith
Regret
Waiting Here (original composition)
ORIGINAL RELEASE: Vitamin AM6KY – 2003
COMMENTS: As a one off, assuming it truly was a tribute, this would be quite the nifty novelty. As just one more in a veritable hailstorm of String Quartet Tributes, however; as a shelfmate to similarly packaged assaults on everyone from Yanni to No Doubt, the Cure to Nirvana, it is clearly just a job of work to the players

involved – and, to be honest, it sounds like it. Kerryn Coulter, Anja Grant, Stephanie Lindner, Richard Dodd, Caerwin Martin, Tom Talley and Guenevere Measham are all gifted musicians. But, when the best performance on a tribute is an original composition, you know something's awry....

(ALBUM) *COOL AS ICE – THE BE MUSIC PRODUCTIONS*
Can't Afford To Let You Go – 52nd Street (Sumner – producer)
Looking From A Hilltop (Megamix) – Section 25 (Sumner – producer)
Reach For Love – Marcel King (Sumner – producer)
Love Tempo – Quando Quango (Sumner – producer)
Cool As Ice – 52nd Street (Sumner – synth programming)
The Only Truth (12-inch mix) – Paul Haig (Sumner – producer)
Atom Rock – Quando Quango (Sumner – producer)
Babcock & Wilcox – Thick Pigeon (Morris/Gilbert – producer)
Fate/Hate – Nyam Nyam (Hook – producer)
Tell Me – Life (Morris/Gilbert – producer)
Beating Heart (12-inch remix) – Section 25 (Sumner – producer)
Theme – Be Music (Hook)
ORIGINAL RELEASE: LTM 2377, 2003
COMMENTS: A fairly representative sampling of New Order/Be Music's production work, undertaken for Factory Records during the 1983-85 period, and leaning towards the team's dancier inclinations. Sadly (but not especially surprisingly), much of what was once so revolutionary sounds a trifle dated today, but the overall imminence of the revolution-to-come remains in sharp focus – with Hook's 'Be Music Theme' an especially powerful piece. Finally, an excellent booklet offers up notes on both Be Music and the artists themselves. (Volume 2 also available 2004.)

(AND FINALLY) *SIX MORE GREAT JOY DIVISION COVERS....*
Ceremony – Galaxie 500 (from *Blue Thunder*, 1990)
Dead Souls – Nine Inch Nails (from *The Crow*, 1994)
Decades – Human Drama (from *Pin-Ups*, 1993; also includes Love Will Tear Us Apart)
Isolation – Die Krupps (from *Odyssey Of The Mind*, 1996)
Love Will Tear Us Apart – PJ Proby (single, 1985)
She's Lost Control/dub version – Grace Jones (single 1980: an early 1990s Peter Hook remix remains unreleased.)

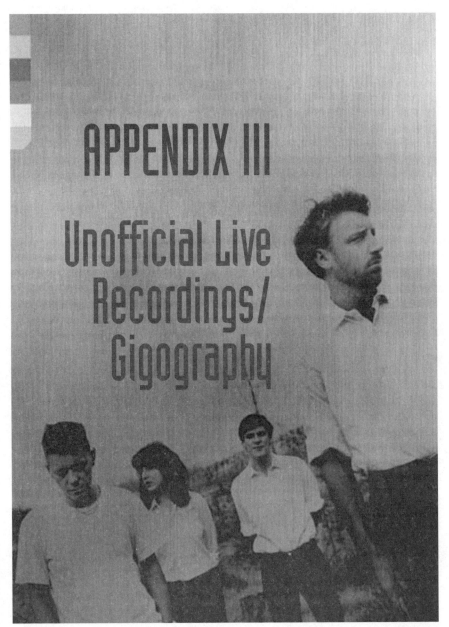

APPENDIX III

Unofficial Live Recordings/ Gigography

No full accounting of every live show that Joy Division and New Order have played has – or, likely, will – ever be published, with attempts at compiling one generally confined to shows either advertised/reviewed in the music press, or preserved on the several hundred live tapes circulating the collectors' underground.

The following is no more complete than any other, and was based in a very large part on that compiled for the worldinmotion.net website (see bibliography). Other material was drawn from *Punk Diary* and *Post-Punk Diary* by George Gimarc, Pollstar Online and individual issues of UK, European and US magazines.

THE STIFF KITTENS/WARSAW
29 MAY 77 The Electric Circus, Manchester

WARSAW/JOY DIVISION
31 MAY 77 Rafters, Manchester
01 JUN 77 The Squat, Manchester
02 JUN 77 Newcastle
03 JUN 77 The Squat, Manchester
16 JUN 77 The Squat, Manchester
30 JUN 77 Rafters, Manchester
?? JUL 77 The Squat, Manchester
27 AUG 77 Eric's, Liverpool (afternoon)
27 AUG 77 The Electric Circus, Manchester (evening)
14 SEP 77 Rock Garden, Middlesbrough
24 SEP 77 The Electric Circus, Manchester
02 OCT 77 The Electric Circus, Manchester
07 OCT 77 Salford Technical College, Salford
08 OCT 77 Manchester Polytechnic, Manchester
19 OCT 77 Piper's Disco, Manchester
?? DEC 77 Rafters, Manchester
31 DEC 77 The Swinging Apple, Liverpool
25 JAN 78 Pip's, Manchester
28 MAR 78 Rafters, Manchester
14 APR 78 Rafters, Manchester
20 MAY 78 The Mayflower, Manchester
09 JUN 78 The Factory I, Manchester
15 JUL 78 Eric's, Liverpool
27 JUL 78 The Fan Club (Roots Club), Leeds
28 JUL 78 The Factory I, Manchester
29 AUG 78 Band On The Wall, Manchester
04 SEP 78 Band On The Wall, Manchester
09 SEP 78 Eric's, Liverpool
10 SEP 78 Royal Standard, Bradford
UK TOUR
02 OCT 78 Institute Of Technology, Bolton

12 OCT 78 Kelly's, Manchester
20 OCT 78 The Factory I, Manchester
24 OCT 78 The Fan Club (Branningan's), Leeds
04 NOV 78 Eric's, Liverpool
14 NOV 78 The Odeon, Canterbury
15 NOV 78 Brunel University, Uxbridge
?? NOV 78 Top Rank, Reading
19 NOV 78 Bristol
20 NOV 78 Check Inn Club, Altrincham
26 NOV 78 New Electric Circus, Manchester
01 DEC 78 The Factory I, Manchester
22 DEC 78 Revolution Club, York
27 DEC 78 The Hope And Anchor, Islington, London
UK TOUR
10 FEB 79 Bolton
16 FEB 79 Eric's, Liverpool
28 FEB 79 Playhouse, Nottingham
01 MAR 79 The Hope And Anchor, Islington, London
04 MAR 79 The Marquee, London
14 MAR 79 Bowden Vale Youth Club, Altrincham
17 MAR 79 University of Kent, Canterbury
30 MAR 79 Youth Centre, Walthamstow
03 MAY 79 Eric's, Liverpool
11 MAY 79 The Factory I, Manchester
17 MAY 79 Acklam Hall, London
23 MAY 79 Bowdon Vale Youth Club, Altrincham
UK TOUR
07 JUN 79 Fan Club, Leeds
13 JUN 79 The Factory / Russell Club, Manchester
16 JUN 79 The Odeon, Canterbury
17 JUN 79 Royalty Theatre, Holborn, London

22 JUN 79 Good Mood, Halifax
25 JUN 79 Free Trade Hall, Manchester
28 JUN 79 The Factory I, Manchester
03 JUL 79 Free Trade Hall, Manchester
05 JUL 79 Limit Club, Sheffield
11 JUL 79 Roots Club, Leeds
13 JUL 79 Russell Club (The Factory),
Manchester
27 JUL 79 Imperial Hotel, Blackpool
28 JUL 79 The Fun House (The
Mayflower), Manchester
02 AUG 79 Prince Of Wales Conference
Centre, YMCA, London
08 AUG 79 Romulus Club, Birmingham
11 AUG 79 Eric's, Liverpool (two shows)
13 AUG 79 Nashville, London
22 AUG 79 Youth Centre, Walthamstow
27 AUG 79 Leigh Pop Festival
31 AUG 79 The Electric Ballroom, London
08 SEP 79 Futurama One, Queen's Hall,
Leeds
22 SEP 79 Nashville Club, London
28 SEP 79 The Factory I, Manchester

BUZZCOCKS TOUR
02 OCT 79 Mountford Hall, University
Of Liverpool, Liverpool
03 OCT 79 Leeds University, Leeds
04 OCT 79 City Hall, Newcastle
05 OCT 79 The Apollo, Glasgow, Scotland
06 OCT 79 Odeon, Edinburgh, Scotland
07 OCT 79 Capitol, Aberdeen, Scotland
08 OCT 79 Caird Hall, Dundee, Scotland
16 OCT 79 Plan K, Brussels, Belgium
18 OCT 79 Bangor University, Bangor
20 OCT 79 Loughborough University,
Loughborough
21 OCT 79 Top Rank, Sheffield
22 OCT 79 Assembly Halls, Derby
23 OCT 79 King George's Hall, Blackburn
24 OCT 79 The Odeon, Birmingham
25 OCT 79 St. George's Hall, Bradford
26 OCT 79 The Electric Ballroom, London
27 OCT 79 Apollo Theatre, Manchester
28 OCT 79 Apollo Theatre, Manchester
29 OCT 79 De Montford Hall, Leicester
30 OCT 79 The New Theatre, Oxford
01 NOV 79 Civic Hall, Guildford
02 NOV 79 Winter Gardens, Bournemouth
03 NOV 79 Sophia Gardens, Cardiff

04 NOV 79 Colston Hall, Bristol
05 NOV 79 Pavilion, Hemel Hempstead
07 NOV 79 Pavilion, West Runton
09 NOV 79 The Rainbow Theatre, London
10 NOV 79 The Rainbow Theatre, London
11 NOV 79 Hemel Hempstead Pavilion
07 DEC 79 Stockport Technical College,
Stockport
08 DEC 79 Eric's, Liverpool
18 DEC 79 Les Bains-Douches Club,
Paris, France
31 DEC 79 Woolworth's, Oldham
Street, Manchester
01 JAN 80 Piccadilly Gardens, Manchester
EUROPEAN TOUR
11 JAN 80 Paradiso, Amsterdam, Holland
12 JAN 80 The Trojan Horse, The
Hague, Holland
13 JAN 80 Doomroosje, Nijmegen,
Holland
14 JAN 80 King Kong, Antwerp,
Belgium
15 JAN 80 The Basement, Cologne,
West Germany
16 JAN 80 Club Lantaren, Rotterdam,
Holland
17 JAN 80 Plan K, Brussels, Belgium
18 JAN 80 Effenaar, Eindhoven,
Holland
19 JAN 80 Vera, Groningen,
Netherlands
21 JAN 80 Kantkino, Berlin, West Germany
07 FEB 80 The Factory II (New
Osbourne Club), Manchester
08 FEB 80 University of London Union,
London
20 FEB 80 Town Hall, High Wycombe
28 FEB 80 The Warehouse, Preston
29 FEB 80 The Lyceum, London
05 MAR 80 Trinity Hall, Bristol
02 APR 80 The Moonlight Club, London
03 APR 80 The Moonlight Club, London
04 APR 80 The Rainbow, London
04 APR 80 The Moonlight Club, London
05 APR 80 The Winter Gardens,
Malvern
08 APR 80 Derby Hall, Bury
11 APR 80 The Factory I (Russell Club),
Manchester

19 APR 80 Ajanta Theatre, Derby
25 APR 80 Scala Cinema, London,
CANCELLED
26 APR 80 Rock Garden,
Middlesbrough, CANCELLED
02 MAY 80 High Hall, Birmingham
University, Birmingham
THE NO NAMES
29 JUL 80 Beach Club, Manchester
NEW ORDER
04 SEP 80 The Warehouse, Preston
05 SEP 80 Scamps, Blackpool
US TOUR
21 SEP 80 Maxwell's, Hoboken, New
Jersey
27 SEP 80 Hurrah's, New York
28 SEP 80 Pier 3, New York
30 SEP 80 The Underground, Boston
UK TOUR
25 OCT 80 The Squat, Manchester
(Gillian Gilbert's first gig)
13 DEC 80 Utopia, Hal 4, Rotterdam,
Holland
19 DEC 80 College of Arts, Rochdale
02 JAN 81 Porterhouse, Retford
03 JAN 81 Tatton Community Centre,
Chorley
04 JAN 81 The Fan Club (Branningan's),
Leeds
11 JAN 81 Rock Garden, Middlesborough
12 JAN 81 Eglinton Toll Plaza,
Glasgow, Scotland
14 JAN 81 Plato's Ballroom (Mr.
Pickwick's), Liverpool
06 FEB 81 Comanche Student Union,
Manchester Polytechnic
07 FEB 81 Road-Menders Club,
Northampton
09 FEB 81 Heaven Ultradisco, London
21 MAR 81 The Boys Club, Bedford
22 MAR 81 Jenkinson's Bar, Brighton
27 MAR 81 Trinity Hall, Bristol
08 APR 81 Rock City, Nottingham
10 APR 81 Cedar Club, Birmingham
16 APR 81 St. Andrews University, Fife,
Scotland
18 APR 81 Victoria Hotel, Aberdeen
19 APR 81 Valintino's, Edinburgh
22 APR 81 Atmosphere (Romeo &

Juliet's), Sheffield
06 MAY 81 Forum Ballroom, Kentish
Town, London
07 MAY 81 Talbot Tabernacle, London
08 MAY 81 University Student Union,
Reading
EUROPEAN TOUR
13 MAY 81 Palais Des Arts, Paris, France
15 MAY 81 L'Ancienne Belgique,
Brussels, Belgium
16 MAY 81 Markthalle, Hamburg,
Germany
17 MAY 81 Saltlagaret, Copenhagen,
Denmark
19 MAY 81 Roxy, Stockholm, Sweden
22 MAY 81 Lobo Disco, Gothenburg,
Sweden
25 MAY 81 Chateau Neuf, Oslo, Norway
27 MAY 81 SO36 Club, Berlin, Germany
20 JUN 81 C.N.D. Festival, Glastonbury
06 SEP 81 Kulttuuritalo, Helsinki,
Finland
23 SEP 81 Phoenix Hall, Sheffield
Polytechnic, Sheffield
25 SEP 81 Assembly Rooms,
Walthamstow
26 SEP 81 Bodiam Castle, England
(cancelled "Mystery Venue" concert)
23 OCT 81 Bradford University, Bradford
26 OCT 81 The Ritz, Manchester
US TOUR
05 NOV 81 Country Club, Reseda,
California
06 NOV 81 Perkins Palace, Pasadena,
California
07 NOV 81 Cinema Club, San Francisco,
California
09 NOV 81 I-Beam Club, San Francisco,
California
10 NOV 81 Berkeley, California
15 NOV 81 The Masonic Temple,
Toronto, Canada
17 NOV 81 The Channel, Boston,
Massachusetts
18 NOV 81 Ritz, New York
19 NOV 81 Ukranian National Home,
New York
20 NOV 81 Peppermint Lounge, New
York

21 NOV 81 Trenton, New Jersey

22 NOV 81 Peppermint Lounge, New York

22 JAN 82 North London Polytechnic, London

23 JAN 82 Imperial Cinema, Birmingham

26 FEB 82 Trinity Hall, Bristol

03 MAR 82 Blue Note, Derby

05 MAR 82 Sir Francis Xavier Hall, Dublin, Ireland

09 MAR 82 Tiffany's, Leeds

10 MAR 82 Tower Cinema, Hull

11 MAR 82 Soul Kitchen (Mayfair Suite), Newcastle

EUROPEAN TOUR

08 APR 82 Glazenzaal, Rotterdam, Netherlands

09 APR 82 Meervaart, Amsterdam, Netherlands

10 APR 82 Stockvishal, Arnhem, Netherlands

11 APR 82 Musiekcentrum, Utrecht, Netherlands

12 APR 82 Staargebouv, Maastricht, Netherlands

14 APR 82 Lido, Leuven, Belgium

15 APR 82 L'Ancienne Belgique, Brussels, Belgium

17 APR 82 Le Palace, Paris, France

05 MAY 82 Kilburn National Ballroom, London

24 MAY 82 Pennies, Norwich

25 MAY 82 Kilburn National Ballroom, London

05 JUN 82 Provinssirock Festival, Seinäjoki, Finland

ITALIAN TOUR

16 JUN 82 Tenax, Florence, Italy

17 JUN 82 Piper, Rome, Italy

18 JUN 82 Tur Sports Centre, Taranto, Italy

21 JUN 82 Palasport, Bologna, Italy

22 JUN 82 Rollingstone, Milan, Italy

26 JUN 82 The Haçienda, Manchester

30 AUG 82 The Venue, Blackpool

11 SEP 82 Futurama Four / Queensferry Leisure Centre – Deeside

19 SEP 82 Sporting Arena, Athens

AUSTRALASIAN TOUR

25 NOV 82 Palais Theatre, Melbourne, Australia

27 NOV 82 The Seaview Ballroom, Melbourne, Australia

03 DEC 82 Mainstreet, Auckland, New Zealand

04 DEC 82 Mainstreet, Auckland, New Zealand

06 DEC 82 Victoria University, Wellington, New Zealand

08 DEC 82 Hillsborough Hotel, Christchurch, New Zealand

14 DEC 82 Old Melbourne Hotel, Perth, Australia

26 JAN 83 The Haçienda, Manchester

29 JAN 83 Great Hall, Joint Student Union, Cardiff, Wales

25 FEB 83 Kolingsborg, Stockholm, Sweden

26 FEB 83 Kolingsborg, Stockholm, Sweden

11 MAR 83 The Ace, Brixton

12 MAR 83 Recreation Centre, Kingston-Upon-Thames, Tolworth

23 MAR 83 The State, Liverpool

24 MAR 83 The State, Liverpool

11 APR 83 Coasters, Edinburgh, Scotland

12 APR 83 Assembly Hall, Edinburgh, Scotland

13 APR 83 St. Andrews University, St. Andrews, Scotland

14 APR 83 Tiffany's, Glasgow, Scotland

15 APR 83 Orient Cinema, Ayr, Scotland

IRISH TOUR

22 APR 83 Savoy, Cork, Ireland

?? APR 83 Aula Maxima, University College Galway

24 APR 83 Rose Hill Hotel, Kilkenny, Ireland

26 APR 83 Sir Francis Xavier Hall, Dublin, Ireland

09 MAY 83 Tower Ballroom, Birmingham

10 MAY 83 Victoria Hall, Hanley

24 MAY 83 Pennies Club, Norwich

US TOUR

17 JUN 83 Club 688, Atlanta, Georgia

19 JUN 83 Nightlife, Austin, Texas

21 JUN 83 Florentine Gardens, Los Angeles, California

23 JUN 83 The Fantasy, Fullerton, California
24 JUN 83 Echo Beach, San Francisco, California
25 JUN 83 I-Beam Club, San Francisco, California
27 JUN 83 The Commodore, Vancouver, Canada
29 JUN 83 First Avenue, Minneapolis, Minnesota
30 JUN 83 The Metro, Chicago, Illinois
02 JUL 83 St. Andrews Hall, Detroit, Michigan
05 JUL 83 The Spectrum, Montreal, Canada
07 JUL 83 Paradise Garage, New York
08 JUL 83 Ontario Theatre, Washington D.C.
09 JUL 83 City Gardens, Trenton, New Jersey
20 JUL 83 The Haçienda, Manchester
01 AUG 83 Beacon Theater, New York
01 DEC 83 The Academy, Brixton
02 DEC 83 Town Hall, Bournemouth
05 DEC 83 London
19 MAR 84 Caesars Palace, Bradford

EUROPEAN TOUR
30 MAR 84 Uni-Mensa, Dusseldorf, Germany
31 MAR 84 Haus Nied, Frankfurt, Germany
02 APR 84 Volkshaus, Zurich, Switzerland
06 APR 84 Wiener Arena, Vienna, Austria
08 APR 84 Metropol, Berlin, Germany
09 APR 84 Sonntage, Berlin, Germany
10 APR 84 Falcon Centrale, Copenhagen, Denmark
12 APR 84 Trinity Hall, Hamburg, Germany
15 APR 84 Galactica, Luneburg, Germany
14 MAY 84 Royal Festival Hall, London
17 MAY 84 Paradiso, Amsterdam, Netherlands
21 MAY 84 Palais, Leicester

UK/EUROPEAN TOUR
03 JUN 84 Powerhouse, Birmingham
04 JUN 84 Palais, Nottingham
05 JUN 84 Studio, Bristol

27 JUN 84 Mayfair Suite, Southampton
01 JUL 84 Roskilde Festival, Denmark
05 JUL 84 Rock-Ola, Madrid, Spain
06 JUL 84 Pacha Auditorium, Valencia, Spain
07 JUL 84 Studio 54, Barcelona, Spain
10 JUL 84 Marbella Moniciple, Marbella, Spain
11 AUG 84 De Panne Seaside Festival, De Panne, Belgium
12 AUG 84 Inside Festival, Luik (Liege), Belgium
15 AUG 84 The Mayfair Suite, Sunderland
16 AUG 84 City Hall, Hull
19 AUG 84 Leisure Centre, Gloucester
20 AUG 84 Winter Gardens, Margate
22 AUG 84 Goldiggers, Chippenham
23 AUG 84 Cornwall Coliseum, St. Austell
26 AUG 84 Guildhall, Portsmouth
27 AUG 84 Heaven Ultradisco, London

UK TOUR
26 JAN 85 St. George's Hall, Blackburn
27 JAN 85 Tiffanys, Leeds
28 JAN 85 Finsbury Park, Michael Sobell Sports Centre, London
05 FEB 85 Caley Palais, Edinburgh, Scotland
06 FEB 85 Barrowlands, Glasgow, Scotland
14 MAR 85 Lancaster University, Lancaster
09 APR 85 Tower Ballroom, Birmingham
10 APR 85 Mayfair, Swansea, Wales
17 APR 85 University, Salford
18 APR 85 Rotters, Doncaster
19 APR 85 Leisure Centre, Macclesfield

FAR EAST/AUSTRALASIAN TOUR
26 APR 85 Canton (club), Hong Kong
01 MAY 85 Kosei Nekin Kaiken Hall, Tokyo, Japan
02 MAY 85 Kosei Nekin Kaiken Hall, Tokyo, Japan
17 MAY 85 The Powerhouse, Melbourne, Australia
18 MAY 85 Briotone Solonic, Sydney, Australia (also listed as Selinas Hotel)
20 MAY 85 East Leagues Club,

Brisbane, Australia
  23 MAY 85 Logan Cambell Centre, Auckland, New Zealand
  16 JUL 85 Haçienda, Manchester
  20 JUL 85 W.O.M.A.D. Festival, Mersea Island, Essex

US TOUR
  01 AUG 85 Felt Forum, New York
  02 AUG 85 Opera House, Boston, Massachusettes
  04 AUG 85 International Centre, Toronto, Canada
  06 AUG 85 Bismark Theatre, Chicago, Illinois
  09 AUG 85 Warner Theatre, Washington D.C.
  11 AUG 85 Fox Theater, Atlanta
  12 AUG 85 McAllistar Auditorium, New Orleans, Louisiana
  14 AUG 85 City Coliseum, Austin, Texas
  16 AUG 85 Rainbow Music Hall, Boulder, Colorado
  17 AUG 85 Salt Lake City, Utah
  19 AUG 85 Henry Kaiser Centre, Oakland, California
  22 AUG 85 Civic Auditorium, Santa Monica, California
  23 AUG 85 Irvine Meadows, Irvine, California

UK TOUR
  22 OCT 85 Guildhall, Preston
  25 OCT 85 University Of London Union, London
  26 OCT 85 Sheffield University, Sheffield
  08 NOV 85 Pavilion, Hemel Hempstead
  10 NOV 85 Hammersmith Palais, London
  03 DEC 85 Haçienda, Manchester (two shows)
  06 DEC 85 Central London Polytechnic, London
  07 DEC 85 Fulcrum, Slough

EUROPEAN TOUR
  10 DEC 85 El Dorado, Paris, France
  11 DEC 85 Salle Villar, Maison De La Culture, Rennes, France
  12 DEC 85 Exo 7, Rouen, France
  13 DEC 85 Salle Du Baron, Orleans, France
  15 DEC 85 Rotterdam Arena, Rotterdam, Netherlands
  17 DEC 85 Manhatten Club, Leuven, Belgium

UK TOUR
  23 JAN 86 Connolly Hall, Cork, Ireland
  24 JAN 86 Sir Francis Xavier, Dublin, Ireland
  25 JAN 86 Sir Francis Xavier, Dublin, Ireland
  27 JAN 86 Queens University, Belfast, Ireland
  08 FEB 86 Royal Court Theatre, Liverpool
  27 FEB 86 Civic Hall, Wolverhampton
  28 FEB 86 St. George's Hall, Bradford
  01 MAR 86 Spectrum Arena, Warrington
  27 MAR 86 Apollo Theatre, Oxford
  28 MAR 86 Brighton Centre, Brighton
  29 MAR 86 Poole Arts Centre, Poole
  14 JUN 86 City Hall, Sheffield
  21 JUN 86 Loughborough University, Lougborough
  19 JUL 86 Manchester Exhibition Centre (GMEX), Manchester
  16 AUG 86 Valby, Copenhagen, Denmark

UK TOUR
  10 SEP 86 Mayfair, Newcastle
  11 SEP 86 Playhouse Theatre, Edinburgh, Scotland
  12 SEP 86 Barrowlands, Glasgow, Scotland
  13 SEP 86 Caird Hall, Dundee, Scotland
  28 SEP 86 Valdarno, San Giovanni, Italy
  02 OCT 86 Tower Ballroom, Birmingham
  03 OCT 86 Winter Gardens, Malvern
  04 OCT 86 Town & Country Club, London
  06 OCT 86 Royal Albert Hall, London
  13 OCT 86 The Haçienda, Manchester

US TOUR
  31 OCT 86 San Diego State University Aztec Bowl, San Diego, California
  01 NOV 86 Irvine Meadows, Irvine, California
  04 NOV 86 Palace, Hollywood, California
  05 NOV 86 Palladium, Hollywood, California
  07 NOV 86 Arlington Theatre, Santa Barbara, California
  08 NOV 86 Berkeley Community Theater, Berkeley, California

?? NOV 86 Salt Lake City, Utah
11 NOV 86 CU Events Center, Boulder, Colorado
14 NOV 86 Maceba Theatre, Houston, Texas
17 NOV 86 City Coliseum, Austin, Texas
20 NOV 86 Oriental Theatre, Milwaukee, Wisconsin
21 NOV 86 Aragon Ballroom, Chicago, Illinois
22 NOV 86 Fox Theatre, Detroit, Michigan
24 NOV 86 Congress Centre, Ottawa, Canada
26 NOV 86 Massey Hall, Toronto, Canada
27 NOV 86 Massey Hall, Toronto, Canada
30 NOV 86 McMaster University (Ivor Wyne), Hamilton, Canada
02 DEC 86 Syria Mosque, Pittsburgh, Pennsylvania
04 DEC 86 University of Pennsylvania, Philadelphia, Pennsylvania
05 DEC 86 1018 Club, New York
06 DEC 86 The Orpheum, Boston, Massachusettes
07 DEC 86 Opera House, Boston, Massachusettes
08 DEC 86 Constitutional Centre, Washington D.C.
09 DEC 86 Felt Forum, New York
12 DEC 86 Fox Theatre, Atlanta, Georgia
13 DEC 86 Tampa Bay Theater, Tampa Bay, Florida

FAR EASTERN/AUSTRALASIAN TOUR
27 JAN 87 Tokyo, Japan
28 JAN 87 Tokyo, Japan
29 JAN 87 Osaka Festival Hall, Osaka, Japan
30 JAN 87 Nagoya, Japan
04 FEB 87 The Galaxy, Auckland, New Zealand
06 FEB 87 Roxy, Brisbane, Australia
07 FEB 87 The Generator, Gold Coast, Australia
09 FEB 87 Byron Bay Arts Centre, Byron Bay, Australia
11 FEB 87 Dee Why Hotel, Sydney, Australia

12 FEB 87 Enmore Theatre, Sydney, Australia
13 FEB 87 Enmore Theatre, Sydney, Australia
14 FEB 87 Selina's, Sydney, Australia
16 FEB 87 Thebarton Town Hall, Adelaide, Australia
17 FEB 87 The Venue, Melbourne, Australia
18 FEB 87 Festival Hall, Melbourne, Australia
20 FEB 87 Canterbury Court, Perth, Australia
21 FEB 87 Red Parrot, Perth, Australia

UK TOUR
02 APR 87 Woolwich Coronet, Woolwich
04 APR 87 The Academy, Brixton
?? MAY 87 Plaza de Toros, Valencia, Spain
16 MAY 87 Mollerussa Pabellon, Mollerussa, Spain
06 JUN 87 Super Tent, Finsbury Park, London
08 JUN 87 The Roxy, Sheffield
09 JUN 87 Barrowlands, Glasgow, Scotland
10 JUN 87 The Haçienda, Manchester
19 JUN 87 C.N.D. Festival, Glastonbury
30 JUN 87 Reading University, Reading

AMERICAN TOUR
13 AUG 87 Northrup Auditorium (Univ of Minn), Minneapolis, Minnesota
15 AUG 87 Pine Knob Amphitheatre, Clarkston, Michigan (Detroit)
16 AUG 87 Poplar Creek Music Theater, Hoffman Estates, Illinois (Chicago)
18 AUG 87 Mansfield G.W.A., Boston, Massachusettes
21 AUG 87 Merriweather Post Pavilion, Columbia, Maryland
22 AUG 87 Nautica Stage, Cleveland, Ohio
24 AUG 87 Mann Music Centre, Philadelphia, Pennsylvania
25 AUG 87 Pier 84, New York
26 AUG 87 Pier 84, New York
31 AUG 87 Jones Beach Theatre, Wantagh, Long Island, New York
01 SEP 87 Montreal University,

Montreal, Canada
03 SEP 87 C.N.E. Grandstand, Toronto, Canada
04 SEP 87 Darien Lakes Amusement Park, Buffalo, New York
05 SEP 87 Civic Centre, Pittsburgh, Pennsylvania
08 SEP 87 Red Rocks Amphitheatre, Denver, Colorado
09 SEP 87 Salt Lake City, Utah
11 SEP 87 San Diego, California
12 SEP 87 Irvine Meadows, Irvine, California (Laguna Hills)
13 SEP 87 The Forum, Los Angeles, California (Inglewood)
15 SEP 87 Compton Terrace, Phoenix, Arizona
18 SEP 87 Greek Theatre, Berkeley, California
19 SEP 87 Greek Theatre, Berkeley, California
06 DEC 87 Philipshalle, Dusseldorf, Germany
08 DEC 87 La Mutualite, Paris, France
10 DEC 87 Wembley Arena, London
SOUTH AMERICAN TOUR
25 NOV 88 Maracanãzinho, Rio De Janeiro, Brazil
28 NOV 88 Gigantinho Gym, Porto Alegre, Brazil
30 NOV 88 Olympia, Sao Paulo, Brazil
01 DEC 88 Ibirapuera, Sao Paulo, Brazil
02 DEC 88 Ibirapuera, Sao Paulo, Brazil
03 DEC 88 Ibirapuera, Sao Paulo, Brazil
17 DEC 88 Manchester Exhibition Centre, Manchester
20 JAN 89 Montpellier Le Zenith
21 JAN 89 Lyon Le Transbordeur
25 MAR 89 Glasgow S.E.C.C. 'SECCstasy', Glasgow, Scotland
26 MAR 89 Birmingham N.E.C., Birmingham
US TOUR
11 APR 89 Knight Center, Miami, Florida
12 APR 89 Bayfront Arena, St. Petersburg, Florida
14 APR 89 O'Connell Center, Gainesville, Florida
15 APR 89 Six Flags Over Georgia, Atlanta, Georgia
16 APR 89 Saenger Theater, New Orleans, Louisiana
20 APR 89 City Coliseum, Austin, Texas
21 APR 89 Astroworld, Houston, Texas
22 APR 89 Starplex Amphitheater, Dallas, Texas
25 APR 89 Mesa Amphitheater, Mesa, Arizona
27 APR 89 Universal Amphitheater, Los Angeles, California
28 APR 89 Universal Amphitheater, Los Angeles, California
30 APR 89 Santa Barbara County Bowl, Santa Barbara, California
02 MAY 89 Civic Auditorium, Portland, Oregon
03 MAY 89 Paramount Theatre, Seattle, Washington
04 MAY 89 Queen Elizabeth Theatre, Vancouver, British Columbia
14 JUN 89 Shoreline Amphitheater, Oakland (Mountain View), California
16 JUN 89 Irvine Meadows Amphitheatre, Irvine, California
17 JUN 89 Aztec Bowl, San Diego, California
18 JUN 89 Irvine Meadows Amphitheatre, Irvine, California
21 JUN 89 Salt Lake City, Utah
23 JUN 89 Red Rocks Amphitheater, Denver, Colorado
25 JUN 89 Sandstone Amphitheater, Bonner Springs, Kansas
27 JUN 89 Minneapolis, Minnesota
29 JUN 89 Marcus Amphitheater, Milwaukee, Wisconsin
30 JUN 89 Poplar Creek Music Theater, Hoffman Estates, Illinois (Chicago)
03 JUL 89 Pittsburgh, Pennsylvania
05 JUL 89 Blossom Music Center, Cuyahoga Falls (Cleveland), Ohio
07 JUL 89 C.N.E. Grandstand, Toronto, Ontario
08 JUL 89 Montreal, Canada
10 JUL 89 Great Woods, Mansfield, Massachusetts
11 JUL 89 Lake Compounce Park, Bristol, Connecticut

12 JUL 89 Jones Beach, New York
15 JUL 89 Merriweather Post Pavilion, Columbia, Maryland
16 JUL 89 Philadelphia, Pennsylvania
17 JUL 89 Detroit, Michigan
19 JUL 89 Brendan Byrne Arena, Meadowlands, New Jersey
25 AUG 89 Reading Festival, Reading
05 JUN 93 Dublin Point Depot, Dublin, Ireland
02 JUL 93 Montreux Jazz Festival, Montreux Switzerland
03 JUL 93 Roskilde Festival, Denmark
10 JUL 93 Loreley Bizarre Festival, St. Goarshausen, Germany

US TOUR
14 JUL 93 Meadowlands, New Jersey
21 JUL 93 Starplex Amphitheatre, Dallas, Texas
24 JUL 93 Shoreline Amphitheatre, Mountain View, California
26 JUL 93 Hollywood Bowl, Hollywood, California
29 JUL 93 World Music Theatre, Tinley Park, Illinois (Chicago)
31 JUL 93 Kingswood Amphitheatre, Toronto, Canada
02 AUG 93 Merriweather Post Pavilion, Columbia, Maryland
04 AUG 93 Brendan Byrne Arena, East Rutherford, New Jersey
05 AUG 93 Great Woods Theater, Mansfield, Massachusetts
29 AUG 93 Reading Festival, Reading
16 JUL 98 Apollo Theatre, Manchester
30 AUG 98 Reading Festival, Reading
29 DEC 98 Manchester Evening News Arena, Manchester
31 DEC 98 Alexandra Palace, London
18 JUL 01 The Olympia, Liverpool
28 JUL 01 Fuji Rock Festival, Japan

US TOUR
31 JUL 01 Shoreline Amphitheater, Mountain View (San Francisco), CA
02 AUG 01 Thunderbird Stadium, Vancouver, BC Canada
03 AUG 01 Gorge Amphitheater, Gorge (Seattle), WA
05 AUG 01 Glen Helen Blockbuster Pavilion, Devore (Los Angeles), CA

UK/EUROPEAN TOUR
11 AUG 01 Müngersdorfer Stadium, Cologne, Germany
04 OCT 01 Apollo Theatre, Manchester
05 OCT 01 Apollo Theatre, Manchester
07 OCT 01 Barrowlands, Glasgow, Scotland
08 OCT 01 Barrowlands, Glasgow, Scotland
10 OCT 01 Brixton Academy, London
11 OCT 01 Brixton Academy, London
12 OCT 01 Brixton Academy, London
11 NOV 01 Olympia, Paris, France
12 NOV 01 Olympia, Paris, France
15 NOV 01 Columbiahalle, Berlin, Germany
16 NOV 01 Palladium, Cologne, Germany
18 NOV 01 Cirkus, Stockholm, Sweden

AUSTRALASIAN TOUR
18 JAN 02 Ericcson Stadium, Auckland, New Zealand
20 JAN 02 Gold Coast Parklands, Gold Coast, Australia
23 JAN 02 Hordern Pavillion, Sydney, Australia
26 JAN 02 Sydney RAS Showgrounds, Sydney, Australia
28 JAN 02 Melbourne Showgrounds, Melbourne, Australia
30 JAN 02 Metro, Melbourne, Australia
01 FEB 02 Adelaide RA&HS Showgrounds, Adelaide, Australia
03 FEB 02 Claremont Showgrounds, Perth, Australia

UK/EUROPEAN TOUR
26 MAY 02 Le Zénith, Paris France
09 JUN 02 Finsbury Park Festival, London
15 JUN 02 Hultsfred Festival, Hultsfred, Sweden
22 JUN 02 Southside Festival, Germany
23 JUN 02 Hurricane Festival, Hamburg, Germany
25 JUN 02 Lansdowne Road, Dublin, Ireland
29 JUN 02 Roskilde Festival, Denmark
13 JUL 02 Old Trafford Cricket Ground, Manchester

ACKNOWLEDGEMENTS
Thanks to everyone whose ideas, thoughts, theories, memories and, most of all, record collections helped to make this book what it is: Amy Hanson, Jo-Ann Greene, Mike Scharman, Ella and Sprocket for filling in some details; and *Singles Going Steady* (Seattle's greatest record store) for filling in some gaps.

To Peter Hook, Bernard Sumner, Stephen Morris, Gillian Gilbert and Rob Gretton for the interviews that form the foundation of this book, and to the library's worth of old magazines that helped confirm my suspicions.

To Sean Body and all at Helter Skelter; and to everybody else who now walks around with 'True Faith' stuck in their heads... Snarleyyowl the Cat Fiend, K-Mart (not the store), Dave Makin, Gaye and Tim, Karin and Bob, Rita, Eric, Sam and Jacob, Anchorite Man, the Bat family (and Crab), Blind Pew, Barb East, Gef the Talking Mongoose, the Gremlins who live in the furnace, Geoff Monmouth, Nutkin, Squirrels, a lot of Thompsons, Turkish Magic Monkey, Neville Viking and the Walrus Ball.

BIBLIOGRAPHY
The printed page...
Curtis, Deborah, *Touching From A Distance,* Faber & Faber, 1995
Flowers, Claude, *Dreams Never End,* Omnibus Books, 1995
Johnson, Mark, et al, *An Ideal For Living,* Proteus, 1984
Middles, Mick, *The Factory Story: From Joy Division To New Order,* Virgin, 1996
Ward, Brian, *Pleasures And Wayward Distractions,* Omnibus Books, 1984
West, Mike, *Joy Division,* Babylon Books, 1984
Wilson, Anthony, *24 Hour Party People,* Channel 4 Books, 2002

The flickering screen...
www.factoryrecords.net Fac421 Your guide to Factory Records on the Internet.
www.worldinmotion.net Fac441 Your guide to Joy Division, New Order, Electronic, Revenge, The Other Two and Monaco on the Internet.
www.cerysmaticfactory.info – all things Factory related, merits a catalogue number all to itself.
www.gerpotze.com – another great discography, Joy Division only.
www.new-order.net Indispensable home to some rare and entertaining archival interviews (mp3) and more.
www.joydiv.com

Other Titles available from Helter Skelter

Coming Soon

Suede: An Armchair Guide
By Dave Thompson
The first biography of one of the most important British Rock Groups of the 90s who paved the way for Blur, Oasis et al. Mixing glam and post-punk influences, fronted by androgynous Bret Anderson, Suede thrust indie-rock into the charts with a string of classic singles in the process catalysing the Brit-pop revolution. Suede's first album was the then fastest selling debut of all time and they remain one of THE live draws on the UK rock circuit, retaining a fiercely loyal cult following.

Paperback	ISBN 1-900924-60-9	234mm X 156mm 256pp, 8pp b/w photos
UK £14.00	US $19.95	

Electric Pioneer: An Armchair Guide to Gary Numan
By Paul Goodwin
From selling 10 million records in 2 years, both with Tubeway Army and solo, to more low key and idiosyncratic releases through subsequent decades, Gary Numan has built up an impressive body of work and retained a hugely devoted cult following. *Electric Pioneer* is the first ever guide to his recorded output, documenting every single and album and featuring sections on his live shows, memorabilia and DVD releases.

Paperback	ISBN 1-900924-95-1	234 X 156mm 256pp, 16pp b/w photos
UK £14.99	US $19.95	

Wheels Out of Gear: Two Tone, The Specials and a World on Fire
By Dave Thompson
When the punks embraced reggae it led to a late 1970s Ska revival that began in Coventry with Jerry Dammers' Two Tone record label and his band, The Specials. Original 60s rude boy fashions – mohair suits, dark glasses and the ubiquitous pork pie hats – along with Dammer's black & white themed logo were the emblems for a hugely popular scene that also comprised hitmaking groups such as Madness, The Beat and The Selector.

Paperback	ISBN 1 900924-84-6	234 X 156mm 256pp, 16pp b/w photos
UK £12.99	US $19.95	

Al Stewart: Lights, Camera, Action – A Life in Pictures
By Neville Judd
Best known for his 70s classic "The Year of The Cat," Al Stewart continues to record and tour and retains a large and loyal international fanbase. This is a unique collection of rare and unpublished photographs, documenting Al's public and private life from early days in 1950s Scotland, through to his success in Hollywood and beyond.

Luxury Paperback	ISBN 1-900924-90-0	192pp 310 X 227mm
All pages photos, 16pp of colour		
UK £25.00	US $35.00	

'77 – The Year of Punk and New Wave
by Henry Bech Poulsen
As, 1967 was to the Haight-Ashbury scene, so 1977 was to punk: a year in which classic singles and albums by all the key bands made it the only musical movement that counted, and before its energy and potential was diluted and dampened by the forces of conservatism and commercialism. '77 tells the story of what every punk and new wave band achieved in that heady year – from The Pistols, Clash and Damned to The Lurkers, The Adverts and The Rezillos, and everyone in between.

Paperback	ISBN 1-900924-92-7	512pp 245 X 174mm
Illustrated throughout		
UK £16.99	US $25.00	

Linda Ronstadt: A Musical Life
By Peter Lewry
Ronstadt's early backing band became The Eagles and she has had success with songs by Neil Young, Jackson Browne and Hank Williams. After a US number 1 single and grammy winning country rock albums in the 1970s, she has continued to challenge preconceptions with albums of Nelson Riddle-produced standards, a record of mariachi songs and a collaboration with Dolly Parton and Emmylou Harris. This is her first ever biography.

Paperback	ISBN 1-900924-50-1	256pp 234 X 156mm
16pp b/w photos		
UK £16.99	US $25.00	

Sex Pistols: Only Anarchists are Pretty
Mick O'Shea
Drawing both on years of research and on creative conjecture, this book, written as a novel, portrays the early years of the Sex Pistols. Giving a fictionalised fly-on-the-wall account of the arguments, in-jokes, gigs, pub sessions and creative tension, it documents the day-to-day life of the ultimate punk band before the Bill Grundy incident and Malcolm McLaren-orchestrated tabloid outrage turned their lives into a media circus.

Paperback   ISBN 1-900924-93-5   234mm X 156mm 256pp 8pp b/w photos
UK £12.99   US $19.95

Action Time Vision: The Story of *Sniffin' Glue*, Alternative TV and Punk Rock
By Mark Perry
The legendary founder-editor of *Sniffin' Glue* – the definitive punk fanzine – gives his own account of the punk years. An eyewitness account of the key gigs; an insider's history of the bands and personalities; the full story of the hugely influential fanzine and the ups and downs of Perry's own recording career with Alternative TV.
Paperback   ISBN 1-900924-89-7   234 X 156mm   16pp b/w photos
UK £14.99   US $21.95

Coming – Spring 2005

Bob Dylan: Like The Night (Revisited)
by CP Lee
Fully revised and updated edition of the hugely acclaimed document of Dylan's pivotal 1966 show at the Manchester Free Trade Hall where fans called him Judas for turning his back on folk music in favour of rock 'n' roll. The album of the concert was released in the same year as the book's first outing and has since become a definitive source.
   "A terrific tome that gets up close to its subject and breathes new life into it... For any fan of Dylan this is quite simply essential." *Time Out*
   "Putting it all vividly in the context of the time, he writes expertly about that one electrifying, widely-bootlegged night." *Mojo*
   "CP Lee's book flushed 'Judas' out into the open." *The Independent*
   "An atmospheric and enjoyable account." *Uncut* (Top 10 of the year)
Paperback   ISBN 1-900924-33-1   198mm X 129mm 224pp 16pp b/w photos
UK £9.99   US $17.95

Everybody Dance
Chic and the Politics of Disco
By Daryl Easlea
Everybody Dance puts the rise and fall of Bernard Edwards and Nile Rodgers, the emblematic disco duo behind era-defining records 'Le Freak', 'Good Times' and 'Lost In Music', at the heart of a changing landscape, taking in socio-political and cultural events such as the Civil Rights struggle, the Black Panthers and the US oil crisis. There are drugs, bankruptcy, up-tight artists, fights, and Muppets but, most importantly an in-depth appraisal of a group whose legacy remains hugely underrated.
Paperback   ISBN 1-900924-56-0   234mm X 156mm 256pp 8pp b/w photos
UK £14.00   US $19.95

Currently Available from Helter Skelter Publishing

The Fall: An Armchair Guide
Dave Thompson
Amelodic, cacophonic and magnificent, The Fall remain the most enduring and prolific of the late-'70s punk and post-punk iconoclasts. *A User's Guide* chronicles the historical and musical background to more than 70 different LPs (plus reissues) and as many singles. The band's history is also documented year-by-year, filling in the gaps between the record releases.
Paperback   ISBN 1-900924-57-9   234mm X 156mm 256pp, 8pp b/w photos
UK £12.99   US $19.95

This Is a Modern Life
by Enamel Verguren
Lavishly illustrated guide to the mod revival that was sparked by the 1979 release of *Quadrophenia*. *This Is a Modern Life* concentrates on the 1980s, but takes in 20 years of a Mod life in London and throughout the world, from 1979 to 1999, with interviews of people directly involved, loads of flyers and posters and a considerable amount of great photos
Paperback   ISBN 1-900924-77-3   264mm X 180mm 224pp
photos throughout
UK £14.99   US $19.95

Smashing Pumpkins: Tales of A Scorched Earth
by Amy Hanson
Initially contemporaries of Nirvana, Billy Corgan's Smashing Pumpkins outgrew and outlived the grunge scene and with hugely acclaimed commercial triumphs like *Siamese Dream* and *Mellon Collie and The Infinite Sadness*. Though drugs and other problems led to the band's final demise, Corgan's recent return with Zwan is a reminder of how awesome the Pumpkins were in their prime. Seattle-based Hanson has followed the band for years and this is the first in-depth biography of their rise and fall.
Paperback   ISBN 1-900924-68-4   234mm X 156mm 256pp   8pp b/w photos
UK £12.99   US $18.95

Be Glad: An Incredible String Band Compendium
Edited by Adrian Whittaker
The ISB pioneered 'world music' on '60s albums like *The Hangman's Beautiful Daughter* – Paul McCartney's favourite album of 1967! – experimented with theatre, film and lifestyle and inspired Led Zeppelin. *Be Glad* features interviews with all the ISB key players, as well as a wealth of background information, reminiscence, critical evaluations and arcane trivia, this is a book that will delight any reader with more than a passing interest in the ISB.

Paperback	ISBN 1-900924-64-1	234mm X 156mm 288pp, b/w photos throughout
UK £14.99	US $22.95	

ISIS: A Bob Dylan Anthology
Ed Derek Barker
ISIS is the best-selling, longest lasting, most highly acclaimed Dylan fanzine. This ultimate Dylan anthology draws on unpublished interviews and research by the *ISIS* team together with the best articles culled from the pages of the definitive Bob magazine. From Bob's earliest days in New York City to the more recent legs of the Never Ending Tour, the *ISIS* archive has exclusive interview material – often rare or previously unpublished – with many of the key players in Dylan's career: friends, musicians and other collaborators, such as playwright Jacques Levy and folk hero Martin Carthy.

Fully revised and expanded edition features additional previously unpublished articles and further rare photos;
"Astounding ... Fascinating... If you're more than mildly interested in Bob Dylan then this is an essential purchase." *Record Collector*
"This book is worth any Dylan specialist's money." Ian MacDonald – **** *Uncut*

Paperback	ISBN 1-900924-82-X	198mm X 129mm 352pp, 16pp b/w photos
UK £9.99	US $17.95	

Waiting for the Man: The Story of Drugs and Popular Music
Harry Shapiro
From Marijuana and Jazz, through acid-rock and speed-fuelled punk, to crack-driven rap and Ecstasy and the Dance Generation, this is the definitive history of drugs and pop. It also features in-depth portraits of music's most famous drug addicts: from Charlie Parker to Sid Vicious and from Jim Morrison to Kurt Cobain. Chosen by the BBC as one of the Top Twenty Music Books of All Time. "Wise and witty." *The Guardian*

Paperback	ISBN 1-900924-58-7	198mm X 129mm 320pp
UK £10.99	US $17.95	

Jefferson Airplane: Got a Revolution
Jeff Tamarkin
With smash hits "Somebody to Love" and "White Rabbit" and albums like *Surrealistic Pillow*, Jefferson Airplane, the most successful and influential rock band to emerge from San Francisco during the 60s, created the sound of a generation. To the public they were free-loving, good-time hippies, but to their inner circle, Airplane were a paradoxical bunch – constantly at odds with each other. Jefferson Airplane members were each brilliant, individualistic artists who became the living embodiment of the ups and downs of the sex, drugs and rock 'n' roll lifestyle.

Tamarkin has interviewed the former band members, friends, lovers, crew members and fellow musicians to come up with the definitive full-length history of the group.
"A compelling account of a remarkable band." *Record Collector*
"A superb chunk of writing that documents every twist and turn in the ever-evolving life of a great American band." *Record Collector*

Paperback	ISBN 1-900924-78-1	234mm X 156mm 408pp, 16pp b/w photos
UK £14.99	US No rights	

Surf's Up: The Beach Boys on Record 1961-1981
Brad Elliott
The ultimate reference work on the recording sessions of one of the most influential and collectable groups.
"... an exhausting, exhilarating 500 pages of discographical and session information about everything anybody connected with the group ever put down or attempted to put down on vinyl." *Goldmine*

Paperback	ISBN 1-900924-79-X	234mm X 156mm 512pp, 16pp b/w photos
UK £25.00	US No rights	

Get Back: The Beatles' Let It Be Disaster
Doug Suply and Ray Shweighardt
Reissued to coincide with the release of *Let It Be ... Naked*, this is a singularly candid look at the greatest band in history at their ultimate moment of crisis. It puts the reader in the studio as John cedes power to Yoko; Paul struggles to keep things afloat, Ringo shrugs and George quits the band.
"One of the most poignant Beatles books ever." *Mojo*

Paperback	ISBN 1-900924-83-8	198mm X 129mm 352pp
UK £9.99	No US rights	

The Clash: Return of the Last Gang in Town
Marcus Gray
Exhaustively researched definitive biography of the last great rock band that traces their progress from pubs and punk clubs to US stadiums and the Top Ten. This edition is further updated to cover the band's induction into the Rock 'n' Roll Hall of Fame and the tragic death of iconic frontman Joe Strummer.

"A must-have for Clash fans [and] a valuable document for anyone interested in the punk era." *Billboard*

"It's important you read this book." *Record Collector*

| Paperback | ISBN 1-900924-62-5 | 234mm X 156mm 512pp, 8pp b/w photos |
| UK £14.99 | US No rights | |

Steve Marriott: All Too Beautiful
by Paolo Hewitt and John Hellier
Marriott was the prime mover behind 60s chart-toppers The Small Faces. Longing to be treated as a serious musician he formed Humble Pie with Peter Frampton, where his blistering rock 'n' blues guitar playing soon saw him take centre stage in the US live favourites. After years in seclusion, Marriott's plans for a comeback in 1991 were tragically cut short when he died in a housefire. He continues to be a key influence for generations of musicians from Paul Weller to Oasis and Blur.

"A riveting account of the singer's life, crammed with entertaining stories of rebellion and debauchery and insightful historical background... Compulsive reading." *The Express*

| Hardback | ISBN 1-900924-44-7 | 234mm X 156mm 352pp 32pp b/w photos |
| UK £20 | US $29.95 | |

Love: Behind The Scenes
By Michael Stuart-Ware
LOVE were one of the legendary bands of the late 60s US West Coast scene. Their masterpiece *Forever Changes* still regularly appears in critics' polls of top albums, while a new-line up of the band has recently toured to mass acclaim. Michael Stuart-Ware was LOVE's drummer during their heyday and shares his inside perspective on the band's recording and performing career and tells how drugs and egos thwarted the potential of one of the great groups of the burgeoning psychedelic era.

| Paperback | ISBN 1-900924-59-5 | 234mm X 156mm 256pp |
| UK £14.00 | US $19.95 | |

A Secret Liverpool: In Search of the La's
By MW Macefield
With timeless single "There She Goes", Lee Mavers' La's overtook The Stone Roses and paved the way for Britpop. However, since 1991, The La's have been silent, while rumours of studio-perfectionism, madness and drug addiction have abounded. The author sets out to discover the truth behind Mavers' lost decade and eventually gains a revelatory audience with Mavers himself.

| Paperback | ISBN 1-900924-63-3 | 234mm X 156mm 192pp |
| UK £11.00 | US $17.95 | |

Pink Floyd: A Saucerful of Secrets
by Nicholas Schaffner
Long overdue reissue of the authoritative and detailed account of one of the most important and popular bands in rock history. From the psychedelic explorations of the Syd Barrett-era to 70s superstardom with *Dark Side of the Moon*, and on to triumph of *The Wall*, before internecine strife tore the group apart. Schaffner's definitive history also covers the improbable return of Pink Floyd without Roger Waters, and the hugely *successful* Momentary Lapse of Reason album and tour.

| Paperback | ISBN 1-900924-52-8 | 234mm X 156mm 256pp, 8pp b/w photos |
| UK £14.99 | No rights | |

The Big Wheel
by Bruce Thomas
Thomas was bassist with Elvis Costello at the height of his success. Though names are never named, *The Big Wheel* paints a vivid and hilarious picture of life touring with Costello and co, sharing your life 24-7 with a moody egotistical singer, a crazed drummer and a host of hangers-on. Costello sacked Thomas on its initial publication.

"A top notch anecdotalist who can time a twist to make you laugh out loud." *Q*

| Paperback | ISBN 1-900924-53-6 | 234mm X 156mm 192pp |
| UK £10.99 | $17.95 | |

www.helterskelterbooks.com

All Helter Skelter, Firefly and SAF titles are available by mail order from

www.helterskelterbooks.com

Or from our office:

Helter Skelter Publishing Limited

South Bank House

Black Prince Road

London SE1 7SJ

Telephone: +44 (0) 20 7463 2204 or Fax: +44 (0)20 7463 2295

Mail order office hours: Mon-Fri 10:00am – 1:30pm,

By post, enclose a cheque [must be drawn on a British bank], International Money Order, or

credit card number and expiry date.

Postage prices per book worldwide are as follows:

UK & Channel Islands	£1.50
Europe & Eire (air)	£2.95
USA, Canada (air)	£7.50
Australasia, Far East (air)	£9.00

Email: info@helterskelterbooks.com